COMPUTATIONAL

INFORMATION

RETRIEVAL

D1716755

SIAM PROCEEDINGS SERIES LIST

Glowinski, R., Golub, G. H., Meurant, G. A., and Periaux, J., First International Conference on Domain Decomposition Methods for Partial Differential Equations (1988)

Salam, Fathi M. A. and Levi, Mark L., Dynamical Systems Approaches to Nonlinear Problems in Systems and Circuits (1988)

Datta, B., Johnson, C., Kaashoek, M., Plemmons, R., and Sontag, E., Linear Algebra in Signals, Systems and Control (1988)

Ringeisen, Richard D. and Roberts, Fred S., Applications of Discrete Mathematics (1988)

McKenna, James and Temam, Roger, ICIAM '87: Proceedings of the First International Conference on Industrial and Applied Mathematics (1988)

Rodrigue, Garry, Parallel Processing for Scientific Computing (1989)

Caflish, Russel E., Mathematical Aspects of Vortex Dynamics (1989)

Wouk, Arthur, Parallel Processing and Medium-Scale Multiprocessors (1989)

Flaherty, Joseph E., Paslow, Pamela J., Shephard, Mark S., and Vasilakis, John D., Adaptive Methods for Partial Differential Equations (1989)

Kohn, Robert V. and Milton, Graeme W., Random Media and Composites (1989)

Mandel, Jan, McCormick, S. F., Dendy, J. E., Jr., Farhat, Charbel, Lonsdale, Guy, Parter, Seymour V., Ruge, John W., and Stüben, Klaus, Proceedings of the Fourth Copper Mountain Conference on Multigrid Methods (1989)

Colton, David, Ewing, Richard, and Rundell, William, Inverse Problems in Partial Differential Equations (1990)

Chan, Tony F., Glowinski, Roland, Periaux, Jacques, and Widlund, Olof B., Third International Symposium on Domain Decomposition Methods for Partial Differential Equations (1990)

Dongarra, Jack, Messina, Paul, Sorensen, Danny C., and Voigt, Robert G., Proceedings of the Fourth SIAM Conference on Parallel Processing for Scientific Computing (1990)

Glowinski, Roland and Lichnewsky, Alain, Computing Methods in Applied Sciences and Engineering (1990)

Coleman, Thomas F. and Li, Yuying, Large-Scale Numerical Optimization (1990)

Aggarwal, Alok, Borodin, Allan, Gabow, Harold, N., Galil, Zvi, Karp, Richard M., Kleitman, Daniel J., Odlyzko, Andrew M., Pulleyblank, William R., Tardos, Éva, and Vishkin, Uzi, Proceedings of the Second Annual ACM-SIAM Symposium on Discrete Algorithms (1990)

Cohen, Gary, Halpern, Laurence, and Joly, Patrick, Mathematical and Numerical Aspects of Wave Propagation Phenomena (1991)

Gómez, S., Hennart, J. P., and Tapia, R. A., Advances in Numerical Partial Differential Equations and Optimization: Proceedings of the Fifth Mexico-United States Workshop (1991)

Glowinski, Roland, Kuznetsov, Yuri A., Meurant, Gérard, Périaux, Jacques, and Widlund, Olof B., Fourth International Symposium on Domain Decomposition Methods for Partial Differential Equations (1991)

Alavi, Y., Chung, F. R. K., Graham, R. L., and Hsu, D. F., Graph Theory, Combinatorics, Algorithms, and Applications (1991)

Wu, Julian J., Ting, T. C. T., and Barnett, David M., Modern Theory of Anisotropic Elasticity and Applications (1991)

Shearer, Michael, Viscous Profiles and Numerical Methods for Shock Waves (1991)

Griewank, Andreas and Corliss, George F., Automatic Differentiation of Algorithms: Theory, Implementation, and Application (1991)

Frederickson, Greg, Graham, Ron, Hochbaum, Dorit S., Johnson, Ellis, Kosaraju, S. Rao, Luby, Michael, Megiddo, Nimrod, Schieber, Baruch, Vaidya, Pravin, and Yao, Frances, Proceedings of the Third Annual ACM-SIAM Symposium on Discrete Algorithms (1992)

Field, David A. and Komkov, Vadim, Theoretical Aspects of Industrial Design (1992)

Field, David A. and Komkov, Vadim, Geometric Aspects of Industrial Design (1992)

Bednar, J. Bee, Lines, L. R., Stolt, R. H., and Weglein, A. B., Geophysical Inversion (1992)

O'Malley, Robert E. Jr., ICIAM 91: Proceedings of the Second International Conference on Industrial and Applied Mathematics (1992)

Keyes, David E., Chan, Tony F., Meurant, Gérard, Scroggs, Jeffrey S., and Voigt, Robert G., Fifth International Symposium on Domain Decomposition Methods for Partial Differential Equations (1992)

Dongarra, Jack, Messina, Paul, Kennedy, Ken, Sorensen, Danny C., and Voigt, Robert G., Proceedings of the Fifth SIAM Conference on Parallel Processing for Scientific Computing (1992)

Corones, James P., Kristensson, Gerhard, Nelson, Paul, and Seth, Daniel L., Invariant Imbedding and Inverse Problems (1992)

Ramachandran, Vijaya, Bentley, Jon, Cole, Richard, Cunningham, William H., Guibas, Leo, King, Valerie, Lawler, Eugene, Lenstra, Arjen, Mulmuley, Ketan, Sleator, Daniel D., and Yannakakis, Mihalis, Proceedings of the Fourth Annual ACM-SIAM Symposium on Discrete Algorithms (1993)

Kleinman, Ralph, Angell, Thomas, Colton, David, Santosa, Fadil, and Stakgold, Ivar, Second International Conference on Mathematical and Numerical Aspects of Wave Propagation (1993)

Banks, H. T., Fabiano, R. H., and Ito, K., Identification and Control in Systems Governed by Partial Differential Equations (1993)

Sleator, Daniel D., Bern, Marshall W., Clarkson, Kenneth L., Cook, William J., Karlin, Anna, Klein, Philip N., Lagarias, Jeffrey C., Lawler, Eugene L., Maggs, Bruce, Milenkovic, Victor J., and Winkler, Peter, Proceedings of the Fifth Annual ACM-SIAM Symposium on Discrete Algorithms (1994)

Lewis, John G., Proceedings of the Fifth SIAM Conference on Applied Linear Algebra (1994)

Brown, J. David, Chu, Moody T., Ellison, Donald C., and Plemmons, Robert J., Proceedings of the Cornelius Lanczos International Centenary Conference (1994)

Dongarra, Jack J. and Tourancheau, B., Proceedings of the Second Workshop on Environments and Tools for Parallel Scientific Computing (1994)

Bailey, David H., Bjørstad, Petter E., Gilbert, John R., Mascagni, Michael V., Schreiber, Robert S., Simon, Horst D., Torczon, Virginia J., and Watson, Layne T., Proceedings of the Seventh SIAM Conference on Parallel Processing for Scientific Computing (1995)

Clarkson, Kenneth, Agarwal, Pankaj K., Atallah, Mikhail, Frieze, Alan, Goldberg, Andrew, Karloff, Howard, Manber, Udi, Munro, Ian, Raghavan, Prabhakar, Schmidt, Jeanette, and Young, Moti, Proceedings of the Sixth Annual ACM-SIAM Symposium on Discrete Algorithms (1995)

Becache, Elaine, Cohen, Gary, Joly, Patrick, and Roberts, Jean E., Third International Conference on Mathematical and Numerical Aspects of Wave Propagation (1995)

Engl, Heinz W., and Rundell, W., GAMM–SIAM Proceedings on Inverse Problems in Diffusion Processes (1995)

Angell, T. S., Cook, Pamela L., Kleinman, R. E., and Olmstead, W. E., *Nonlinear Problems in Applied Mathematics* (1995)

Tardos, Éva, Applegate, David, Canny, John, Eppstein, David, Galil, Zvi, Karger, David R., Karlin, Anna R., Linial, Nati, Rao, Satish B., Vitter, Jeffrey S., and Winkler, Peter M., *Proceedings of the Seventh Annual ACM-SIAM Symposium on Discrete Algorithms* (1996)

Cook, Pamela L., Roytburd, Victor, and Tulin, Marshal, *Mathematics Is for Solving Problems* (1996)

Adams, Loyce and Nazareth, J. L., *Linear and Nonlinear Conjugate Gradient-Related Methods* (1996)

Renardy, Yuriko Y., Coward, Adrian V., Papageorgiou, Demetrios T., and Sun, Shu-Ming, *Advances in Multi-Fluid Flows* (1996)

Berz, Martin, Bischof, Christian, Corliss, George, and Griewank, Andreas, *Computational Differentiation: Techniques, Applications, and Tools* (1996)

Delic, George and Wheeler, Mary F., *Next Generation Environmental Models and Computational Methods* (1997)

Engl, Heinz W., Louis, Alfred, and Rundell, William, *Inverse Problems in Geophysical Applications* (1997)

Saks, Michael, Anderson, Richard, Bach, Eric, Berger, Bonnie, Blum, Avrim, Chazelle, Bernard, Edelsbrunner,Herbert, Henzinger, Monika, Johnson, David, Kannan, Sampath, Khuller, Samir, Maggs, Bruce, Muthukrishnan, S., Ruskey, Frank, Seymour, Paul, Spencer, Joel, Williamson, David P., and Williamson, Gill, *Proceedings of the Eighth Annual ACM-SIAM Symposium on Discrete Algorithms* (1997)

Alexandrov, Natalia M. and Hussaini, M. Y., *Multidisciplinary Design Optimization: State of the Art* (1997)

Van Huffel, Sabine, *Recent Advances in Total Least Squares Techniques and Errors-in-Variables Modeling* (1997)

Ferris, Michael C. and Pang, Jong-Shi, *Complementarity and Variational Problems: State of the Art* (1997)

Bern, Marshall, Fiat, Amos, Goldberg, Andrew, Kannan, Sampath, Karloff, Howard, Kenyon, Claire, Kierstead, Hal, Kosaraju, Rao, Linial, Nati, Rabani, Yuval, Rödl, Vojta, Sharir, Micha, Shmoys, David, Spielman, Dan, Spinrad, Jerry, Srinivasan, Aravind, and Sudan, Madhu, *Proceedings of the Ninth Annual ACM-SIAM Symposium on Discrete Algorithms* (1998)

DeSanto, John A., *Mathematical and Numerical Aspects of Wave Propagation* (1998)

Tarjan, Robert E., Warnow, Tandy, Amenta, Nina, Benham, Craig, Corneil, Derek G., Edelsbrunner, Herbert, Feigenbaum, Joan, Gusfield, Dan, Habib, Michel, Hall, Leslie, Karp, Richard, King, Valerie, Koller, Daphne, McKay, Brendan, Moret, Bernard, Muthukrishnan, S., Phillips, Cindy, Raghavan, Prabhakar, Randall, Dana, and Scheinerman, Edward, *Proceedings of the Tenth ACM-SIAM Symposium on Discrete Algorithms* (1999)

Hendrickson, Bruce, Yelick, Katherine A., Bischof, Christian H., Duff, Iain S., Edelman, Alan S., Geist, George A., Heath, Michael T., Heroux, Michael H., Koelbel, Chuck, Schrieber, Robert S., Sincovec, Richard F., and Wheeler, Mary F., *Proceedings of the Ninth SIAM Conference on Parallel Processing for Scientific Computing* (1999)

Henderson, Michael E., Anderson, Christopher R., and Lyons, Stephen L., *Object Oriented Methods for Interoperable Scientific and Engineering Computing* (1999)

Shmoys, David, Brightwell, Graham, Cohen, Edith, Cook, Bill, Eppstein, David, Gerards, Bert, Irani, Sandy, Kenyon, Claire, Ostrovsky, Rafail, Peleg, David, Pevzner, Pavel, Reed, Bruce, Stein, Cliff, Tetali, Prasad, and Welsh, Dominic, *Proceedings of the Eleventh ACM-SIAM Symposium on Discrete Algorithms* (2000)

Bermúdez, Alfredo, Gómez, Dolores, Hazard, Christophe, Joly, Patrick, and Roberts, Jean E., *Fifth International Conference on Mathematical and Numerical Aspects of Wave Propagation* (2000)

Kosaraju, S. Rao, Bellare, Mihir, Buchsbaum, Adam, Chazelle, Bernard, Graham, Fan Chung, Karp, Richard, Lovász, László, Motwani, Rajeev, Myrvold, Wendy, Pruhs, Kirk, Sinclair, Alistair, Spencer, Joel, Stein, Cliff, Tardos, Eva, Vempala, Santosh, *Proceedings of the Twelfth Annual ACM-SIAM Symposium on Discrete Algorithms* (2001)

Koelbel, Charles and Meza, Juan, *Proceedings of the Tenth SIAM Conference on Parallel Processing for Scientific Computing* (2001)

Grossman, Robert, Kumar, Vipin, and Han, Jiawei, *Proceedings of the First SIAM International Conference on Data Mining* (2001)

Berry, Michael, *Computational Information Retrieval* (2001)

COMPUTATIONAL

INFORMATION

RETRIEVAL

Edited by   Michael W. Berry
The University of Tennessee
Knoxville, Tennessee

Society for Industrial and Applied Mathematics
Philadelphia

COMPUTATIONAL INFORMATION RETRIEVAL

Proceedings of the Computational Information Retrieval Conference (CIR '00) held October 22, 2000, at North Carolina University, Raleigh, North Carolina.

Library of Congress Cataloging-in-Publication Data
Computational Information Retrieval Conference (2000 : Raleigh, N.C.)
   Computational information retrieval / edited by Michael W. Berry.
      p. cm.
   "Proceedings of the Computational Information retrieval Conference (CIR '00) held October 22, 2000, at North Carolina University, Raleigh, North Carolina"–CIP t.p. verso.
   ISBN 0-89871-500-8 (pbk. : alk. paper) *7045748*
     1. Database management–Congresses. 2. Information storage and retrieval systems.–Congresses. I. Berry, Michael W. II. Society for Industrial and Applied Mathematics. III. Title.
QA76.9.D3 C655 2000
005.74–dc21   2001032069

The cover art appears courtesy of William M. Pottenger and Russell H. Bader. This figure first appeared in "The Role of the HDDI® Collection Builder in Hierarchical Distributed Dynamic Indexing," in Proceedings of the Text Mine '01 Workshop, April 7, 2001, Chicago, IL, an unpublished volume of papers from the workshop compiled and bound by the Army High Performance Computing Research Center (AHPCRC), Minneapolis, MN. The cover art is a corrected version of the figure appearing in the contribution authored by William M. Pottenger and Ting-Hao Yang in this volume.

CONTENTS

List of Contributors

Haesun Park, Moongu Jeon, and J. Ben Rosen
University of Minnesota

Fredrick B. Holt and Yuan-Jye Jason Wu
The Boeing Company

Katarina Blom and Axel Ruhe
Chalmers Institute of Technology and the University of Göteborg

Younes Chahlaoui and Paul Van Dooren
Université catholique de Louvain

Kyle A. Gallivan
Florida State University

Chris H.Q. Ding
Lawrence Berkeley National Laboratory

Michael W. Berry and Xiaoyan Zhang
University of Tennessee

Padma Raghavan
The Pennsylvania State University

William M. Pottenger
Lehigh University

Ting-Hao Yang
National Center for Supercomputing Applications

Jacob Kogan
University of Maryland Baltimore County

Elizabeth R. Jessup and James H. Martin
University of Colorado, Boulder

Parry Husbands, Horst Simon, and Chris H.Q. Ding
Lawrence Berkeley National Laboratory

John Caron
University Corporation for Atmospheric Research and University of Colorado, Boulder

Marco Lizza and Flavio Sartoretto
Università "Ca' Foscari" di Venezia

Preface

As digital libraries and the World Wide Web (WWW) continue to grow exponentially, the ability to find useful information will greatly depend on the associated underlying framework of the indexing infrastructure or search engine. The push to get information on-line must be mediated by the design of automated techniques for extracting that information for a variety of users and needs. What algorithms and software environments are plausible for achieving both accuracy and speed in text searching today? This was one of the fundamental questions addressed at the first annual "Computational Information Retrieval Workshop" (CIR'00) held on Sunday, October 22, 2000 in Raleigh, NC. This workshop was held at the Jane S. McKimmon Center on the campus of North Carolina State University, and was held the day before the Seventh SIAM Conference on Applied Linear Algebra. The workshop attendees numbered close to 70 and represented numerous universities, industrial corporations, and government laboratories. Invited and contributed talks focused on the use of linear algebra, computational statistics, and computer science in the development of algorithms and software systems for information (particularly text) retrieval. The workshop was graciously funded by SIAM, National Science Foundation, Boeing, M-CAM, Inc., and Telcordia Technologies, Inc.

The invited and contributed papers compiled in this proceedings are organized into four areas:

1. Reduced Rank Subspace Models,

2. Probabilistic IR Models and Symbolic Techniques,

3. Clustering Algorithms and Applications, and

4. Case Studies of Latent Semantic Analysis (Indexing).

Many of the papers presented at the workshop focused on the use of Latent Semantic Indexing/Analysis (LSI/A) and alternative vector space models for Information Retrieval (IR). Some progress has been made in reducing the SVD-based costs of LSI using symbolic techniques common to sparse matrix factorization research and graph theory (Berry, Raghavan, and Zhang). A different approach to SVD-complexity reduction based on fast bi-diagonalization (using short Krylov subspaces) was presented (Blom and Ruhe). An efficient method for incrementally computing dominant singular subspaces (exploited by LSI/A) was discussed (Chahlaoui,

Gallivan, and Van Dooren), and a novel two-step approach for document clustering was also presented (Kogan).

Demonstrating optimal performance of LSI/A across different text collections, however, remains inconsistent (Jessup and Martin), and workshop discussions on a paradigm shift from *noise reduction* associated with low-rank subspace modeling to *noise addition* with more emphasis on the statistical significance of additive subspace dimensionality emerged (Ding). Rare terms (limited use) have been shown to have little or no effect on the final LSI representation of documents (Husbands, Simon, and Ding), and the exploitation of *phrase-indexing* has been shown to improve average retrieval precision up to 9% on certain collections (Sartoretto). Examples of complete IR systems based on LSI/A include the BIRDS project at Minnesota (Park, Jeon, and Rosen) and the TRUST system at Boeing (Wu). New applications areas such as the automatic detection of warranty repair claims (Pottenger and Yang) and technical support (Caron) were presented as well.

The workshop was quite successful in outlining future research in vector space IR modeling and there is considerable interest in holding a follow-up workshop (CIR'01) in 2001. Special thanks to Rick Thursby, Donna Bodenheimer, Dorsey Bottoms, and Gloria Turner in the Department of Computer Science at the University of Tennessee for their diligent efforts with all the local arrangements and workshop materials for CIR'00.

Michael W. Berry
University of Tennessee

Part I

Reduced Rank Subspace Models

Lower Dimensional Representation of Text Data in Vector Space Based Information Retrieval

Haesun Park[*], *Moongu Jeon*[†], *and J. Ben Rosen*[‡]

1   Introduction

Today's exponential growth of internet and computing power make it possible to add tremendous amount of data to an information retrieval system everyday, and users demand more efficient techniques to get useful information from floods of data. The data in information retrieval takes various forms such as text, image and multimedia, but in this paper we will concentrate on text or document retrieval, and especially on vector space based method. The vector space based information retrieval system, originated by G. Salton [30, 31], represents documents as vectors in a vector space. Specifically, a term-document matrix $A \in \mathbb{R}^{m \times n}$ is formed with the collection of the documents, where m is the total number of terms in the document collection and n is the number of total documents. Each column of A represents a document, and in the matrix $A = (a_{ij})$, a_{ij} are weighted frequencies of each word in a specific document,

[*]The work of this author was supported in part by the National Science Foundation grants CCR-9509085 and CCR-9901992. Department of Computer Science and Engineering, University of Minnesota, Minneapolis, MN 55455. E-mail: hpark@cs.umn.edu.

[†]The work of this author was supported in part by the National Science Foundation grants CCR-9509085 and CCR-9901992. Department of Computer Science and Engineering, University of Minnesota, Minneapolis, MN 55455. E-mail: jeon@cs.umn.edu.

[‡]The work of this author was supported in part by NSF grants CCR-9527151, CCR-9509085 and CCR-9901992. Department of Computer Science and Engineering, University of Minnesota, Minneapolis, MN 55455 and Department of Computer Science and Engineering, University of California, San Diego, La Jolla, CA 92093. E-mail: jbrosen@cs.ucsd.edu.

i.e., a_{ij} is a weight or importance of term i of document j. The simplest a_{ij} is binary, but to improve the retrieval performance, various weighting methods have been developed [12, 31]. For other related topics such as stemming and removing stop lists, see [12, 31]. SMART system [31] is one of the most influential test beds where the vector based method is successfully implemented. Latent semantic indexing [2, 3, 4, 9, 13, 28] is an example of vector space based method where the singular value decomposition of the term-document matrix is utilized to remove noise in the matrix and achieve lower dimensional representation of the data. One major advantage of the vector space based method is that the algebraic structures of the term-document matrix can be exploited using the techniques developed in linear algebra. In particular, we believe that incorporation of a priori knowledge in the data in its vector space representation is important in building an effective information retrieval system.

The modern document sets are huge. In order to achieve higher efficiency and effectiveness in manipulating these data, it will be necessary to find lower dimensional representation of the data. A vector space based information retrieval system needs to solve largely the following three problems frequently: document retrieval, classification, and clustering. Document retrieval is to extract relevant documents from a text database given a query. Classification is the process of assigning new data to its proper group. The group is also called class or category. The classification problem may be complicated by imperfect class definitions, overlapping categories, and random variations in the new data [1]. A common classification system is composed of data collection, feature generation, feature selection, classifier design, and finally, system evaluation and feedback [15, 27, 32]. Among them feature selection is of great importance for the quality of classification and computational cost of the classifier. Dimension reduction can be considered as a task of feature selection process in vector space based method. Clustering is the special case of classification, and the process to find out homogeneous groups (clusters) of data based on the values of their vector components and predefined measure [20]. While the category structure is known in classification, in cluster analysis little or nothing is known about the category structure. All that is available is a collection of data whose category memberships are unknown. The objective is to discover a category structure of data set [1].

In document retrieval, classification, and in some clustering algorithms, the kernel of the computation involves comparison of two vectors, which will be affected by different weighting schemes and the similarity measures [21, 31]. With dimension reduction of the given text collection, the complexity of subsequent computations involved in these problems can be substantially reduced. To achieve higher efficiency in computation, often it is necessary to reduce the dimension severely, and in the process, we may lose too much information which was available in the original data. Therefore, it is important to achieve *better representation* of data in the lower dimensional space rather than simply reducing the dimension of the data to best approximate the full term-document matrix. The significance of this has been recognized by Hubert, et.al. [19], for example. The difficulty involved is that it is not easy to measure how well a certain dimension reduction method gives a good representation of the original data. It seems that this can only be estimated using experimental results.

The dimension reduction methods that we will discuss in this paper are based on the vector subspace computation in linear algebra. Unlike other probability and frequency based methods where a set of representative words are chosen, the vector subspace computation will give reduction in the dimension of term space where for each dimension in the reduced space we cannot easily attach corresponding words or a meaning. The dimension reduction by the optimal lower rank approximation from the SVD has been successfully applied in numerous applications, e.g. in signal processing. In these applications, often what the dimension reduction achieves is the effect of getting rid of noise in the data. In case of information retrieval, often the term-document matrix has either full rank or close-to full rank. Also the meaning of *noise* in the data collection is not well understood, unlike in other applications such as signal processing [29] or image processing. In addition, in information retrieval, the lower rank approximation is not only a tool for rephrasing a given problem into another one which is easier to solve, but the data representation in the lower dimension space itself is important [19].

In this paper, we propose a mathematical framework for lower dimensional representation of text data using the tool of minimization and matrix rank reduction formula. In our method, a lower dimensional representation of the original data is achieved by finding a lower rank approximate decomposition of the data matrix. This approximation is realized as a minimization problem, or by using a matrix rank reduction formula. When the minimization is achieved using matrix Frobenius norm, the lower dimensional representation of the data becomes the projected representation. How successfully we choose the projection will certainly influence the quality of the lower dimensional representation of the data. In particular, it will be important to choose the projection so that a priori knowledge on the data collection is reflected as much as possible. However, it is not always clear how to represent a priori knowledge mathematically to obtain better lower dimensional data. We attempt to present general mathematical framework of dimension reduction in vector space based information retrieval, and illustrate the importance of incorporating a priori knowledge of the cluster structure in the data.

2 Lower Dimensional Representation of Term-Document Matrix

In a vector space based text retrieval system, each document is treated as a vector where each term corresponds to one component in the vector, therefore, occupies one dimension in the Cartesian coordinate system. This means that implicitly, it is assumed that the terms are independent from each other. In fact, this assumption is not necessarily true, for some words are closely related than others. In addition, in handling the vast amount of today's data, allowing one extra dimension for each term, even after proper preprocessing such as stemming and removing the stop lists [12, 23], will make the computation complexity extremely high. Therefore, the dimension reduction in vector space based information retrieval is important for higher efficiency and effectiveness.

To mathematically understand the problem of lower dimensional representation of the given document sets, we will first assume that the reduced dimension, which we will denote as $k(k << min(m, n))$, is given or determined in advance. Then given a term-document matrix $A \in \mathbb{R}^{m \times n}$, and an integer k ($k << min(m, n)$), the problem is to find a transformation that maps each column a_i of A in the m dimensional space to a column y_i in the k dimensional space :

$$a_i \in \mathbb{R}^{m \times 1} \rightarrow y_i \in \mathbb{R}^{k \times 1}, 1 \le i \le n. \tag{1}$$

Rather than looking for the mapping that achieves this explicitly, One can rephrase this as an approximation problem where the given matrix A has to be decomposed into two matrices B and Y as

$$A \approx BY \tag{2}$$

where both $B \in \mathbb{R}^{m \times k}$ with rank$(B) = k$ and $Y \in \mathbb{R}^{k \times n}$ with rank$(Y) = k$ are to be found. This lower rank approximate factorization is not unique since for any nonsingular matrix $Z \in \mathbb{R}^{k \times k}$,

$$A \approx BY = (BZ)(Z^{-1}Y),$$

and $rank(BZ) = k$ and $rank(Z^{-1}Y) = k$. This problem can be recast in two different but related ways. The first is in terms of matrix rank reduction formula and the second is as a minimization problem. The matrix rank reduction formula has been studied substantially in numerical linear algebra as well as psychometrics and applied statistics [7, 8, 16, 17, 19]. Here, we summarize the results that are relevant to our problem of lower dimensional representation of term-document matrix.

Theorem 1. *(Matrix Rank Reduction Theorem) Let $A \in \mathbb{R}^{m \times n}$ be a given matrix with rank$(A) = r$. Then the matrix*

$$E = A - (AS)(PAS)^{-1}(PA) \tag{3}$$

where $P \in \mathbb{R}^{k \times m}$ and $S \in \mathbb{R}^{n \times k}$, $k \le r$, satisfies

$$rank(E) = rank(A) - rank((AS)(PAS)^{-1}(PA)) \tag{4}$$

if and only if $PAS \in \mathbb{R}^{k \times k}$ is nonsingular.

The only restriction on the premultiplier P and the postmultiplier S is on their dimensions and that the product PAS be nonsingular. It is this choice for P and S that makes the dimension reduction flexible and makes incorporation of a priori knowledge possible. For our purpose, we will concentrate mostly on Eqn (3), which we call *matrix rank reduction formula*. In fact, in [7] it is shown that many of the matrix decompositions can be derived using the matrix rank reduction formula. It is easy to see that the rank k approximation from the truncated SVD of A provides a solution that minimizes $||E||_2$ or $||E||_F$ [5, 14]. We will discuss more on this in the next subsection. Minimizing the error matrix E in a certain norm is equivalent to solving a minimization problem

$$\min_{B,Y} \|A - BY\|_l \tag{5}$$

where $B \in \mathbb{R}^{m \times k}$ with $\text{rank}(B) = k$ and $Y \in \mathbb{R}^{k \times n}$ with $\text{rank}(Y) = k$, and in this case, Eqn (3) and Eqn (5) are related since

$$BY = (AS)(PAS)^{-1}PA.$$

It is well known that with $n = 2$ or F, the best approximation is obtained from the singular value decomposition of A. The commonly used latent semantic indexing exploits the SVD of the term-document matrix [2, 3, 9, 11]. We emphasized that for successful rank reduction scheme, it is important to exploit a priori knowledge. The incorporation of a priori knowledge can be translated to choosing the matrix P and S in (3), or adding a constraint in the minimization problem (5). However, mathematical formulation of the a priori knowledge as a constraint is not always easy or even possible.

In the following, we discuss various ways to choose the matrices B and Y. In Section 3, we also show some interesting test results that illustrate that although the singular value decomposition (SVD) of A gives the best approximation in terms of minimizing the distance between A and BY for $l = 2$ or F, some other choices of B and Y based on the clustering of the data matrix A may give far superior reduced dimension representation of original documents in tasks such as document retrieval and classification. The choice of reduced dimension k will be discussed in future and for now we will assume that the integer k is given. There have been active research on Latent Semantic Indexing in the research community in numerical linear algebra [2, 3, 25]. In much of this work, the common ground is the singular value decomposition, and the efforts have been made to essentially facilitate the usage of the SVD by either parallelizing the SVD preserving sparsity of the term-document matrix in the SVD or finding a faster decomposition that can approximate the SVD. The SVD certainly gives the best lower rank approximation and it can be explained using our mathematical model. We summarize the LSI with SVD in the next subsection.

2.1 Latent Semantic Indexing by SVD

It is well known that for any matrix $A \in \mathbb{R}^{m \times n}$, its singular value decomposition (SVD) exists [5, 14]. The SVD is defined as

$$A = U\Sigma V^T \tag{6}$$

where

$$U \in \mathbb{R}^{m \times m}, \quad \Sigma \in \mathbb{R}^{m \times n}, \quad V \in \mathbb{R}^{n \times n}$$

$$U^T U = I_m, \quad V^T V = I_n, \quad \Sigma = diag(\sigma_1 \cdots \sigma_p)$$

with $p = min(m, n)$, $\sigma_1 \geq \sigma_2 \geq \cdots \sigma_p \geq 0$ which are the singular values, and the columns of U and V are left and right singular vectors, respectively. The SVD is useful for determining the rank of a matrix thanks to the diagonality of Σ, where the rank of a matrix is the same as the number of nonzero singular values. It is also widely known that the noise in data can be filtered by truncated SVD. If we eliminate the portion of Σ and corresponding left and right singular vectors, then the reduced rank representation can be obtained as

$$A \approx A_k = (U_k \hat{U}) \begin{pmatrix} \Sigma_k & 0 \\ 0 & 0 \end{pmatrix} \begin{pmatrix} V_k^T \\ \hat{V}^T \end{pmatrix} = U_k \Sigma_k V_k^T, \qquad (7)$$

where $U_k \in \mathbb{R}^{m \times k}, \Sigma_k \in \mathbb{R}k \times k, \text{and} V_k \in \mathbb{R}^{n \times k}$. The LSI uses the SVD to filter the noise and improve the efficiency in retrieval performance [2]. The rank k approximation (7) can also be obtained when the matrix E in the matrix rank reduction formula shown in (3) is minimized using matrix L_2 norm or Frobenius norm. It can be easily shown that the minimum error is obtained with $P = U_k^T$ and $S = V_k$, which gives

$$\begin{aligned} (AS)(PAS)^{-1}(PA) &= (AV_k)(U_k^T A V_k)^{-1}(U_k^T A) \\ &= (U_k \Sigma_k)(\Sigma_k)^{-1}(\Sigma_k V_k^T) \\ &= U_k \Sigma_k V_k^T. \end{aligned}$$

The LSI is based on the assumption that there is some underlying latent semantic structure in the data of term-document matrix that is corrupted by the wide variety of words used in documents and queries for the same objects (because of the different background knowledge of the author and the users, for example [9]). It is claimed that the SVD and statistics of the frequency of association terms make it possible that even though two documents of similar topic do not share the same keywords, they can belong to the same cluster or be retrieved simultaneously for a query including that keyword [2]. In other words, the basic idea of LSI with SVD is that if two document vectors represent the same topic, they will share many associating words with a keyword, and they will have very close semantic structures after dimension reduction via SVD.

The LSI with SVD breaks the original relationship of the data into linearly independent components [9], and the original term vectors are represented by left singular vectors as shown in (8), and document vectors by right singular vectors as shown in (9):

$$\text{Range}(A) = \text{Range}(U) \qquad (8)$$

$$\text{Range}(A^T) = \text{Range}(V). \qquad (9)$$

Reduced approximation space is used for filtering the noise as well as reducing the computational cost. The error of the approximate matrix is given as

$$\|A - A_k\|_2 = \sigma_{k+1}, \qquad \text{with} \qquad A_k = U_k \Sigma_k V_k^T \qquad (10)$$

and approximation dimension k in the range of 100 to 300 has been reported to give good precision of retrieval [11].

In all three major tasks in information retrieval of classification, clustering, and document retrieval, the fundamental operation is to compare a document (or pseudo-document) to another document (or pseudo-document). In this, the choice of similarity measure plays an important role [21]. In the vector space based information retrieval, the most commonly used similarity measures are, L_2 norm (Euclidean distance), inner product, cosine, or variations of these [21]. When inner product is used as a measure, the documents are compared as,

$$A^T A \approx A_k^T A_k = V_k \Sigma_k^T U_k^T U_k \Sigma_k V_k^T$$
$$= (V_k \Sigma_k^T)(\Sigma_k V_k^T).$$

Therefore, the inner product between a pair of columns of A can be approximated by the inner product between a pair of columns of $\Sigma_k V_k^T$. Accordingly, $V_k \Sigma_k^T$ is considered as a representation of the document vectors in the reduced dimension. This argument holds for the cosine similarity measure as well when the vectors are properly normalized. In general the above derivation is valid only for the inner product measure.

For document retrieval, a query vector $q \in \mathbb{R}^{m \times 1}$ needs to be represented in a space with dimension k. Consider the inner product between the query vector and document vectors :

$$q^T A \approx q^T A_k = (q^T)(U_k \Sigma_k V_k^T) \tag{11}$$
$$= (q^T U_k)(\Sigma_k V_k). \tag{12}$$

Eqn (12) shows that the query vector can be represented as

$$\hat{q} = U_k^T q \tag{13}$$

after it is adjusted to be in the k dimensional space, since the columns of $\Sigma_k V_k^T$ represent the document vectors in the reduced dimension. In some other cases, it has been proposed that q be reduced to a vector in $\mathbb{R}^{k \times 1}$ as

$$\hat{q} = \Sigma_k^{-1} U_k^T q. \tag{14}$$

In the next subsection, we give a different derivation and interpretation of the transformations (13) and (14) of q to $\hat{q}$. In fact, our derivation will clearly illustrate how one can obtain $\hat{q}$ represented in Eqn (14).

2.2   Dimension Reduction of Cluster Structured Data

Although the SVD gives the approximation BY of A that gives the minimum distance when $l = 2$ or F in Eqn (5), the SVD does not take it into account that the data matrix A is often *structured*. Here, we say that a matrix has a *cluster structure* when its columns can be grouped into a number of clusters. In other words, in a cluster structured matrix, we can recognize that each column is more closely related to a certain set of columns than to others. We will show that there are other approximation schemes that are often superior to the SVD in producing better reduced dimension representation of the text data when the data has a cluster structure.

Representation of Each Cluster

First we will assume that the data set is cluster structured and already grouped into certain clusters. This assumption is not a restriction since we can cluster the data set if it is not already clustered using one of the several existing clustering algorithms such as k-means [10, 20]. Also especially when the data set is huge, we can assume that the data has a cluster structure and it is often necessary to cluster the data to utilize the tremendous amount of information, in an efficient way. For example, with clustered WebPages or documents, search can retrieve items similar to an input item without any additional overhead [23].

Suppose we are given a data matrix A whose columns are grouped into k clusters $C_1, C_2, \ldots, C_k$, where $C_i \in \mathbb{R}^{m \times n_i}$, and $\sum_{i=1}^{k} n_i = n$. Instead of treating each column of the matrix A equally regardless of its membership in a specific cluster, which is what is done in the SVD, we want to find the matrices B and Y with k columns and k rows, respectively, so that the k clusters are represented in the space with reduced dimension. For this purpose, we want to choose each column of B so that it *represents* the corresponding cluster. To answer the question of which vector can represent each cluster well, we first consider an easier problem with scalar data. For any given scalar data set $\alpha_1, \alpha_2, \cdots, \alpha_n$, the *mean* value

$$m_\alpha = \frac{1}{n} \sum_{i=1}^{n} \alpha_i \tag{15}$$

is often used to represent the data set. The use of mean value is justified since it is the one that gives the minimum variance

$$\sum_{i=1}^{n} (\alpha_i - m_\alpha)^2 = \min_{\delta \in \mathbb{R}} \sum_{i=1}^{n} (\alpha_i - x)^2 = \min_{\delta \in \mathbb{R}} \|(\alpha_1 \cdots \alpha_n) - \delta(1 \cdots 1)\|_2^2. \tag{16}$$

The mean value is often extended to the data sets in a vector space as follows. Suppose $a_1, a_2, \cdots, a_n \in \mathbb{R}^{m \times 1}$. Then its *centroid* defined as

$$c_a = \frac{1}{n} \sum_{i=1}^{n} a_i = \frac{1}{n} A e \tag{17}$$

where $e = (1, 1, \cdots, 1)^T \in \mathbf{R}^{n \times 1}$, is used as a vector that represents the vector data set, where $A = [a_1 a_2 \cdots a_n]$. The centroid is the vector which achieves the minimum variance in the following sense:

$$\sum_{i=1}^{n} \|a_i - c_a\|_2^2 = \min_{x \in \mathbb{R}^{n \times 1}} \sum_{i=1}^{n} \|a_i - x\|_2^2 = \min_{x \in \mathbb{R}^{n \times 1}} \|A - x e^T\|_F^2. \tag{18}$$

It is clear from (18) that the centroid vector gives the smallest distance in Frobenius norm between the matrix A and the rank one approximation $x e^T$ where x is to be determined. Since one of the vectors in this rank one approximation is fixed to be e, this distance cannot be smaller than the distance obtained from rank one approximation from the SVD: the rank one approximation from the SVD would choose *two* vectors $y \in \mathbb{R}^{m \times 1}$ and $z \in \mathbb{R}^{n \times 1}$ such that $\|A - yz^T\|_F$ is minimized, and

$$\min_{y,z} \|A - yz^T\|_F \leq \min_x \|A - xe^T\|_F.$$

However, the centroid vector has the advantage that for each cluster, we can find *one* vector to represent it instead of *two* vectors. In the following three subsections, we describe how we find the approximation BY that exploits the cluster structure, and also illustrate that the LSI with SVD is a special case of our model.

Minimization with Centroid Vectors

First, we set the columns of B to be the centroids of the k clusters, and then find a lower dimensional representation Y by solving the least squares problem

$$\min_{y \in \mathbb{R}^{k \times 1}} \|By - a_i\|_2, \tag{19}$$

for each of the solution vectors $y_i \in \mathbb{R}^{k \times 1}$, $1 \leq i \leq n$, i.e.

$$\min_{Y \in \mathbb{R}^{k \times n}} \|BY - A\|_F.$$

Then Y is the representation of A in the k dimensional space. It is easy to see that Y is the projected representation of A in the range space of the matrix B. This shows that the choice of columns of B plays an important role. The above can also be explained using the matrix rank reduction formula as follows.

Defining a *grouping* matrix $H \in \mathbb{R}^{n \times k}$ as

$$H = F \cdot (diag(diag(F^T F)))^{-1}$$

$$\text{where} \quad F(i,j) = \begin{cases} 1 & \text{if document } i \text{ belongs to cluster } j, \\ 0 & \text{otherwise} \end{cases} \quad \text{and} \quad F \in \mathbb{R}^{n \times k}, \tag{20}$$

it is easy to see that the matrix B whose columns are the centroids of each cluster can be represented as

$$B = AH. \tag{21}$$

In addition, the solution Y for

$$\min_Y \|BY - A\|_F$$

obtained with $B = AH$ can be represented as $Y = (B^T B)^{-1} B^T A$, which in turn, gives the matrix rank reduction expression (3) as

$$E = A - BY = A - (AH)(B^T B)^{-1} B^T A \tag{22}$$

$$= A - (AH)(H^T A^T AH)^{-1}(H^T A^T A). \tag{23}$$

Eqn. (22) shows the prefactor $P = H^T A^T$ and the postfactor $S = H$ in our method.

After obtaining the decomposition $A \approx BY$ as discussed above, any new document q that is not a column of the matrix A, can be transformed to the lower dimension by solving the minimization problem

$$\min_{y \in \mathbb{R}^{k \times 1}} \|By - q\|_2. \tag{24}$$

In text retrieval, a query is first represented as a vector in m dimensional space, then transformed into the vector y which is a solution for (24). Comparison of documents or pseudo documents is achieved by comparing two vectors in full space or reduced space using a specific similarity measure. The commonly used similarity measures are based on cosine or Euclidean norm. In case of cosine measure in full dimensional space, to compare any two vectors $a \in \mathbb{R}^{n \times 1}$ and $q \in \mathbb{R}^{n \times 1}$,

$$Cos(a, q) \equiv \frac{a^T q}{\|a\|_2 \|q\|_2} \tag{25}$$

is computed. Using the approximation $A \approx BY$, (25) is approximated by

$$Cos(B\hat{a}, B\hat{q}) = \frac{\hat{a}^T B^T B \hat{q}}{\|B\hat{a}\|_2 \|B\hat{q}\|_2} \tag{26}$$

where $\hat{a} \in \mathbb{R}^{k \times 1}$ and $\hat{q} \in \mathbb{R}^{k \times 1}$ are the k-dimensional representation of a and q, respectively. Defining a new vector norm as

$$\|y\|_B \equiv \|By\|_2$$

and the corresponding inner product as

$$< x, y >_B \equiv x^T B^T By,$$

Eqn (26) becomes

$$Cos(B\hat{a}, B\hat{q}) = \frac{< \hat{a}, \hat{q} >_B}{\|\hat{a}\|_B \|\hat{q}\|_B} . \tag{27}$$

A similar argument holds for L_2 norm or inner product measures. According to our experiments [21], although there is no clear winner among many existing similarity measures, the L_2 norm based similarity measures consistently perform worse in handling text documents. This is also shown in our test results, which are presented in Section 3.

In Section 3, we also present the results where the measures from the full dimensional space are applied to the lower dimensional representation of the data, without the matrix B, e.g., $Cos(a, q)$ is approximated with $Cos(\hat{a}, \hat{q})$:

$$Cos(a, q) \approx Cos(\hat{a}, \hat{q}) = \frac{\hat{a}^T \hat{q}}{\|\hat{a}\|_2 \|\hat{q}\|_2} .$$

This can be interpreted as either discarding the matrix B after projection, or using the norm $\| \cdot \|_2$ instead of $\| \cdot \|_B$ in the reduced space. Surprisingly, at least on the data we tested, this straight forward application of the cosine measure to the projected representation of data works well. It also has the following several interesting properties. For the minimization problems

$$min\|By - b_i\|_l \tag{28}$$

where b_i is the ith column of B, $1 \leq i \leq k$, the solution y is the unit vector $e_i \in \mathbb{R}^{k \times 1}$ which is the ith column of the identity matrix of order k. This means that in the k dimensional space, the columns of B are projected to the unit vectors, and therefore, they are orthogonal. The independence of the vectors that represent the clusters is maximized as a result of projection to the space spanned by the columns in the matrix B.

In a simple classification algorithm, the similarity between a vector q to be classified and the vectors b_i, $1 \leq i \leq k$ that represent the clusters (they are often the centroids) would be compared. In the reduced dimensional space, this means that after q is projected to the reduced dimension to be $\hat{q}$, it is simply compared to the unit vectors e_i, $1 \leq i \leq k$ which are the centroids of the vectors represented as Y. When the Euclidean distance is used as the similarity measure, we look for

$$arg \min_{1 \leq i \leq k} \|\hat{q} - e_i\|_2. \tag{29}$$

The minimum will be achieved when i is the index of the largest component of $\hat{q}$. Therefore, the computation of k of the 2-norms in (29) becomes unnecessary. We simply need to find out where the largest component of q lies and it will be the cluster where it belongs. The situation is similar when the cosine measure is used: We will look for

$$arg \max_{1 \leq i \leq k} \frac{\hat{q}^T e_i}{\|\hat{q}\|_2 \|e_i\|_2}, \tag{30}$$

which is obtained when i is the index of the largest component of $\hat{q}$. Therefore, the result of classification will be the same whether we use 2-norm or cosine as similarity measures. The computational complexity is lower since the computation of k of the 2-norm (or cosine) will be replaced by searching for the largest of the k values.

Minimization with an Orthogonal Basis of the Cluster Representatives

After we obtain a rank k approximation $A \approx BY$, if the first factor B has orthonormal columns, then the matrix Y by itself can give a good approximation for A in the sense that the correlation of A can be approximated with the correlation of Y:

$$A^T A \approx Y^T B^T B Y = Y^T Y, \quad B^T B = I .$$

In addition, most of the common similarity measures can directly be inherited from the full dimensional space to the reduced dimensional space, since

$$\|y\|_B = \|By\|_2 = \|y\|_2,$$

14

where B has orthonormal columns. Accordingly,

$$Cos(a,q) \approx Cos(B\hat{a}, B\hat{q}) = Cos(\hat{a}, \hat{q})$$

and

$$||a - q||_2 \approx ||B\hat{a} - B\hat{q}||_2 = ||\hat{a} - \hat{q}||_2.$$

Therefore, for comparing two vectors in the reduced space, the matrix B does not need to be involved. No matter how the matrices B and Y are chosen, this can be achieved by computing the reduced QR decomposition of the matrix B if it does not already have orthonormal columns. With the reduced QR decomposition on B,

$$B = QR \quad \text{with} \quad Q \in \mathbb{R}^{m \times k}, R \in \mathbb{R}^{k \times k}.$$

the solution for

$$\min_z ||QZ - A||_F$$

is $Z = Q^T A = RY$ where Y is the solution for

$$\min_Y ||BY - A||_F .$$

In both expressions $A \approx BY$ and $A \approx Q(RY)$, since $BY = QRY$, the error E_d in data approximation is

$$E_d = A - BY = A - AH(H^T A^T AH)^{-1} H^T A^T A,$$

which is in matrix reduction formula. The error in correlation from approximation $A \approx Q(RY) = QZ$ is

$$\begin{aligned} E_c &= A^T A - ZZ^T \\ &= A^T A - Q^T AAQ^T \\ &= A^T A - (A^T AH)(H^T A^T AH)^{-1}(H^T A^T A). \end{aligned}$$

It is interesting to note that when the columns of B are the centroids of the clusters, the columns of the upper triangular matrix R in the reduced QR decomposition of B are the centroids projected through the matrix Q.

Minimization with the Basis of Term-Document Matrix

Now we explain how the LSI with SVD can be explained using our model, and achieve the results in (13) and (14). One solution for the minimization problem (5) can be obtained from the SVD of A as $B = U_k$ and $Y = \Sigma_k V_k^T$. In fact, this is the optimal solution when $l = 2$ or F. Then solving the least squares problem

$$min \ || \ B\hat{q} - q \ ||_2 = min \ || \ U_k \hat{q} - q \ ||_2 \tag{31}$$

we obtain

$$\hat{q} = U_k^T q. \tag{32}$$

This produces the same result as Eqn (13) and shows that the reduced dimension representation of the query vector is the projection of q onto the range space of U_k, $range(U_k)$. In LSI with SVD, $\hat{q}$ is compared with the document vectors in the reduced dimension, which are $\Sigma_k V_k^T$. Note that the columns of $\Sigma_k V_k^T$ are the solution vectors $\hat{y}_i$ that we would obtain from solving

$$\min_y \| U_k y - a_i \|_2 \tag{33}$$

for $1 \leq i \leq n$.

Using our minimization model, it can easily be shown that the representation for $\hat{q}$ in Eqn (14) is the solution for

$$\min_y \| U_k \Sigma_k \hat{y} - q \|_2, \tag{34}$$

therefore, in this case, the matrix B is considered to be $\Sigma_k U_k$ and accordingly, the document vectors in the reduced dimension are the columns of V_k^T. (This is when the SVD for rank k reduction is factored into $U_k \Sigma_k$ and V_k^T). Our derivation also makes it possible for any similarity measure such as cosine and L_2 norm to be used in comparing the vectors in the reduced dimension, and it is not restricted only to the inner product for similarity measure as in the original derivation.

The LSI with SVD shows by experiment that the dimension between 100 to 300 gives best performance in text retrieval systems [2]. Considering the size of the text documents these days, even this range of 100 to 300 seems to be quite a dramatic reduction of the dimension. In fact, the reduced dimension will rarely be the numerically estimated dimension of the original data, unlike in the majority of signal processing applications where the SVD is often utilized.

3 Experimental Results

In this section, we present several experimental test results that illustrate advantages of the methods we presented in earlier sections, as well as comparison of our centroid based methods to the SVD based method in classification. A few small test results we present are performed in MATLAB. We also have built our own information retrieval test bed system (BIRDS) which was used for tests (Figure 1).

The main purpose of the BIRDS is to flexibly test and compare various methods of weighting, dimension reduction, similarity measure, as well as classification, clustering and document retrieval algorithms. To make this possible, it is designed so that each module presented in Figure 1 can be incorporated into other modules seamlessly. Our information retrieval system consists of four main parts, Graphical user interface(GUI), text preprocessor, clustering and classification, and retrieval system. Currently preprocessor, classification, and retrieval system are complete, and GUI and what is marked with the dotted line in Figure 1 are being constructed.

16

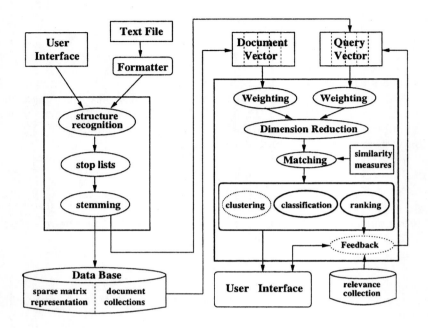

Figure 1. *Basic Information Retrieval Development System(BIRDS)*

In the preprocessor unit, data documents are converted to a file with words and frequencies, and other statistics like the total number of words (dimension), and total number of documents. In the preprocessing stage some words such as *the, a,* etc. which are called stop words and appear in almost every document, are eliminated, since they are not considered as important words for differentiating documents from each other. Other meaningful words are processed into stems to reduce vector dimension and increase the recall of document retrieval. For example, *computer, computation,* and *computing* are processed into one stem word like *comput* by a certain stemming algorithm. In our preprocessing stage, Porter's algorithm [12] is applied.

In the first very small test, the objective was to check how well classification in the reduced space by LS with centroids (Centroid) performs compared to that in the full space. The data set is such that the items 1 to 4 belong to cluster A, items 5 to 11 belong to cluster B, and the rest belong to cluster C. In Table 1, the first column represents the item number, and the columns with L_2 and *cosine* show the distance between the item and the centroid of each cluster computed with L_2 norm and cosine measures in the reduced space of dimension 3, respectively. The smaller L_2 norm or the larger cosine value means that the item is closer to that class. The test shows that the classification in the reduced space reproduced the result in full space, exactly.

In the next experiment, three data sets are tested using L_2 norm and cosine measures, and using the dimension reduction methods by least squares with centroid

item	with class A		with class B		with class C	
	L_2	cosine	L_2	cosine	L_2	cosine
1	0.09	0.999	1.48	0.000	1.49	0.000
2	0.25	0.967	1.55	0.000	1.31	0.000
3	0.19	0.981	1.27	0.000	1.45	0.000
4	0.05	0.998	1.37	0.000	1.42	0.000
5	1.45	0.032	0.12	0.997	1.53	0.000
6	1.28	0.180	0.18	0.984	1.40	0.000
7	1.66	0.000	0.27	0.975	1.44	0.000
8	1.21	0.143	0.22	0.983	1.23	0.000
9	1.58	0.000	0.18	0.992	1.56	0.000
10	1.29	0.000	0.24	0.993	1.19	0.000
11	1.44	0.044	0.16	0.991	1.57	0.000
12	1.49	0.000	1.48	0.000	0.09	1.000
13	1.35	0.078	1.44	0.000	0.09	0.996
14	1.36	0.000	1.31	0.073	0.10	0.997
15	1.58	0.000	1.59	0.000	0.22	0.993
16	1.29	0.093	1.25	0.155	0.19	0.983

Table 1. *Distance between an item and the cluster centroids in the reduced space of dimension 3 using L_2 and cosine measure*

(Centroid) and least square with the orthogonal factor in the QR decomposition of the centroids (CentroidQR).

For the first data set, three data sets from the SMART system are chosen from documents of computer and information science (ADI) with 82 documents, aerospace engineering (CRANFIELD) with 1400 documents, and medical science (MEDLINE) with 1033 documents.

The second data set consists of 5 categories, which are all from the MEDLINE database. Each category has 500 documents, and the total number of terms are 22,095 after preprocessing with stopping and stemming algorithm. The categories have many common words related to a cancer.

The last data set is an extension of the second data set to 8 categories of MEDLINE data. Like the second data set, 500 documents are chosen from each category, and the total number of terms (dimension of system) is 29,152 (see Table 2) .. In this test, our algorithms (Centroid and CentroidQR) are verified by self-classification again, and two different similarity measures are examined to determine which measure is more appropriate for classifying electronic text data. By self-classification we mean that classification results are already known, and we classify all data in the classes, and verify they are classified into correct classes. Classifying new data is just an extension of this procedure. The test procedure is exactly the same as that in the previous test.

The test results are shown in Table 3, where we compare the classification results based on comparison of each document to the centroid in the full space, and

No	Data set A category	Data set B category	Data set C category
1	ADI	heart attack	heart attack
2	CRANFIELD	colon cancer	colon cancer
3	MEDLINE	diabetes	diabetes
4		oral cancer	oral cancer
5		tooth decay	tooth decay
6			prostate cancer
7			breast cancer
8			diet weight loss
Full Dimension	12140×2515 $(82+1400+1033)$	22095×2500 (500 / categ.)	29152×4000 (500 / categ.)

Table 2. *Input data sets*

	Data set A (in %)		
	Full	Centroid	CentroidQR
Dimension	12140×2515	3×2515	3×2515
L_2	10.97	3.14	10.97
Cosine	1.59	3.14	1.59
	Data set B (in %)		
	Full	Centroid	CentroidQR
Dimension	22095×2500	5×2500	5×2500
L_2	11.76	8.52	11.76
Cosine	7.80	8.52	7.80
	Data set C (in %)		
	Full	Centroid	CentroidQR
Dimension	29152×2500	8×2500	8×2500
L_2	22.62	16.63	22.62
Cosine	16.00	16.63	16.00

Table 3. *Misclassification Rate*

also in two reduced dimensional spaces, one obtained by projection through the centroids, and the other obtained by projection through the orthogonal factor in the reduced QR decomposition of the centroids. We also compared the performance of the different similarity measures, L_2 norm and cosine measures.

In all three cases of data sets, the classification with the cosine measure performed better. This is consistent with other substantial test results we obtained comparing several similarity measures in text processing [22]. As shown earlier, since the result of cosine and L_2 norm measures becomes the same when in the reduced space obtained by the centroids, the classification in the reduced space

reduced dim	Centroid (in %)		CentroidQR (in %)		SVD (in %)	
	self	new	self	new	self	new
5	2.0	17.0	3.5	16	25.5	27.5
10					10.5	19.5
20					6.5	17
50					6.0	16.5
100					6.0	14.5
200					3.5	15.5
full(7519)					3.5	16.0

Table 4. *Misclassification Rate. Training data set of* 7519×200, *and new data set of* 7519×200, *are classified*

appears to outperform that in the full space, when L_2 norm is used.

The classification result for the data set A is better than that for two other data sets due to the fact that the clusters in data set A are almost disjoint, while the data set B and C have more and more documents that may belong to more than one cluster.

Another interesting fact is that the results in the full space and the reduced space obtained by CentroidQR were identical when the classification is achieved by simply comparing the document to the centroids. We have observed the same phenomenon in several other tests.

The last experiment was conducted on the small set of MEDLINE database to compare the performance of Centroid, CentroidQR, and SVD based reduction methods with the cosine measure. In this test, there are 5 clusters like in data set B. The training set of 200 documents from 5 clusters were used in computing the centroids. The classification of the training data set in the reduced space was compared and presented under the columns denoted as *self*. In addition, 200 new documents were classified.

It is remarkable that in all our tests, even though the dimension reduction is quite severe, the two centroid based methods presented in this paper works extremely well. On the other hand, when the dimension reduction is severe, the SVD based method is far inferior to the others at the dimension. However, as the reduced dimension is increased, the performance of the SVD based method increases.

4 Future Research

Although our experimental test results clearly illustrate that the new approaches proposed in this paper are promising, there are several questions yet to be answered. We have illustrated our new dimension reduction model and its use for clustered data assuming that the data have already been clustered and the reduced dimension is the same as the number of clusters. An important question which remains to be answered, is the choice of the clustering algorithm when the data set is not already clustered as well as the reduced dimension k. In terms of reducing the computational complexity, the smaller k is the better. However, severe reduction in dimension may cause loss of information in the original data, and the optimal choice of the dimension needs to be determined.

Our scheme fixes reduced dimension k as the number of clusters. If a different value of k is desired, the existing clusters can either be combined or further clustered to decrease or increase the values k, respectively.

In the matrix B that consists of the centroids of the clusters, we assumed that B has full column rank. This assumption cannot be guaranteed although we have not experienced any counter example in practice. Especially when the number of the clusters is relatively small compared to the full dimension, the matrix B was always well conditioned. Two important components of a modern information system are retrieval and classification. Our current paper shows only classification results, and we plan to report retrieval in reduced space in the future. For the similarity measure of distance, this time only the 2 or F norm is used due to its computational simplicity, but we will investigate the effect of different a norm such as medoid, in future research.

Acknowledgement The work of the first author was conducted in part when she was visiting Department of Mathematics, Linkoping University, Linkoping, Sweden, during August, 2000. She would like to thank the department and Professor Lars Elden for their kind invitation to visit the department. She would also like to thank Professor Gene Golub who was also visiting the department in August, for valuable discussions and the references which made this work more interesting.

Bibliography

[1] M. R. ANDERBER, <u>Cluster Analysis for Applications</u>, Academic Press, New York and London, 1973.

[2] M.W. BERRY, S.T. DUMAIS, AND G.W. O'BRIEN, *Using Linear Algebra for Intelligent Information Retrieval*, SIAM Review 37:573-595, 1995.

[3] M.W. BERRY, Z. DRMAČ, AND E.R. JESSUP, *Matrices, Vector Spaces, and Information Retrieval*, SIAM Review 41:335-362, 1999.

[4] M.W. BERRY, R.D. FIERRO, *Low-Rank Orthogonal Decompositions for Information Retrieval Applications*, Numerical Linear Algebra with Applications 1:1-27, 1996.

[5] A. BJÖRCK, *Numerical Methods for Least Squares Problems.* SIAM, Philadelphia, PA, 1996.

[6] J.R. COLON AND S.J. COLON, *Optimal Use of an Information Retrieval System*, J. of the American Society of Information Science 47(6):449-457, 1996.

[7] M.T. CHU, R.E. FUNDERLIC, AND G.H. GOLUB, *A Rank-Reduction Formula and its Applications to Matrix Factorizations*, SIAM Review 37:512-530, 1995.

[8] R.E. CLINE AND R.E. FUNDERLIC, *The Rank of a Difference of Matrices and Associated Generalized Inverses*, Linear Algebra Appl. 24:185-215, 1979.

[9] S. DEERWESTER, S.T. DUMAIS, G.W. FURNAS, T.K. LANDAUER, AND R. HARSHMAN, *Indexing by Latent Semantic Analysis*, J. of the Society for Information Science 41:391-407, 1990.

[10] I. S. DHILLON, *Concept Decompositions for Large Sparse Text Data using Clustering*, IBM Research Report, RJ 10147, 1999.

[11] S.T. DUMAIS, *Improving the Retrieval of Information from External Sources*, Behavior Research Methods, Instruments, & Computers 23:229-236, 1991.

[12] W.B. FRAKES AND R. BAEZA-YATES <u>Information Retrieval, Data Structures and Algorithms</u>, Prentice Hall PTR, 1992.

[13] M.D. GORDON, *Using Latent Semantic Indexing for Literature Based Discovery*, J. of the American Society for Information Science 49(8):674-685, 1998.

[14] G.H. Golub and C.F. Van Loan. *Matrix Computations*, third edition. Johns Hopkins University Press, Baltimore, 1996.

[15] E. Gose, R. Johnsonbaugh and S. Jost. Pattern Recognition and Image Analysis. *Prentice Hall Ptr*, 1996.

[16] L. GUTTMAN, *A Necessary and Sufficient Formula for Matrix Factoring*, Psychometrika 22:79-81, 1957.

[17] S. HARTER, *Psychological Relevance and Information Science*, J. of the American Society of Information Science 43(9):602-615, 1992.

[18] H.S. HEAPS, Information Retrieval, Computational and Theoretical Aspects, Academic Press, 1978.

[19] L. HUBERT, J. MEULMAN, AND W. HEISER, *Two Purposes for Matrix Factorization: A Historical Appraisal*, SIAM Review 429(1):68-82, 2000.

[20] A.K. JAIN, AND R.C. DUBES, Algorithms for Clustering Data, Prentice Hall, 1988.

[21] Y. JUNG, H. PARK, AND D. DU, *An Effective Term-Weighting Scheme for Information Retrieval*, Technical Report TR00-008. Department of Computer Science and Engineering, University of Minnesota.

[22] Y. JUNG, H. PARK, AND D. DU, *A Balanced Term-Weighting Scheme for Improved Document Comparison and Classification*, preprint.

[23] G. KOWALSKI, Information Retrieval System: Theory and Implementation, Kluwer Academic Publishers, 1997.

[24] T. G. KOLDA, *Limited-Memory Matrix Methods with Applications*, Dissertation, Applied Mathematics, University of Maryland, 1997.

[25] T. G. KOLDA AND D. P. O'LEARY, *A Semi-Discrete Matrix Decomposition for Latent Semantic Indexing in Information Retrieval*, ACM Transactions on Information Systems, 1996.

[26] R. KROVETZ AND W.B. CROFT, *Lexical Ambiguity and Information Retrieval*, ACM Transactions on Information Systems 10(2):115-241, 1992.

[27] M. NADLER AND E.P. SMITH, Pattern Recognition Engineering, John Wiley & Sons, 1993.

[28] A.M. PEJTERSEN, *Semantic Information Retrieval*, Communications of the ACM 41(4):90-92, 1998.

[29] J.B. ROSEN, H. PARK, AND J. GLICK, *Total Least Norm Formulation and Solution for Structured Problems*, SIAM Journal on Matrix Anal. Appl. 17(1):110-128, 1996.

[30] G. SALTON, The SMART Retrieval System, Prentice Hall, 1971.

[31] G. SALTON, AND M.J. MCGILL, Introduction to Modern Information Retrieval, McGraw-Hill, 1983.

[32] S. THEODORIDIS AND K. KOUTROUSMBAS, Pattern Recognition, Academic Press, 1999

[33] D. ZHANG, R. RAMAKRISHAN, AND M. LIVNY, *An Efficient Data Clustering Method for Very Large Databases*, Proc. of the ACM SIGMOD conference on management of data, Montreal, Canada, June 1996.

Information Retrieval and Classification with Subspace Representations

Fredrick B. Holt and Yuan-Jye Jason Wu[*]

1   Introduction

In this report, we describe our recent achievement on information retrieval from a text data collection. For the purpose of current discussion, a *document* means a unit of free text (or semi-structured text). This body of free text might actually be the entire content of a document, or some delimited portion of it, such as the title or summary, or it might also be a paragraph within some document, or the contents of a structured field. It can be text generated from images, graphics or audio/video objects, with a certain level of errors. Our method also handles both static and dynamic collections of text data effectively.

A *term* typically is a single word. However, it can also consist of several words that are commonly used together as a fixed phrase in the domain. For example, we might want to treat *landing gear* as one term and not two. Terms might also be obtained by acronym and abbreviation expansion, word stemming, spelling normalization, or from a list of synonyms of words found in the document. While terms typically consist of letters, a term may also contain numbers and symbols such as hyphens or slashes depending on the application.

A *vector space model* [10, 8] of a text data collection is represented by a sparse non-negative $t \times d$ matrix D in which each of the t rows corresponds to a term, each of the d columns corresponds to a document in the collection, and the ij^{th} entry of D is the raw count of the occurrences of the ith term in the jth document. Some sequence of pre-processing or indexing steps is typically applied to this raw data

[*]The Boeing Company P.O. Box 3707, M/S 7L-21, Seattle, WA 98124. E-mail: {fred.b.holt,jason.wu}@boeing.com.

matrix D to form a more useful term-document matrix.

In the context of representing a text data collection in a vector space, Boeing's text mining technology TRUST [2] (*T*ext *R*epresentation *U*sing *S*ubspace *T*ransformation) provides a subspace interpretation of Latent Semantic Indexing (LSI) beyond the traditional principal components analysis [3, 1]. The LSI has traditionally been identified with the singular value decomposition. In the TRUST technology, we obtain a *subspace representation* for the term-document matrix via a two-sided orthogonal matrix decomposition. However, we emphasize the importance of the concept of a subspace representation regardless of the particular numerical methods used.

Furthermore, queries for information retrieval are traditionally treated as pseudo-documents in any method based on a vector space model [4, 5, 9]. We have discovered that a vector-space model naturally admits two types of queries, each with different properties.

The report is organized as follows: In Section 2, we describe a general definition of subspace representation for a term-document matrix. We then introduce two types of queries, *query-by-example* and *query-by-keyword* in Section 3. A new term weighting factor for queries is given in Section 4. In Section 5, we show some preliminary experimental results. Finally, in Section 6, we show how to extend this method of information retrieval to text classification.

2 Subspace representation

In TRUST, we obtain our $t \times d$ working matrix A by normalizing the columns of matrix D to have unit sum, stabilizing the variance of terms via a nonlinear function, and then centering with respect to the mean vector of the columns. Hence we abbreviate our current preprocessing as $A = f(D) - ce^T$ in which c is the mean vector and e is a d-vector all of whose components are 1, so that the average of the columns of A is now $\mathbf{0}$. Each ij^{th} entry in A is a score indicating the relative occurrence of the ith term in the jth document. We use f to indicate the preprocessing applied either to D or to a single document vector. Traditionally, f is defined as a two-sided weighting function, i.e.,

$$f(D) = (W_t D)W_d, \tag{1}$$

where W_t and W_d are two diagonal scaling matrices for weighting terms and documents respectively. In our applications, we apply

$$f(D) = \sin^{-1}(\text{sqrt}(DW_d)) \tag{2}$$

without row-scaling factor W_t. In Section 4 we will introduce row-scaling when evaluating queries; the advantages of this approach will be addressed then.

To capture some of the semantics latent in this corpus of documents, we use an orthogonal decomposition of A to obtain a rank-k $t \times d$ matrix A_k approximating A. Our discussion will work explicitly with the truncated URV decomposition (TURV) [7]. Thus the discussion applies directly to both LSI and TRUST, and the material extends easily beyond this to other matrix decompositions.

The foundation for TURV is the Lanczos iteration and two-sided orthogonal decomposition. For a given dimension k, the TURV computes bases of salient subspaces (matrices U_k and V_k with orthonormal columns) satisfying the equation

$$AV_k = U_k R_k, \tag{3}$$

where R_k is a triangular matrix of order k. Then an approximate term-document matrix A_k is defined as

$$A_k \equiv U_k R_k V_k^T. \tag{4}$$

For the approximation A_k, just as for A, each row corresponds to a term and each column corresponds to a document. The ij^{th} entry of A_k provides a relative occurrence of the ith term in the jth document, but this relative occurrence has now been filtered by the approximation which, by design, tries to capture semantics latent in the corpus. The factor U_k captures variation in vocabulary while the factor V_k^T brings out latent structure in the corpus of documents.

Coming from orthogonal decompositions, these rank-k approximations have natural maps associated with them. By orthogonality we have

$$\begin{aligned} U_k^T U_k &= I_k, & U_k U_k^T &= P_t, \\ V_k^T V_k &= I_k, & V_k V_k^T &= P_d, \end{aligned}$$

in which I_k is the identity matrix of order k and P_t and P_d are projection matrices for the k dimensional subspaces $\mathcal{R}(U_k)$ and $\mathcal{R}(V_k)$, respectively. Note that the projections P_t and P_d are not independent of each other. For example, in (3), we first compute matrix V_k such that AV_k has rank k, hence the projection P_d is defined. Then columns of U_k are computed as an orthonormal basis for the k dimensional subspace $\mathcal{R}(AV_k)$. Therefore, the projections P_t are constrained to project any vector x in the subspace $\mathcal{R}(AV_k)$ onto itself, i.e., $P_t x = x$. A similar constraint applies to P_d if the TURV is set to satisfy

$$U_k^T A = R_k V_k^T \tag{5}$$

instead of (3). Furthermore, with the projection P_d, we could redefine A_k in (4) as a *subspace representation* of A by $A_k \equiv AP_d$, or in (5) by $A_k \equiv P_t A$.

3 Keyword and document queries

One of the primary goals of any representation of a corpus is that it be searchable. We would like to submit a query and have returned to us those documents which are most relevant to the given query. In traditional vector-space as well as LSI approaches [8, 3, 6], a query is treated as a pseudo-document and could be represented as a vector q of length t. Like columns of the corpus matrix D, each component of q records the occurrence of the correspondent term in the query. A query could be another document, like those in the original corpus, or it may contain just a few terms called keywords.

Suppose that we have A_k, a subspace representation of A. Mechanically, we wish to compare each document (each column of A_k) to the given query and assign a score based on this comparison, i.e., calculating a $1 \times d$ score vector s as

$$s = \delta(P_t(f(q) - c), A_k), \qquad (6)$$

where δ is a measurement function applied to $P_t(f(q) - c)$ and each column of A_k. Traditionally, δ could be inner product, cosine of angle, or Euclidean distance of vectors. Then a sorting process will return several of the best scoring documents as the most relevant documents (to this query, given this scoring function).

It can be shown that for some traditional choices for δ, the projection P_t won't alter the sorting result. For example, since $P_t^T = P_t$ and $P_t A_k = A_k$, the score resulting from inner product is not changed if we remove P_t in (6). Therefore, it is more common to define the score-vector as

$$s = \delta(f(q) - c, A_k).$$

However, from our observation, this traditional approach does not perform satisfactorily on queries with keywords. We have identified two conditions which can undermine any system which naively treats a query with keywords as a pseudo-document. A query vector resulting from few keywords contains only few nonzero components; hence, distance calculations δ may be polluted by each document's entries for terms that are *not* of interest. When a user queries by terms, the terms not present in the queries should be treated as *don't care*. However, when queries are treated as pseudo-documents, it is assumed that the proportion of term frequencies in the query is significant, and the absence of certain terms means those terms should occur below average in the returned documents. Also, if there is more than one keyword, the distance calculations may penalize a document for disproportionate use of the keywords. In our experiments we witnessed both of these effects. The problem is not finding a different δ but instead treating such kind of queries differently. In this report, we propose to distinguish these two types of queries, query-by-example and query-by-keyword, associated with different scoring methods.

3.1 Query-by-example

A query-by-example or document-query ranks the columns of A_k by a score which reflects each column's proximity to a given query vector in term space. If the inner product is chosen as the function δ in (6), the score vector is similar to rows of $A_k^T A_k$ which is commonly used for document-document analysis. If the columns of A_k have roughly equal norm – often the columns are normalized to unit length or unit sum to compensate for document length – then this inner product is essentially calculating the cosine of the angular separation.

For a raw query vector q to be a pseudo-document, it must be comparable to the current projection of the corpus, the columns of A_k, and so q must pass through the preprocessing steps. Not only must it pass through the map f, but in particular, the query-by-example must be centered in the same way the other documents were.

3.2 Query-by-keyword

A query-by-keyword or term-query ranks the columns of A_k by a score ranking each column by the magnitude of its entries in the rows indicated by the keywords. A term-query is given by a short list of keywords. Its vector is usually much simpler, consisting of few nonzero entries. Despite some heuristics to distinguish extreme cases, it suffices at this time to leave to users the decision whether to process a query as document-like or keyword-like.

While a document-query requires a document-document comparison, a term-query focuses on a term-document relationship. As we mentioned before, the approximation A_k has already accounted for the semantics latent in the corpus. Thus, if we want a score vector for a term-query consisting a single term, we could directly pick out the corresponding row of A_k and read off the entries as scores for the documents. This process suggests a different scoring formula from (6) for document-query since we apply neither the preprocessing function f nor the centering to the query vector.

The term-query is treated as a selection of terms rather than as a document. For queries on multiple keywords, we first pick out those rows of A_k corresponding to the keywords. The question that remains is how to synthesize these rows into a score vector.

4 Query weighting factors

Having identified two distinct types of queries, we turn our attention below primarily to the term-query. One of the most notable differences between the term-query and the document-query is that the term-query looks directly at the rows of the approximation A_k to exploit the latent semantics captured in this subspace representation, while a query-by-example is brought explicitly into the same subspace populated by the projections of the other documents.

Suppose that we have a subspace representation A_k. Without loss of generality, we assume that a given query only contains two keywords, term i and term j, with equal importance, i.e., the vector $q = e_i + e_j$, where e_i and e_j are the ith and j^{th} unit vectors respectively. The goal in processing this query is to identify those documents in which both terms exist semantically.

The simplest (and traditional) way to form a score vector is to calculate the inner product

$$s = q^T A_k \tag{7}$$
$$= (e_i + e_j)^T A_k$$
$$= a_i + a_j,$$

where a_i and a_j are the ith and j^{th} rows of A_k, respectively. A few experiments reveal that this naive approach is severely flawed by the lack of any row-scaling factor W_t in (2). Without some sort of row-weighting, the terms that are more frequent in this corpus will swamp those terms which appear infrequently.

In one of our examples from work at the Boeing Company, we submitted the keywords **engines** and **idle** to a data set of Boeing Service Bulletins, containing

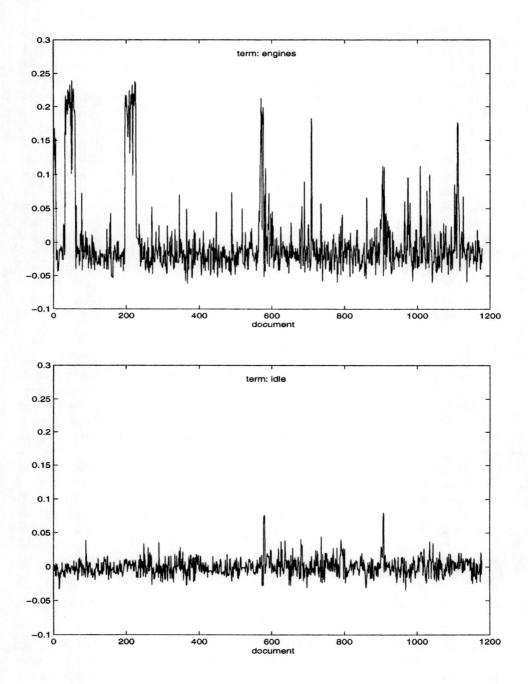

Figure 1. *Component sizes of row a_i (engines) and row a_j (idle). Without some normalization, when both terms occur in a query, e.g.* engines idle, *the term* idle *contributes minimally to the scoring result.*

1178 documents indexed by 3514 terms. Figure 1 shows the component sizes of a_i (term `engines`) and a_j (term `idle`) in one subspace representation of this corpus. Obviously, the entries in a_i will dominate the calculation of the score.

Indeed, this is the reason that the term weighting factor W_t is traditionally included in the preprocessing function f to reduce the impact of high-frequency terms. However, the term weighting factor W_t makes updating (adding new documents to collection) and downdating (removing old documents from collection) algorithms more complicated. This type of weighting scheme is a global weighting. It has to be calculated based on the entire document set. The updating and downdating will thus involve modifications of all the previously represented documents. In addition, the row weighting will change the actual importance of certain terms in a document so that the resulting subspace representation A_k will not be suitable for other applications, such as the assignment of topic words (words automatically generated to summarize a document or group of documents).

Therefore, at the time of querying by keywords we apply term-weighting as a specific compensation for the various frequencies of terms for A_k. This term-weighting is unnecessary in the preprocessing function f, and it complicates the task of maintaining the subspace representation for a dynamic corpus of documents.

Again we emphasize that the approximation A_k has already accounted for the semantics latent in the corpus. It is our intention to use A_k as a surrogate for the raw term-document matrix D in the vector space model. Therefore, we apply the term weighting factor W_t to A_k for information retrieval, i.e., we amend the above score formula (7) as

$$
\begin{aligned}
s &= q^T W_t A_k \\
  &= (e_i + e_j)^T W_t A_k \\
  &= \omega_i a_i + \omega_j a_j,
\end{aligned}
\tag{8}
$$

where $W_t = \mathrm{diag}(\omega_1, \dots, \omega_t)$ is a matrix with row weighting scalars in its diagonal. Traditionally, people use TFIDF (term frequency / inverse document frequency) [9] or log entropy [4, 5] for these weights. Both methods compute the row-weighting scalars based on the raw term-document matrix D. In this report, we suggest first that the weights be calculated from the A_k and also that the following simple calculations be used for the weights:

- inverse infinity norm: $\omega_i = 1/\|a_i\|_\infty$,

- inverse 1-norm: $\omega_i = 1/\|a_i\|_1$,

- inverse 2-norm: $\omega_i = 1/\|a_i\|_2$.

Since our W_t is computed based on A_k directly, these row-weighting scalars are easy to maintain, and no extra work is required during updating and downdating.

Geometrically, we can project the documents down to the 2-D plane spanned by the ith and j^{th} terms, i.e., a_i and a_j are x- and y-coordinate of documents, respectively. The scoring method using inner product could be interpreted as a line with slope -1 that moves from the far upper-right corner to the lower-left one. The

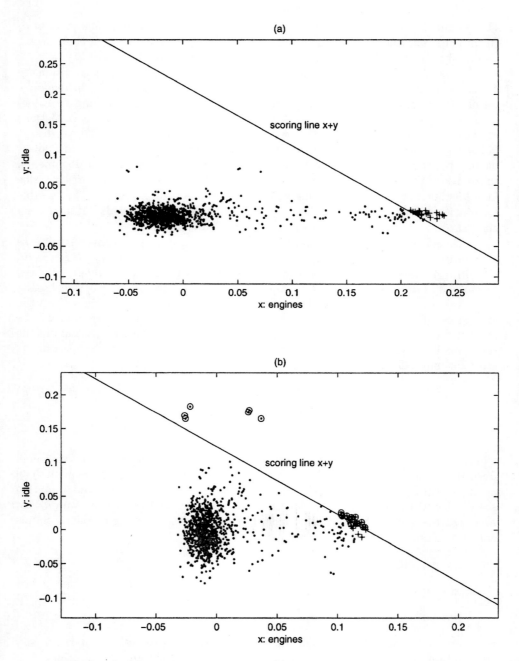

Figure 2. *Document projections are marked with '•'. Scoring line stops after passing 20 documents. (a) On unweighted plane, top 20 picks are marked with '+'. (b) On weighted plane, previous top 20 are still marked with '+', and the new top 20 picks are marked with '○'.*

sorting result is equivalent to the order in which the documents are touched by this moving line.

Figure 2 illustrates how our weighting scalars work. All projected documents are initially represented by '•'. In Figure 2(a), we mark the top 20 documents resulting from unweighted scores with '+', and draw the scoring line where it has separated these first 20 documents from the rest of the corpus. In Figure 2(b), we again mark those top 20 for the unweighted score with '+' for reference, but we now apply term-weights (in this example we used the inverse 2-norm) and mark the top 20 documents for this weighted score with 'o'. It is clear that our weighting scalars boost the contribution of a_j, giving it parity with a_i. We will examine these results in the next section.

The above framework extends immediately to handle queries containing more than two keywords and advanced queries in which the keywords are assigned weights indicating their relative importance to the user. One will see that the equations (7, 8) have a quite general expression.

5 Experimental results

In this section, we will demonstrate the performance of our new query categorization and weighting factor. The text corpus is from Boeing Service Bulletin data and contains 1178 unique documents indexed on 3514 terms. Each document consists of two parts: subject and body. We applied preprocessing and indexing only to the bodies of the documents, and we obtained a subspace representation A_k via TURV with $k = 55$. The subject lines are used as queries later.

Since A_k is a dense matrix, it is never formed explicitly. Using the matrices R and V and partial rows of U, we compute the rows of A_k when needed. That is, only those rows which correspond to terms in the query are computed and saved for further uses. Thereafter the corresponding weighting scalars ω are calculated.

Rank	engines	engines + idle
1	52	245
2	245	52
3	247	238
4	46	247
5	238	57
6	56	40
7	40	229
8	229	46
9	42	42
10	57	221

Table 1. *The indices for the top 10 documents returned by the unweighted scoring function for the two queries* engines *and* engines+idle.

652 ENGINE FUEL AND CONTROL (XXXX ENGINES) - FUEL CONTROL SYSTEM - MINIMUM IDLE
REVISION

654 ENGINE CONTROL (XXXX ENGINES) - ENGINE IDLE CONTROL SYSTEM - INSPECTION

653 ENGINE FUEL AND CONTROL (XXXX ENGINE) - FUEL CONTROL SYSTEM - MINIMUM IDLE
REVISION

656 ENGINE CONTROL (XXXX FADEC ENGINES) - ENGINE IDLE CONTROL SYSTEM - INSPECTION

1022 IGNITION (XXXX ENGINES) - IGNITION GENERAL - ENGINE IGNITION CONTROL - MINIMUM
IDLE REVISION

1023 IGNITION (XXXX ENGINES) - IGNITION GENERAL - ENGINE IGNITION CONTROL - MINIMUM
IDLE REVISION

1024 ENGINE CONTROL (XXXX ENGINES) - ENGINE IDLE CONTROL SYSTEM - INSPECTION

Table 2. *The document indices and subject lines for the documents deemed relevant to the query* engines+idle.

Rank	unweighted score	weighted score	IDF
1	245	**1024**	**1022**
2	52	**656**	240
3	238	**654**	**1024**
4	247	**1023**	**1023**
5	57	**652**	**653**
6	40	**653**	**652**
7	229	**1022**	**654**
8	46	57	39
9	42	238	236
10	221	221	**656**

Table 3. *The document indices for the top 10 returns to the query* engines+idle *by three different methods. The 7 relevant documents are indicated by the boldface indices.*

We first test the unweighted scoring method with two queries,

- {engines(566)} and
- {engines(566), idle(76)},

in which the numbers indicate the raw term frequencies in the collection. From Table 1 we see that the lists of the top 10 documents returned by these two queries are almost identical. There is some difference in the order of the documents, but the keyword **engines** clearly dominates the result. The data tabulated here is illustrated in Figure 2(a).

Next we tested the unweighted and weighted scoring functions on the query {engines(566), idle(76)}. By manual screenings, we found that 7 documents are most relevant to this query. Table 2 shows the document ID's and subject lines of these 7 relevant documents. In Table 3, we list the top 10 picks returned from using unweighted scoring method and inverse 2-norm weighted scoring method. For comparison, we also generated a subspace representation for term-document matrix resulting from applying traditional two-sided weighting function (1) with IDF term weighting factor. The top 10 picks using unweighted scoring methods on this IDF weighted matrix are also given. The weighted score returns all 7 relevant documents (marked with boldface) in top 7 picks and has better performance than the other two methods. This example of using inverse 2-norm row-weighting on the term-query is illustrated in Figure 2(b).

For our next query we chose the following subject line:

```
airplane general - airplane systems modification for high
altitude airfield operation - JT-XXXX series engines.
```

Removing stop words (*airplane* is considered a stop word in this domain), we have the following 10 keywords.

JT(957)	high(168)
engines(566)	altitude(89)
operation(272)	general(51)
modification(250)	series(23)
systems(220)	airfield(12)

Through manual screenings, we know that documents with ID's 1 to 7 are relevant to this query. Table 4 shows the top 10 picks for inverse 2-norm weighted score and IDF, and marks relevant documents with boldface. Again, weighted score outperforms IDF.

Rank	weighted score	IDF
1	**3**	240
2	**6**	39
3	**4**	236
4	**7**	42
5	**2**	**2**
6	**1**	52
7	**5**	45
8	648	232
9	651	235
10	56	43

Table 4. *The document indices for the top 10 returns by two methods to a query consisting of a subject line. The 7 relevant documents are indicated by boldface indices.*

Finally, we used 1026 unique subject lines as queries and defined success if the top 10 picks include their corresponding bodies. The average length of the subject lines is 13.1 words. This time we set subspace dimension $k = 100$ and compared the query-by-example with three different weighted scoring methods. Table 5 gives total numbers of successful queries and rates. In general, weighted scores give better results.

Method	successful queries	success rate
query-by-example	741	72.2%
inverse infinity-norm	843	82.2%
inverse one-norm	846	82.5%
inverse two-norm	856	83.4%

Table 5. *Results for 1026 queries by unique subject lines. A query is successful if the document body was in the top 10 returns for the query on its subject-line.*

6 Text Classification

In this section we will show how the query-by-keyword method can be extended to text classification.

Text classification, also known as text categorization, is a text mining application which classifies or categorizes a new document into one or more of a set of pre-defined classes or categories based on a set of training examples that have already been classified. All classification applications require that

- there is a set of pre-defined classes, and

- there is training data consisting of samples of data for each class.

The query-by-keyword method we presented above can be directly applied in text classification. In this case, in addition to a term-document matrix D from the training data, we need a document-class matrix B whose ijth entry is one if the ith document is assigned to the jth class or zero otherwise. Then we obtain a term-class matrix C, where

$$C = D * B.$$

Note that each class is essentially constructed by concatenating all the documents in the training data which belong to that class (a sort of *super-document*).

After preprocessing and computing a subspace representation C_k, the features of each class are represented by term frequencies in the class, as in the case of information retrieval. To classify a new document, we do a query-by-keyword against this transformed term-by-class matrix C_k using the new document as the query. This document is assigned to each class for which its score is above some threshold.

Preliminary experiments show good returns similar to those for information retrieval, and we are in the process of designing a threshold for this approach.

7 Conclusion

In this report, we first defined a subspace representation of a text corpus and elaborated the relationship between term and document projections. Second, we identified two distinct types of queries, query-by-example and query-by-keyword, and the different processing required in scoring these. Third, we proposed several new weighting factors to make the scoring process more accurate and more efficient. Finally, we explained how to extend this method of information retrieval to text classification. We have presented this material within a systematic view of vector-space methods: corpus preprocessing, subspace representations, queries and scoring methods.

Among our next steps will be further comparisons of the weighting factors, experiments with scoring methods other than inner product, an implementation of Boolean operators in our keyword queries, and design of threshold for text classification.

Acknowledgements

We thank the Boeing Large Text Analysis team for supporting this research. We offer our appreciation to Steve Poteet and Grace Cho in particular for running experiments on our behalf.

Bibliography

[1] M.W. BERRY, S. DUMAIS, AND G. O'BRIEN, *Using Linear Algebra for Intelligent Information Retrieval*, SIAM Review 37(4):573-595, 1995.

[2] A. BOOKER, M. CONDLIFF, M. GREAVES, F.B. HOLT, A. KAO, D.J. PIERCE, S. POTEET, AND Y.-J.J. WU, *Visualizing Text Data Sets*, Computing in Science & Engineering 1(4):26-35, 1999.

[3] S. DEERWESTER, S. DUMAIS, G.W. FURNAS, T.K. LANDAUER, AND R. HARSHMAN, *Indexing by Latent Semantic Analysis*, Journal of the American Society for Information Science 41(6):391-407, 1990.

[4] S. DUMAIS, *Improving the Retrieval of Information from External Sources*, Behavior Research Methods, Instrument, & Computers 23:229-236, 1991.

[5] W.B. FRAKES AND R. BAEZA-YATES, Information Retrieval: Data Structures and Algorithms, Prentice-Hall, Englewood Cliffs, NJ, 1992.

[6] T. KOLDA AND D.P. O'LEARY, *A Semi-Discrete Matrix Decomposition for Latent Semantic Indexing in Information Retrieval*, ACM Transactions on Information Systems 16:322-346, 1998.

[7] D. J. PIERCE AND Y.-J. J. WU, *Incomplete URV for Data Analysis*, Shared Service Group Report SSGTECH-98-009, the Boeing Company, 1998.

[8] G. SALTON, editor. The Smart Retrieval System–Experiments in Automatic Document Processing, Prentice-Hall, Englewood Cliffs, NJ, 1971.

[9] G. SALTON AND C. BUCKLEY, *Term Weighting Approaches in Automatic Text Retrieval*, Information Processing and Management 24:513-523, 1988.

[10] G. SALTON, A. WONG, AND C.S. YANG, *A Vector Space Model for Information Retrieval*, Journal for the American Society for Information Retrieval 18(11):613-620, 1975.

Information Retrieval Using Very Short Krylov Sequences

Katarina Blom and Axel Ruhe[*]

1 Introduction

The task is to search among the *documents* in a large data base for those that contain information of interest stated in a *query*. We summarize the contents of the data base as an $m \times n$ *term document* matrix X, where each column represents one document and each row one *term*, in the simplest case just a specific word. An element x_{ik} is nonzero whenever term i is present in document k.

The query is now q, an m vector of terms, and we may form the scalar product

$$p^T = q^T X \tag{1}$$

to get p a *choice vector* whose nonzero elements indicate which of the documents that contain any of the terms in the query.

This is the way one looks at it in the *vector space methods* of information retrieval [9], each document is regarded as a column vector x_k in m space and the query q is another. In the simplest case, we retrieve those documents k whose angle to the query is smallest, say that we take those for which the cosine

$$c_k = \cos \angle(q, x_k) = \frac{q^T x_k}{\|q\|_2 \|x_k\|_2}$$

is largest.

[*]Department of Mathematics, Chalmers Institute of Technology and the University of Göteborg, S-41296 Göteborg, Sweden. Email: {blom,ruhe}@math.chalmers.se. Support to the first author from Chalmers University Graduate Students Travel Fund and to the second from the Royal Society for Arts and Sciences in Göteborg is gratefully acknowledged.

39

2 Latent Semantic Indexing

The Latent Semantic Indexing (LSI) method has become rather well established, see the works of Berry, Dumais et. al. [8, 1, 4]! Its aim is to find the global structure in the data by computing the leading part of the singular value decomposition of the term document matrix,

$$X = U\Sigma V^T$$

containing the r leading components and look at

$$X^{(r)} = U_r \Sigma_{rr} V_r^T \, . \tag{2}$$

Here we let the superscript in $X^{(r)}$ signify that we take a rank r matrix of full size, $m \times n$, while subscripts like U_r mean that we take the r first columns of U and double subscripts in Σ_{rr} that we take the leading rows and columns of Σ.

The reason for doing the SVD is that the leading singular vectors contain the global information of the data base, and we filter out local peculiarities as, e.g., spelling errors and nonstandard use of terms.

The rank r is chosen as a much smaller number than m or n, but is still quite large, typically values like $r = 100$ to $r = 300$ are reported. One uses the singular vectors computed to find a choice vector,

$$p^{(r)T} = q^T X^{(r)} = q^T U_r \Sigma_{rr} V_r^T = \left[U_r^T q \right] \left[\Sigma_{rr} V_r^T \right] = \hat{q}_r{}^T \hat{X}_{rn} \, , \tag{3}$$

now with a r dimensional transformed query vector $\hat{q}_r$ and a $r \times n$ transformed term document matrix $\hat{X}_{rn}$, the latter can be regarded as some kind of catalogue of the document collection, where relevant information is gathered.

One can avoid computing this transformed term document matrix $\hat{X}_{rn}$ by instead computing a projected query vector, noting that

$$p^{(r)T} = q^T U_r \Sigma_{rr} V_r^T = q^T U_r U_r^T U_r \Sigma_{rr} V_r^T = \left[U_r U_r^T q \right]^T U_m \Sigma_{mn} V_n^T = \tilde{q}^T X \, , \tag{4}$$

a product between the *projected* query vector $\tilde{q}$ and the *original* term document matrix X.

In LSI, the choices are determined by angles between the transformed query $\hat{q}_r$ and the transformed document vectors $\hat{x}_k$, which is the same as between the projected query $\tilde{q}$ and the projected document vectors $\tilde{x}_k$ in the leading singular subspace spanned by U_r,

$$\tilde{c}_k^1 = \cos(\tilde{q}, \tilde{x}_k) = \frac{p_k^{(r)}}{\|\tilde{q}\|_2 \|\tilde{x}_k\|_2} \, . \tag{5}$$

But we will still need to get all the norms of the projected documents $\tilde{x}_k$.

We may avoid this extra computation, by instead, letting the angles between the *projected* query $\hat{q}_r$ and the *original* documents x_k determine the scoring,

$$\tilde{c}_k^2 = \cos(\tilde{q}, x_k) = \frac{p_k^{(r)}}{\|\tilde{q}\|_2 \|x_k\|_2} \, . \tag{6}$$

This is simpler, since now we only need to compute the norms of the original sparse x_k and can use the simpler multiplication (4) to compute p_k. This simplified choice gives a preference to documents that are closer to the leading singular subspace of the document space X. We will see that this is of advantage when we deal with Krylov subspaces later in this contribution.

One drawback of LSI is that the computation of several hundred singular values of a huge matrix is a rather time consuming task. We also need to store a large amount of singular vectors in the form of real numbers, while the original matrix X is a very sparse matrix of small integers. It is also nontrivial to determine the most appropriate rank r, and changes in the data base. Additions and deletions of terms and documents will require some kind of update of the SVD.

3   Our approach

We have tried a simpler way to find the global information in the data base. Run Lanczos, or more properly the Golub Kahan bidiagonalization algorithm [2, 7], starting with the query vector q, and look at what you can get from the Krylov subspaces thus computed.

Take the normalized query vector q as a start, $q_1 = q/\|q\|$, and compute a bidiagonal representation,

$$X^T Q_j = P_j B_{j,j}^T, \quad X P_j = Q_{j+1} B_{j+1,j} \tag{7}$$

with P and Q orthonormal bases of dimensions indicated by the subscripts and B a lower bidiagonal matrix, see [3, Section 9.3.3].

The bases Q and P are computed, adding one column in each step j using the following:

ALGORITHM BIDIAG
Start with $q_1 = q/\|q\|_2$, $\beta_1 = 0$
For $j = 1, 2, \ldots$ *do*

1. $\alpha_j p_j = X^T q_j - \beta_j p_{j-1}$

2. $\beta_{j+1} q_{j+1} = X p_j - \alpha_j q_j$

End

The quantities α_j and β_{j+1} are computed to give the vectors p_j and q_{j+1} unit Euclidean norm.

After step j we have got the bidiagonal matrix,

$$B_{j+1,j} = \begin{bmatrix} \alpha_1 & 0 & & & 0 \\ \beta_2 & \alpha_2 & 0 & & \\ 0 & \beta_3 & \alpha_3 & & \\ & & \ddots & \ddots & \\ & & & \beta_j & \alpha_j \\ & & & 0 & \beta_{j+1} \end{bmatrix}$$

We can show that P_j is an orthonormal basis of the Krylov subspace $K^j(X^T X, X^T q)$ and Q_j of $K^j(XX^T, q)$. A Krylov space $K^j(A, x)$ is a j dimensional subspace of a starting vector x and successive applications of the matrix operator A to x,

$$K^j(A, x) = \text{span}\left(x, Ax, A^2x, \ldots, A^{j-1}x\right).$$

Interpretation   The columns of Q have the dimension of a kind of query, while those of P can be interpreted as choices among the documents in the collection X. The first column p_1 contains those documents that contain terms in the query, say its brothers and sisters, and the next p_2 can similarly be interpreted as cousins and so on. The number of documents reached will grow in a chain letter fashion, so we can hope that rather few steps j will be sufficient to reach all documents that have any connection to the original query.

Each step j can be interpreted as first applying the current query q_j, in matrix language doing $X^T q_j$, giving a new choice p_j that is strongly different from previous choices. In matrix language, we say that it is orthogonal. Then all terms from the chosen documents are combined in the multiplication Xp_j, to give a new query q_{j+1} strongly different (orthogonal) to all previous queries $q_1, \ldots, q_j$. After j steps we have made j queries to the data base, all of them strongly different from each other. Some readers may remember the children's game "master mind".

Measuring progress   We are interested in the *reached subspace* spanned by all the documents that are combinations of all choices up to step j,

$$XP_j = Q_{j+1}B_{j+1,j} = Q_{j+1}H_{j+1,j}R_{j,j}, \tag{8}$$

where H and R are the results of a QR-factorization of B. Note that H is both orthogonal and Hessenberg, i.e., it is upper triangular with just one subdiagonal added and can be computed as a product of j elementary Givens rotation matrices. The matrices

$$W_j = Q_{j+1}H_{j+1,j}$$

will be orthogonal bases of these interesting subspaces for a sequence of steps j. Let us project the query onto this subspace

$$\tilde{q}^{(j)} = W_j W_j^T q = W_j H_{j+1,j}^T e_1 = W_j \begin{pmatrix} h_{1,1} \\ h_{1,2} \\ \vdots \\ h_{1,j} \end{pmatrix},$$

and we see that the first row of H gives the coordinates of the query in the basis W. When we run several steps j of our algorithm, new columns are added to H, but it is only the last column that is modified.

In step j the distance between the query q and the projected query $\tilde{q}^{(j)}$ is

$$
\begin{aligned}
r^{(j)} &= q - \tilde{q}^{(j)} \\
&= Q_{j+1}e_1 - Q_{j+1}H_{j+1,j}H_{j+1,j}^T e_1 \\
&= Q_{j+1}(I - H_{j+1,j}H_{j+1,j}^T)e_1 \\
&= Q_{j+1}h_{j+1}^{(j)}h_{j+1}^{(j)T}e_1 \\
&= Q_{j+1}h_{j+1}^{(j)}h_{1,j+1}^{(j)}
\end{aligned}
\tag{9}
$$

and its norm is just

$$
\|r^{(j)}\| = |h_{1,j+1}^{(j)}|.
\tag{10}
$$

It decreases as we let j grow, but will not tend to zero unless the query is a linear combination of the documents in X.

We will get a quantity that tends to zero, if we follow the normal equation residual,

$$
\begin{aligned}
X^T r^{(j)} &= X^T Q_{j+1}h_{j+1}^{(j)}h_{1,j+1}^{(j)} \\
&= P_{j+1}B_{j+1,j+1}^T h_{j+1}^{(j)}h_{1,j+1}^{(j)} \\
&= P_{j+1}\begin{pmatrix} B_{j+1,j}^T \\ 0 \quad \alpha_{j+1} \end{pmatrix} h_{j+1}^{(j)}h_{1,j+1}^{(j)} \\
&= P_{j+1}\begin{pmatrix} 0 \\ \alpha_{j+1}h_{j+1,j+1}^{(j)} \end{pmatrix} h_{1,j+1}^{(j)}
\end{aligned}
\tag{11}
$$

which has the norm

$$
\|X^T r^{(j)}\| = |\alpha_{j+1}h_{j+1,j+1}^{(j)}h_{1,j+1}^{(j)}|.
\tag{12}
$$

Scoring documents   There are several possible ways to use the quantities obtained from our algorithm to score documents for relevance with respect to the query q. It is natural to mimic LSI and choose the angles either between the query and documents projected into the reached subspace (5),

$$
c_k^1 = \cos(\tilde{q}, \tilde{x}_k) = \frac{p_k}{\|\tilde{q}\|_2 \|\tilde{x}_k\|_2},
\tag{13}
$$

or between the projected query and the original documents (6),

$$
c_k^2 = \cos(\tilde{q}, x_k) = \frac{p_k}{\|\tilde{q}\|_2 \|x_k\|_2}.
\tag{14}
$$

It is easy to find these from quantities computed in ALGORITHM BIDIAG. Apply an elementary orthogonal transformation $S_{j,j}$ from the right to the Hessenberg matrix $H_{j+1,j}$ so that the resulting $H_{j+1,j}S_{j,j}$ has only its leading element nonzero in the first row. Then $Q_{j+1}H_{j+1,j}S_{j,j}$ is a new basis of the reached subspace. Premultiply the document vector x_k with this basis and,

$$y_k = S_{j,j}^T H_{j+1,j}^T Q_{j+1}^T x_k$$

will give the component of x_k along $\tilde{q}^{(j)}$ as its first coordinate $y_{1,k}$, and the rest of the projected $\tilde{x}_k$ as the norm of the remaining $(y_{2,k}, \ldots, y_{j,k})^T$.

Our experiments have shown that the second choice (14) gave a better precision. We will use this choice as our standard.

4   Illustrations

We have tested our algorithm on several widely circulated test sets coming from a. o. the TREC conferences [6]. Here we choose to report results on the well known MEDLINE collection [5]. It is admittedly a toy problem, but since it has been tested by a wide range of people, it is good for comparison and illustration purposes.

Our original matrix X is of size $m \times n = 7014 \times 1033$, with $x_{ik} = 1$ if term i is present in document k, then no counting of appearances is done. Instead we *scale* the matrix in a way that is natural in the analysis of general data. First all rows are scaled to have Euclidean norm (sum of squares) equal to unity. This is sensible, since it deemphasizes common terms, as is done in most weighting schemes. Then we scale the columns to have unit length. This disturbs the row scaling somehow, but is good for illustration purposes; we get the same length on all vectors and can let the length of a projection tell how close the vector is to a subspace it is projected into. Moreover, we will most often let angles between vectors and spaces determine choices, and those are independent of the length of the vectors. We plot the row (term) and column (document) norms in Figure 1. The lines are the row and column norms in the original matrix X. After the row scaling, all rows have unit norm, so we do not plot them, but we plot the column norms as points in the right plot. After the column scaling, all columns have unit norm, but the rows have the norms indicated by the dots on the left plot. We see that the row norms are no longer strictly equal but reasonably equilibrated.

There are 30 queries supplied with the test matrix, together with indices k of relevant documents for each query. This gives between 9 and 39 relevant documents for each query, altogether 696 documents are relevant to some query and no document is relevant to more than one query. We compare our results to these correct answers, and are interested to know whether any quantities obtained during the computation can be used to determine if a query is a difficult or a simple one to handle with our method.

Let us list results for some typical and interesting queries. First take query 1. It has rather many, 37 relevant documents, and is on the easy side for our algorithm. In Figure 2 we follow the progress in linear algebra terms, as we execute the algorithm for steps $j = 1, \ldots, 12$. Circles are the residual norms $\|r^{(j)}\|$, (10). They decrease unnoticeably slowly from 1 to 0.892. This means that the query q is at a rather large angle to the reached subspace, and has a projection of length 0.451. We plot the normal equation residuals $\|X^T r^{(j)}\|$, (12), as pluses, and note that they

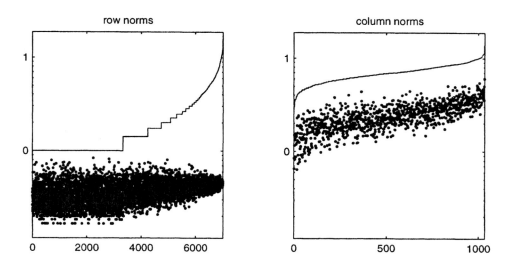

Figure 1. *Medline matrix row and column norms, before and after scaling. Sorted before scaling.*

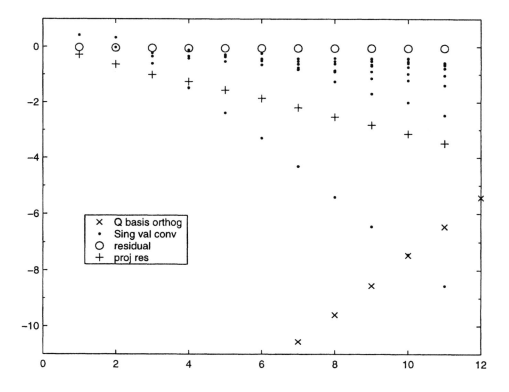

Figure 2. *Medline matrix, follow convergence of bidiagonalization procedure.*

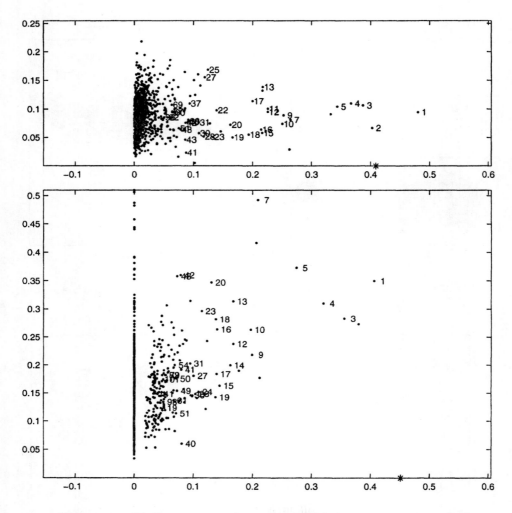

Figure 3. *Medline matrix, Query 1, upper half step $j = 2$, lower half step $j = 12$, numbers scores of relevant documents.*

decrease fast enough at a linear rate. After 12 steps, we have found the projection of the query into the document space spanned by X to at least 3 decimals. We were curious to see how the singular values converged and plotted estimates of their accurracies as points. Note that the leading singular value converged very fast. After 12 steps, its vector is accurate to 9 decimals, and the singular value to full machine precision. It is well known that the basis vectors Q_j keep orthogonal until one of the singular values converges, to verify that we plotted the orthogonality of each basis vector q_j to its predecessors Q_{j-1} as crosses and, true to theory, the crosses and points intersect at half the machine accuracy level during step 10.

Let us now turn to a view of all the documents, and see how well we find the relevant documents for query 1. We plot them in a two dimensional coordinate system in Figure 3. The x axis is along the projected query $\tilde{q}^{(j)}$. The y axis is used to plot the component of each x_k in the reached subspace (8) orthogonal to $\tilde{q}^{(j)}$. This makes up two of the three components of each x_k vector. We can infer the length of the third component, which is orthogonal to the reached subspace, by remembering that all vectors x_k were normalized to unit length, so the distances of the points plotted to the origin indicate how close the vectors are to the reached subspace. Those close to the origin are far from the reached subspace. If we continue the bidiagonalization to full length $j = n$, most of the vectors will get unit length, because then the reached subspace is the whole span of X, except in the rare case when the query is totally unrelated to a part of the document collection.

If we use our standard scoring method (14), taking angles between the original documents and the projected query, we would choose documents from right to left as plotted in Figure 3, and we can check how well we find the relevant documents. We show this by giving the score number beside each relevant document. Look at the lower part of Figure 3. First comes document 1 which is a relevant. Then comes an unnumbered point down to the left. It is not numbered since it is not relevant. Then come 3, 4, 5 all relevant, while 6 is missing. Again 7 is relevant but 8 is not, then 9 and 10 are good. Now our algorithm has given us 10 suggestions, of which we find that 7 are relevant. We say that the *precision* is 0.7 now when the *recall* is 7 out of 37, that is 0.2. APR, the averaged precision over all relevant documents [6], is slightly lower at 0.634 since the last relevant documents are found much later, we see that the last one scores as number 141. This is still not too bad! We had 1033 documents to score.

Let's take a final look at the lower half of Figure 3. There are many points along the y axis, which denote documents that are orthogonal to the projected query, and will be the last ones scored. Actually, all but 234 of the 1033 documents are orthogonal to both the original and the projected first query.

Our experiments have shown that it is overkill to run the algorithm as far as $j = 12$. The APR reaches its maximum already after $j = 2$ steps. Look at the upper part of Figure 3. The projected query is slightly shorter, 0.408 compared to 0.451 at step 12, and all the x_k points are quite a bit closer to the origin, indicating that the components of the document vectors in the reached plane are smaller. On the other hand, there is one more relevant document among the first 10 scored, and the last relevant document is now scored as number 96, which brings up the APR to 0.762.

When scoring documents by angles in the reached plane (13), these can be seen as angles to the x axis in Figure 3. It did not differ much from the standard scoring (14). Actually it gave slightly worse precision in this case APR 0.621 for $j = 2$. The third scoring choice, angles to Krylov subspace, cannot be directly seen in the plots in Figure 3. It amounts somehow to choosing those documents plotted far from the origin and gives about the same choices, but with still somewhat lower precision (in this case APR 0.495).

We have performed this kind of analysis for all the 30 queries given. Some give better and some give worse results than this first query. See Figure 4, where the APR is plotted against the step j for some of the queries, and Figure 5 gives a

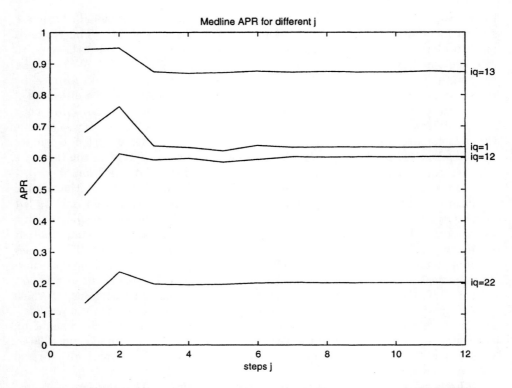

Figure 4. *Medline matrix, averaged precision recall for different steps j and some queries iq.*

(noninterpolated) precision recall diagram for these same queries at step $j = 2$.

Let us study a good question: query 13 in Figure 6. It gives full score for the first 16 documents scored, and the 21st and last relevant document is scored as number 32. We do not show the figure corresponding to Figure 2 for this query. It is very similar. This query actually deteriorates if we run up to 12 steps. See the lower half of Figure 6. Now we see that no less than 941 of the documents are orthogonal to the query, including one relevant document that is scored as 582. This needs to be studied further. One advantage claimed for LSI is that it can handle synonymy (see [1]), and return documents that are orthogonal to the original query. Here it looks like our method has this property at step $j = 2$, but loses it when $j = 12$ is reached.

The final query we will examine is 22, the worst performer. See Figure 7. Here, one relevant document is the first to be scored, but then we have to look until number 6 and 13 to find the next relevant documents. The 25th and last does not appear until number 292, and at 0.237. The APR is not that impressive. There does not seem to be anything wrong with the query. Its projection is 0.46, which is not smaller than the others.

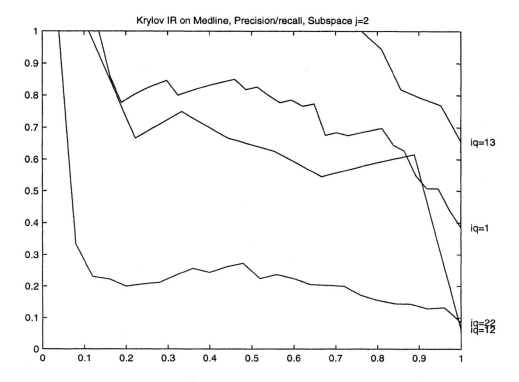

Figure 5. *Medline matrix, precision recall at step $j = 2$ and some queries iq.*

One might believe that it should be difficult to distinguish relevant document vectors from irrelevant ones, but that appears far from true. Plot the cosines of the angles between all the document vectors x_k and those relevant to query 22 in the left half of Figure 8. The relevant documents form a 25 dimensional subspace. That is remarkably well since it is separated from all the other vectors. The closest irrelevant vector has a cosine of 0.277 to the subspace of relevant vectors. The query vector is at a cosine of 0.3, which is not very close either. But this is true also for the lucky query 13, where it is 0.43. We see in the right half of Figure 8, that now the relevant document vectors get good scoring cosines. The first points are higher, and the later lower than those for query 22. So, after the fact, we can see that the separation is better for query 13 than for query 22.

Let us once more point out that the information needed for Figure 8 is only available when we know which documents are relevant. It cannot be used in the information retrieval process.

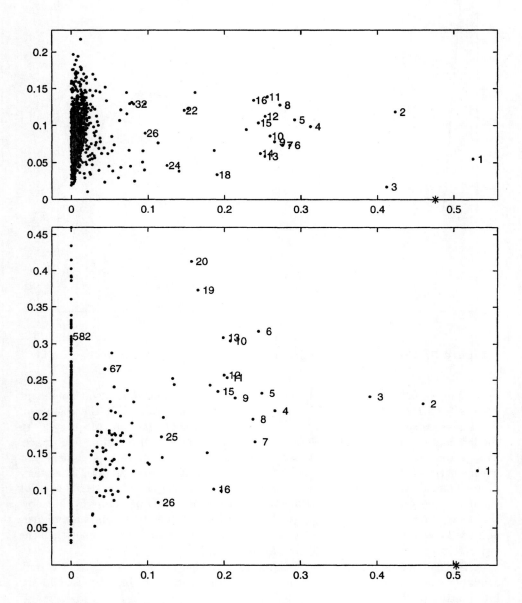

Figure 6. *Medline matrix, Query 13, upper half step $j = 2$, lower half step $j = 12$, numbers scores of relevant documents.*

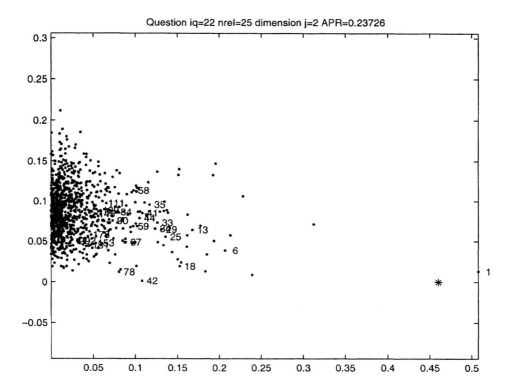

Figure 7. *Medline matrix, Query 22, j = 2, numbers scores of relevant documents.*

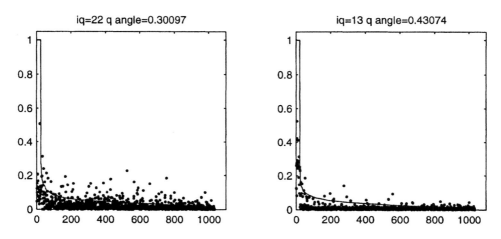

Figure 8. *Medline matrix, lines cosines of angles to subspace of relevant documents, points cosines of angles to projected query. Sorted after angle to subspace.*

Bibliography

[1] M. W. BERRY, S. T. DUMAIS, AND G. W. O'BRIEN, *Using Linear Algebra for Intelligent Information Retrieval*, SIAM Review, 37 (1995), pp. 573–595.

[2] G. H. GOLUB AND W. KAHAN, *Calculating the Singular Values and Pseudo-inverse of a Matrix*, SIAM Journal on Numerical Analysis, 2 (1965), pp. 205–224.

[3] G. H. GOLUB AND C. F. VAN LOAN, Matrix Computations, Johns Hopkins University Press, Baltimore, Maryland, 3 ed., 1996.

[4] K. LOCHBAUM AND L. STEETER, *Comparing and Combining the Effectiveness of Latent Semantic Indexing and the Ordinary Vector Space Model for Information Retrieval*, Information Processing and Management, 25(6) (1989), pp. 665–76.

[5] Medline collection. See ftp://ftp.cs.cornell.edu/pub/smart/med.

[6] NIST SPECIAL PUBLICATION 500-246, *The Eighth Text REtrieval Conference (TREC 8), November 16-19, 1999*, 2000. (Available at URL: http://trec.nist.gov/pubs/trec8/t8_proceedings.html).

[7] C. C. PAIGE AND M. A. SAUNDERS, *LSQR. an Algorithm for Sparse Linear Equations and Sparse Least Squares*, ACM Transactions on Mathematical Software, 8 (1982), pp. 43–71.

[8] S. DEERWESTER, S. DUMAIS, G. FURNAS, T. LANDAUER, AND R. HARSHMAN, *Indexing by Latent Semantic Analysis*, Journal of the American Society for Information Science, 41 (1990), pp. 391–407.

[9] G. SALTON, Automatic Text Processing the Transformation, Analysis, and Retrieval of Information by Computer, Addison-Wesley, Reading, Mass., 1989.

An Incremental Method for Computing Dominant Singular Spaces*

Younes Chahlaoui[†], Kyle A. Gallivan[‡], and Paul Van Dooren[§]

1 Introduction

In many problems one needs to compute a projector on the dominant subspace of a given data matrix A of dimension $m \times n$. One can interpret the columns of the matrix A as *data vectors* with some *energy* equal to their 2-norm. Finding the dominant space of dimension $k < \min(m,n)$ amounts to finding the k first columns of the matrix U in the singular value decomposition of A:

$$A = U\Sigma V^T, \quad U^T U = I_n, \quad VV^T = V^T V = I_n, \quad \Sigma = \text{diag}\{\sigma_1, \ldots \sigma_n\}, \quad (1)$$

and where the diagonal elements σ_i of Σ are non negative and non increasing. This decomposition in fact expresses that the orthogonal transformation V applied to the columns of A yields a new matrix $AV = U\Sigma$ with orthogonal columns of non increasing norm. The *dominant* columns of this transformed matrix are obviously the k leading ones. A block version of this decomposition makes this more explicit :

$$A = U\Sigma V^T = \begin{bmatrix} U_1 & U_2 \end{bmatrix} \begin{bmatrix} \Sigma_{1,1} & \\ & \Sigma_{2,2} \end{bmatrix} \begin{bmatrix} V_1 & V_2 \end{bmatrix}^T, \quad (2)$$

---

*This work was supported in part by the National Science Foundation through grants CCR-9796315 and ASC-9872140, and by the Belgian Programme on Inter-university Poles of Attraction.

[†]Department of Mathematical Engineering, Université catholique de Louvain, Belgium, E-mail: chahloui@csam.ucl.ac.be

[‡]School of Computational Science and Information Technology, The Florida State University, Tallahassee, FL, 32306, E-mail: gallivan@csit.fsu.edu.

[§]Department of Mathematical Engineering, Université catholique de Louvain, Belgium, E-mail: vdooren@csam.ucl.ac.be

where U_1 and V_1 have k columns and $\Sigma_{1,1}$ is $k \times k$. An orthogonal basis for the corresponding space is then clearly given by U_1 which is also equal to $AV_1\Sigma_{1,1}^{-1}$. The cost of this decomposition including the construction of U is $14mn^2 + O(n^3)$. For an additional $O(n^3)$ operations it is also possible to compute an orthogonal basis for the columns of V_1, which is required in several applications.

In this paper we are interested in problems where m is very large, and $m >> n >> k$, and where column operations on A or on the basis U are not only costly in computations but also involves swapping data from the main memory. For such problems, computing the entire decomposition and then truncating to k basis vectors is unacceptable. We would like the complexity to be essentially linear in the size of the data or $O(mnk)$.

In addition, we assume that the matrix A is produced incrementally, i.e., all of the columns are not available simultaneously. Several applications have this property. For example, representing in this fashion a sequence of large images via the approximation of A where each column of A is an image is essentially the Karhunen-Loeve compression technique [6]. Such an approximation is also used in the context of observation-based model reduction for dynamical systems. The so-called **proper orthogonal decomposition** (POD) approximation uses the dominant left space of a matrix A where a column consists of a time instance of the solution of an evolution equation, e.g., the flow field from a fluid dynamics simulation. Since these flow fields tend to be very large, only a small number can be stored efficiently during the simulation and therefore an incremental approach is useful. As each time step is solved the basis for the space is updated to track the dominant left space. Each vector is used as a discrete approximation of a basis function of space only to approximate the state $x(t) \approx U_k a(t)$. The evolution equation $\dot{x} = F(x)$ is replaced by a reduced order equation $\dot{a} = U_k^H F(U_k a) = f(a)$. State information is recovered by integrating the reduced order equation rather than interpolating between saved states, thereby trading space for computation. The cost of the production of the reduced order system is dependent on the form of the differential equation which strongly influences the efficiency of applying the technique. Finally, the dominant space approximation is also used in text retrieval to encode document/term information, and avoid certain types of semantic noise. The incremental form is required when documents are added or when the entire matrix is not available at one point in time and space.

In this paper, we summarize an algorithm that yields an approximation to one or both of the dominant singular spaces by working incrementally on the columns of A. It requires $8mnk + O(nk^3)$ operations if only the left space is tracked and $10mnk + O(nk^3)$ if both spaces are tracked.

2 An incremental procedure

In this section, we summarize an incremental procedure to estimate the dominant subspaces of a given matrix A. The procedure processes a sliding window across the columns of the matrix. Each iteration consists of two steps. On the first step, we add l columns to the current window of k vectors into the matrix A. The second step deflates the $k + l$ vectors to k. At the end of each iteration, we have a factorization that yields bases of the left and right dominant singular spaces. In the description of the algorithm that follows, we assume for simplicity $l = 1$.

To start the procedure, we assume that we have a QR factorization of the first k columns of A denoted $A(:, 1 : k) = QR$ (using MATLAB notation). We initialize the right space basis to $V^T = I_k$. The vectors e_{i+1}^T and e_{k+1} are appended to expand the $k \times i$ matrix V^T by a row and column. The next column of A, denoted a, is used to expand Q and R via a Gram-Schmidt procedure:

$$r = Q^T a$$
$$\hat{a} = a - Qr$$
$$\rho = \|\hat{a}\|$$
$$\hat{a} = q\rho.$$

This produces a new factorization

$$\hat{Q}\hat{R}\hat{V}^T. \tag{3}$$

The structure of the expand step is shown in Figure 1 for $l = 1$.

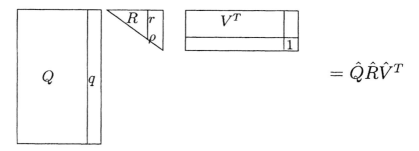

Figure 1. *The expand step for $l = 1$.*

The deflation step uses knowledge of the smallest singular value and the corresponding left singular vector of $\hat{R}$ in order to define transformations that place the factorization into a form that isolates the approximate bases for the dominant left and right singular spaces. We first compute the smallest singular value μ_{k+1} and corresponding singular vector u_{k+1} of the $(k+1) \times (k+1)$ matrix $\hat{R}$. An orthogonal matrix, G_u^T, constructed such that

$$G_u^T u_{k+1} = e_{k+1},$$

is applied to $\hat{R}$. Of course the matrix $G_u^T \hat{R}$ is not in triangular form, so we restore the triangular form by constructing an orthogonal matrix G_v such that

$$R_{up} = G_u^T \hat{R} G_v$$

56

is upper triangular. In order to isolate the dominant spaces, the matrices G_u and G_v must be used appropriately to deflate μ_{k+1} from R_{up}.

Given that R_{up} is upper triangular and $G_u^T u_{k+1} = e_{k+1}$ we have

$$e_{k+1}^T R_{up} e_{k+1} = \mu_{k+1}$$
$$G_v^T v_{k+1} = e_{k+1}$$
$$R_{up} e_{k+1} = \mu_{k+1} e_{k+1}.$$

It follows immediately from this that

$$R_{up} = \begin{bmatrix} R_+ & 0 \\ 0 & \mu_{k+1} \end{bmatrix} \tag{4}$$

where R_+ is upper triangular. Applying G_u and G_v in (3) yields

$$\hat{Q}\hat{R}\hat{V}^T = (\hat{Q}G_u)(G_u^T \hat{R} G_v)(G_v^T \hat{V}^T)$$
$$= (\hat{Q}G_u) R_{up} (G_v^T \hat{V}^T)$$
$$= \bar{Q} R_{up} \bar{V}^T$$

whose structure is shown in Figure 2. The column $\bar{q}$, row $\bar{v}^T$, and the last column and row in R_{up} are deleted to yield Q_+, R_+, and V_+^T, which are $m \times k$, $k \times k$, and $k \times i$ respectively after the i-th step. These are used as the factorization that is expanded by the $i + 1$-st column of A during the next iteration.

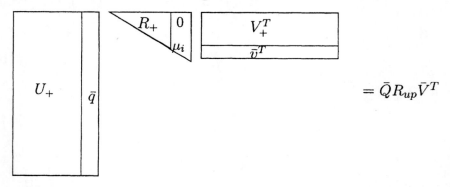

Figure 2. *The deflate step for $l = 1$.*

All columns of A are *passed* through once and *compared* with the current best estimate of the dominant subspace before deflating to maintain the k vectors in each basis. The derivations of the algorithms are very empirical but, in fact, good bounds can be obtained for the quality of the bases. These are summarized in Section 4.

3 Computational cost

The one-sided algorithm that produces a basis for the left dominant singular subspace (Q_+) and an estimate of the singular values (from R_+) has a complexity of $8mnk + O(nk^3)$. The Gram-Schmidt expansion of Q requires approximately $4mk$ per iteration. In the deflate step, the computation of $\hat{Q}G_u$ also requires approximately $4mk$ operations if G_u is formed from Householder transformations or modified Givens rotations. The construction of G_v via a QR factorization, the computation of u_{k+1} and μ_{k+1}, and the computation of $G_u^T \hat{R} G_v$ together require $O(k^3)$ operations.

The two-sided algorithm that tracks $Q_+, R_+,$ and V_+ requires more careful consideration to achieve our $O(mnk)$ target. As before the Gram-Schmidt portion contributes $4mk$ per iteration. If the QR factorization-based formation of G_v is used then the computation of $G_v^T \hat{V}^T$ requires $O(ik^2)$ per iteration resulting in an overall complexity term of $O(n^2k^2)$ which is unacceptable. However, using Givens rotations implies that, given u_{k+1} and μ_{k+1}, G_u and G_v can be determined and $G_u^T \hat{R} G_v$ computed in $O(k^2)$ operations. The matrices G_u and G_v are computed and applied simultaneously to a matrix, T, formed by appending u_{k+1} to $\hat{R}$ as the final column:

$$G_u^T T G_v = P_k P_{k-1} \cdots P_1 T Z_1 \cdots Z_{k-1} Z_k$$

where P_j is a rotation of rows j and $j+1$ and Z_j is a rotation of columns j and $j+1$. The nonzero elimination and fill pattern is shown in Figure 3 for $k = 3$. ρ is used to mark the positions of original elements of $\hat{R}$ that are updated, η_j is used to mark the element of u_{k+1} that is eliminated by P_j (with the exception of η_4), and ϕ_j is used to denote the fill-in caused by P_j and eliminated by Z_j.

$$P_3 P_2 P_1 \begin{pmatrix} \rho & \rho & \rho & \rho & \eta_1 \\ \phi_1 & \rho & \rho & \rho & \eta_2 \\ 0 & \phi_2 & \rho & \rho & \eta_3 \\ 0 & 0 & \phi_3 & \rho & \eta_4 \end{pmatrix} Z_1 Z_2 Z_3 = \begin{pmatrix} \rho & \rho & \rho & 0 & 0 \\ 0 & \rho & \rho & 0 & 0 \\ 0 & 0 & \rho & 0 & 0 \\ 0 & 0 & 0 & \mu_4 & 1 \end{pmatrix}$$

Figure 3. *The elimination and fill-in structure for the two-sided algorithm with $k = 3$.*

The computation of $\hat{Q}G_u$ requires the application of k Givens rotations and $6km$ operations and the computation of $G_v^T \hat{V}^T$ requires the application of k Givens and $6ki$ operations on the i-th iteration. Including the $O(k^3)$ on each step to find u_{k+1} and μ_{k+1}, the total operation count is $10mnk + 3kn^2 + O(nk^3)$. This is the most efficient algorithm for tracking dominant singular spaces of which we are aware. The closest approach is that of Chandrasekaran et al. [2].

4 Accuracy and orthogonality

In [1], the effect of truncating the SVD on the spaces and singular values as well as the consequences of finite precision are analyzed in detail. The results of those analyses are summarized in this section.

The analysis of the effect of the truncation on each iteration starts with the observation that there exists an orthogonal column transformation G_n that relates A and the intermediate results of the algorithm :

$$AG_n = \begin{bmatrix} Q_{(n)}R_{(n)} & \nu_{(k+1)}z_{k+1} & \cdots & \nu_{(n)}z_n \end{bmatrix}. \tag{5}$$

G_n consists of the product of the G_v matrices from each iteration and appropriately chosen permutations. $Q_{(n)}$ and $R_{(n)}$ are the basis for the left dominant space and the $k \times k$ triangular matrix whose singular values are used as approximations to the dominant singular values of A. The $\nu_{(j)}$ and z_j are the value μ_{k+1} and vector $\bar{q}$ dropped on the j-th iteration.

Using the singular value decomposition of $R_{(n)}$:

$$R_{(n)} = \hat{U}_n \hat{\Sigma} \hat{V}_n^T$$

we construct:

$$AG_n \begin{bmatrix} \hat{V}_n & 0 \\ 0 & I \end{bmatrix} = \begin{bmatrix} Q_{(n)}\hat{U}_n & Q_{(n)}^\perp \end{bmatrix} \begin{bmatrix} \hat{\Sigma} & A_{1,2} \\ 0 & A_{2,2} \end{bmatrix} = WM,$$

where the columns of $A_2 \doteq \begin{bmatrix} A_{1,2} \\ A_{2,2} \end{bmatrix}$ have 2-norms $\nu_{(i)}$ and the Frobenius norm of this submatrix is $\| \begin{bmatrix} \nu_{(k+1)}, \dots, \nu_{(n)} \end{bmatrix} \|_2$.

The singular values of A are also those of

$$M \doteq \begin{bmatrix} \hat{\Sigma} & A_{1,2} \\ 0 & A_{2,2} \end{bmatrix}.$$

Bases of the true left dominant subspace and the approximated subspace (that is generated by setting $A_2 = 0$ in M) can be normalized so the subspaces are $\text{Im} \begin{bmatrix} I_k \\ P_u \end{bmatrix}$ for the true subspace and $\text{Im} \begin{bmatrix} I_k \\ 0 \end{bmatrix}$ for the approximation. The largest canonical angle θ_k between the subspaces satisfies $\tan \theta_k = \|P_u\|$ [7]. We therefore want $\|P_u\| \approx 0$. A similar construction is possible for the right space and using results from [4] the following is shown in [1].

Theorem 2. *Let $\hat{\mu} = \max_i \nu_{(i)}$, σ_i be the singular values of A, $\hat{\sigma}_i^{(n)}$ be the singular values of $R_{(n)}$,*

$$\hat{M} = \begin{bmatrix} \hat{\Sigma} & 0 \\ 0 & 0 \end{bmatrix}, \quad M = \begin{bmatrix} \hat{\Sigma} & A_{1,2} \\ 0 & A_{2,2} \end{bmatrix}, \quad \mu \doteq \| \begin{bmatrix} A_{1,2} \\ A_{2,2} \end{bmatrix} \|_2.$$

The left and right canonical angles θ_k and ϕ_k and the singular values satisfy the following bounds.

$$|\sigma_i - \hat{\sigma}_i^{(n)}| \approx \frac{\hat{\mu}^2}{(\sigma_i + \hat{\sigma}_i^{(n)})} \leq \frac{\hat{\mu}^2}{2\hat{\sigma}_i^{(n)}}.$$

If $\mu < \hat{\sigma}_k^{(n)}/\sqrt{3}$ then

$$\tan\theta_k \le \tan\hat{\theta}_k = \frac{\hat{\mu}^2}{(\hat{\sigma}_k^{(n)})^2 - \hat{\mu}^2},$$

and if $\mu < 7(\hat{\sigma}_k^{(n)})^2/16\|A\|_2$ then

$$\tan\phi_k \le \tan\hat{\phi}_k = \frac{\hat{\mu}\hat{\sigma}_1^{(n)}}{(\hat{\sigma}_k^{(n)})^2 - \hat{\mu}^2}.$$

Note that the estimates are all quadratic in $\hat{\mu}$ and should give quite accurate results if $\hat{\mu} << \hat{\sigma}_i^{(n)}$. This is the case when the gap, γ, between σ_k and σ_{k+1} is large.

We therefore have that in exact arithmetic the algorithm can track well the dominant spaces given a sufficient gap in the spectrum. The algorithm, however, has the flavor of classical Gram-Schmidt and therefore raises concerns about the numerical reliability of the algorithm. We have shown that the concerns are unfounded [1]. A backward error analysis yields the following theorem.

Theorem 3. *The incremental algorithm produces approximate matrices $\bar{V}_{(i)}, \bar{Q}_{(i)}$ and $\bar{R}_{(i)}$ that satisfy exactly the perturbed equation*

$$[A(:, 1:i) + E]\bar{V}_{(i)} = \bar{Q}_{(i)}\bar{R}_{(i)}, \quad (\bar{V}_{(i)} + F)^T(\bar{V}_{(i)} + F) = I_k,$$

with the bounds (up to $O(\epsilon_{unit}^2)$ terms where ϵ_{unit} is the unit roundoff) :

$$\|E\|_F \le \epsilon_e \|A\|_2, \quad \epsilon_e \le 26k^{3/2}n\epsilon_{unit}, \quad \|F\|_F \le \epsilon_f \le 9k^{3/2}n\epsilon_{unit}.$$

and in practice

$$\epsilon_e \le 26k^2\epsilon_{unit}, \quad \epsilon_f \le 9k^2\epsilon_{unit}.$$

Note these bounds do not depend on m, largest dimension of A, and in practice they do not depend strongly on n and therefore the result scales well for the large problems encountered in the applications discussed above.

Given the backward error result, we have also considered the implications for the loss of orthogonality in the bases. If the loss is proportional to the condition number of A, the results could be disastrous. If, however, the loss is proportional to the condition number of A restricted to the dominant space, the algorithms are satisfactory in practice. This is in fact the case, and using results from [3] and [5] the following theorem can be proven.

Theorem 4. *Let (a given matrix) $\bar{V} \in \mathcal{R}^{n \times k}$ select k columns of the matrix $A \in \mathcal{R}^{m \times n}$, and let*

$$A\bar{V} = QR, \quad Q^T Q = I_k,$$

with R upper triangular, be its exact QR factorization. Let

$$A\bar{V} + G = \bar{Q}\bar{R}, \quad \|G\|_F = \epsilon_g\|A\|_2 \approx u\|A\|_2, \tag{6}$$

be a computed version, where $\bar{Q} = Q + \Delta_Q$, $\bar{R} = R + \Delta_R$. Then under a mild assumption, we can bound the loss of orthogonality in $\bar{Q}$ as follows:

$$\|\bar{Q}^T\bar{Q} - I_k\|_F \leq \sqrt{2}\epsilon_g\kappa_2(R)\kappa_R(A\bar{V}) \leq 2\epsilon_g\kappa_2^2(R), \quad \epsilon_g \approx u.$$

$\kappa_R(M)$ refers to the refined condition number of [3]. The implication is that there is no disastrous loss of orthogonality and this is consistent with our empirical observations [1].

5   Example

We have tested the algorithms with random matrices of dimension $m = 1000$ and $n = 50$. The matrices were normalized so that the singular values were all between 0 and 1. The number of dominant singular values and vectors was taken to be $k = 5$. We illustrate the potential of the incremental algorithm with a single experiment with a fairly large gap of $\gamma = 0.7448$. The complete set of experiments is given in [1]. In Figure 4, we plot the true singular values σ_i as a solid line, the approximations, $\sigma_i^{(n)}$, of the k leading singular values as stars, and the dismissed singular values $\nu_{(i)}$ as circles. Details of the predicted and actual singular values and canonical angles are presented in Tables 1 and 2.

σ_i	$\hat{\sigma}_i^{(n)}$	$|\sigma_i - \hat{\sigma}_i|$	$\hat{\mu}^2/(2\hat{\sigma}_i^{(n)})$	$\cos\theta_i$	$\cos\phi_i$
0.9820	0.9817	0.0003	0.0091	1.0000	0.9999
0.9544	0.9541	0.0003	0.0096	1.0000	0.9999
0.9461	0.9458	0.0003	0.0098	1.0000	0.9999
0.9442	0.9440	0.0003	0.0098	1.0000	0.9996
0.9302	0.9301	0.0002	0.0101	1.0000	0.9992

Table 1. *Errors in singular values, predicted bound, and true canonical cosines.*

$\mu = 0.1857$	$\hat{\mu} = 0.1323$
$\|P_u\|_2 = 0.0047$	$\|\hat{P}_u\|_2 = 0.0413$
$\|P_v\|_2 = 0.0396$	$\|\hat{P}_v\|_2 = 0.3066$
$\cos\hat{\theta}_k = 0.9991$	$\cos\hat{\phi}_k = 0.9561$

Table 2. *Predicted cosines, and true and predicted tangents, true and predicted first dismissed singular value.*

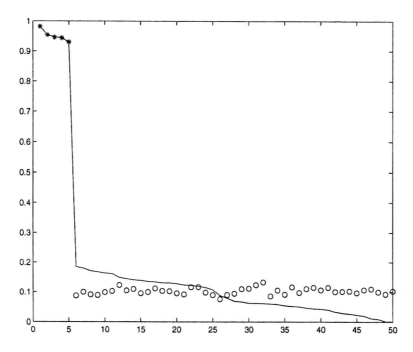

Figure 4. —- *true sv's $\sigma_i(A)$, $*$ approximated sv's $\hat{\sigma}_1^{(n)}, \ldots, \hat{\sigma}_k^{(n)}$, $\circ$ dismissed sv's $\nu_{(k+1)}, \ldots, \nu_{(n)}$.*

6 Conclusions

In this paper we have summarized our recent work on the design and analysis of incremental algorithms for determining dominant singular spaces. The proposed one- and two-sided algorithms are efficient and effective. They are reasonably robust with acceptable loss of orthogonality and accuracy related to the gap in the spectrum. The algorithms seem to have potential for large problems due to the practical error bounds that are essentially independent of m and n given certain simplifying assumptions.

Bibliography

[1] Y. CHAHLAOUI, K. A. GALLIVAN, AND P. VAN DOOREN, *Recursive Calculation of Dominant Singular Subspaces*, submitted for publication.

[2] S. CHANDRASEKARAN, B. MANJUNATH, Y. WANG, J. WINKELER AND H. ZHANG, *An Eigenspace Update Algorithm for Image Analysis*, submitted for publication.

[3] X.-W. CHANG, C. PAIGE AND G. STEWART, *Perturbation Analyses for the QR Factorization*, SIAM J. Matr. Anal. Appl., 18 (1997), pp. 775–791.

[4] S. GEMAN, *A Limit Theorem for the Norm of Random Matrices*, Annals of Probability, 8 (1908), pp. 252–261.

[5] N. HIGHAM, *Accuracy and Stability of Numerical Algorithms*, SIAM Publications, Philadelphia, 1996.

[6] A. ROSENFELD AND A. C. KAK, *Digital Picture Processing*, Academic Press, New York, 1982.

[7] G. W. STEWART AND J.-G. SUN, *Matrix Perturbation Theory*, Academic Press, San Diego, 1990.

Part II

Probabilistic IR Models and Symbolic Techniques

A Probabilistic Model for Latent Semantic Indexing in Information Retrieval and Filtering

*Chris H.Q. Ding**

1 Introduction

Information retrieval systems typically match the keywords in a user's query to the index words for all documents in the database, ranks the matched documents by some relevance or similarity score and returns them to the user. However, the lexical matching has the well-known problems of using individual keywords to identify the content of documents, the synonymy problem, the polysemy problem, etc.

Latent semantic indexing (LSI) [5, 6, 2] is a successful method to go beyond lexical matching to address these problems. LSI is a dimensionality reduction method, which automatically computes a much smaller semantic subspace from the original text collection, and experiments show LSI improves the effectiveness in information retrieval and information filtering (or text classification). A number of studies for a theoretical understanding of LSI appeared, including a multi-dimensional scaling interpretation [1], a probabilistic corpus model based on singular values cutoff [11], a low-rank- plus- shift structure based on minimum description length principle [16], a concept vector sparse data decomposition from spherical K-means clustering [4], and an aspect model dealing with probabilities directly [7]. However, many open questions remain.

Here we outline a dual probabilistic model based on the fundamental document-document and word-word similarity concepts in information retrieval, and show LSI is the optimal solution of the model. Using the likelihood as a quantitative measure of the statistical significance of the semantic subspace, we calculated likelihood

*NERSC Division, Lawrence Berkeley National Laboratory University of California, Berkeley, CA 94720. Email: chqding@lbl.gov.

curves of four standard document collections and found they all exhibit the *optimal semantic subspace*, a key concept in any effective dimensionality reduction methods. The statistical significance of the LSI vectors are found to be directly related to their eigenvalues and are found to follow the Zipf-distribution, indicating LSI vectors represent some hidden concepts. This establishes a framework upon which LSI and similar projection methods can be analyzed and further improved.

2 Latent Semantic Indexing

We begin with a brief description of LSI. The word matching scheme in informal retrieval (IR) is typically implemented in a vector-space spanned by d indexing words [16, 12]. Each document $\mathbf{x}_i$ is represented by a vector, containing the frequences of index words occurring in the document, properly weighted by other factors. Collecting all n document vectors into a word-document matrix

$$X \equiv (\mathbf{x}_1 \cdots \mathbf{x}_n) \equiv (\mathbf{t}^1 \cdots \mathbf{t}^d)^T, \tag{1}$$

X then uniquely defines the words to documents associative relations. (Here subscripts denote column vectors, representing documents; superscripts denote row vectors, such as $\mathbf{t}^1$, representing words.) Given a user query $\mathbf{q}$, consisting of a set of keywords, the retrieval system calculates a list of scores $s_i = \mathbf{q}^T \mathbf{x}_i$ as the relevance of each document to the query. (We assume both documents and query are normalized to 1 without loss of generality. Thus, cosine similarity is equivalent to dot-product similarity.) The relevant documents are sorted according to the score and returned to user.

LSI re-represents both words and documents in a much smaller k-dim subspace. This is done through the truncated singular value decomposition [10],

$$X = \sum_{i=1}^{r} \mathbf{u}_i \sigma_i \mathbf{v}^i \simeq \sum_{i=1}^{k} \mathbf{u}_i \sigma_i \mathbf{v}^i = U_k \Sigma_k V_k^T, \tag{2}$$

where $\Sigma_k \equiv \mathrm{diag}(\sigma_1 \cdots \sigma_k)$ are the singular values, $U_k \equiv (\mathbf{u}_1 \cdots \mathbf{u}_k)$ and $V_k \equiv (\mathbf{v}^1 \cdots \mathbf{v}^k)$ are left and right singular vectors, which span the k-dim subspace. The query is transformed to $\mathbf{q}^T U_k$, the documents are represented as $\Sigma_k V_k^T$, and the relevance score is computed as $\mathbf{s} = (\mathbf{q}^T U_k)(\Sigma_k V_k^T)$. Typically taking $k = 200$ (far less than original dimensions), LSI increases the precision for retrieval and accuracy for classification [5, 6, 1, 16, 15]. The success of LSI is attributed to that LSI subspace which captures the essential associative semantic relationships better than the original document space, and thus partially resolves the word choice problem.

Clearly, a theoretical and quantitative understanding is important. Mathematically, the truncated SVD is the best approximation of X in the reduced k-dim subspace [10]. But are there reasons beyond mathematical approximation? Although dimensions with smaller singular values are less important, but *less important* does not automatically imply *noise* or *redundancy*. How small does a singular value has to be for its corresponding dimension to be noise? In addition, since LSI/SVD is a *pure* numerical procedure, the central question becomes how to quantitatively measure the associative semantic relationships and see if it becomes negative for those *noisy/redundant* dimensions.

Is there an optimal or intrinsic semantic subspace for a given document collection? If yes, could it be determined theoretically rather than by exhaustive experiments? Although several studies have appeared [1, 11, 16, 4, 7], these fundamental questions remain unresolved. In the following, we outline a probabilistic approach that gives clear answers to these questions.

3 Dual Probability Model

Traditional IR probabilistic models, such as the binary independence retrieval model [12, 8] focus on relevance to queries. There, relevance to a specific query is predetermined or iteratively determined in the relevance feedback, on individual query basis. Our new approach focuses on the data, the word-document matrix X, using a generative model, i.e., the probability of occurrence of documents.

We start with the matrices $X^T X$ and XX^T , since they determine the SVD and give arise to latent semantic vectors. It is widely accepted in IR that the cosine or dot-product between two documents vectors best measures the correlation or similarity of word usages in the two documents, therefore the similarity between the two documents. $X^T X$ contains similarities between all pairs of documents, and is the similarity matrix between documents. The dot-product between two word vectors measures their co-occurrences through all documents in the collection, therefore their closeness or similarity. XX^T contains similarities between all pairs of words and is the word-word similarity matrix, also called word co-occurrence matrix. These similarity matrices are of fundamental importance in IR. Note that document-document similarity is defined in the word-space, while word-word similarity is defined in document-space. This strong dual relationship between documents and words is a key feature of the model.

If we view each document as a data entry in the d-dimensional word-space (index space), there are reasons to believe that documents do not occur entirely randomly. We assume they are generated according to certain probability distribution. To find the optimal distribution, we assume (1) the probability distribution is governed by k characteristic document vectors $c_1 \cdots c_k$ (collectively denoted as C_k), which will be later identified as the latent semantic index vectors in LSI. (2) The occurrence of a document x_i is proportional to its similarity to $c_1 \cdots c_k$. (3) $c_1 \cdots c_k$ are statistically independent factors. (4) Their contribution to total probability for a document is additive. With these assumptions, and further motivated by Gaussian distribution, we consider the following generative model:

$$p(\mathbf{x}_i | \mathbf{c}_1 \cdots \mathbf{c}_k) = e^{(\mathbf{x}_i \cdot \mathbf{c}_1)^2} \cdots e^{(\mathbf{x}_i \cdot \mathbf{c}_k)^2} / Z(C_k) \tag{3}$$

where $Z(C_k)$ is the normalization constant:

$$Z_k = \int \cdots \int e^{(\mathbf{x} \cdot \mathbf{c}_1)^2 + \cdots + (\mathbf{x} \cdot \mathbf{c}_k)^2} dx^1 \cdots dx^d. \tag{4}$$

To obtain $\mathbf{c}_1 \cdots \mathbf{c}_k$ as the optimal parameter for the probability model, we use the maximum likelihood estimation (MLE) that maximizes the log-likelihood function: $\ell(C_k) = \log \prod_{i=1}^{n} p(\mathbf{x}_i)$. After some algebra,

$$\ell(C_k) = \sum_{j=1}^{k} \mathbf{c}_j^T X X^T \mathbf{c}_j - n\log Z(C_k). \tag{5}$$

The word-word similarity matrix $X X^T$ arises as natural consequence of MLE. Note that due to the duality relationship, it is the word similarity matrix, rather than the document similarity matrix, that appears here. Since documents are data which live in the index space (word space), $X X^T$ measures the *correlation* between components of data when properly normalized, and would not change much if more data are included, thus serving a role similar to the covariance matrix in principal component analysis.

In general, finding C_k that maximizes $\ell(C_k)$ involves a rather complicated numerical procedure, primarily because $Z(C_k)$ (see Eq.4) is a high ($d = 10^3 - 10^5$) dimensional integral which is analytically intractable. However, note that $n\log Z(C_k)$ is a very slow changing function in comparison to $\sum_j \mathbf{c}_j^T X X^T \mathbf{c}_j$: (1) In essence, $\mathbf{c}_j$ is similar to the mean vector μ in Gaussian distribution, where the normalization constant is independent of μ. Thus, $Z(C_k)$ should be nearly independent of $\mathbf{c}_j$. (2) The logarithm of a slow changing function is even slower. Thus $n\log Z(C_k)$ can be regarded as fixed, and we concentrate on maximizing the first term. The optimal solution is $(\mathbf{c}_1 \cdots \mathbf{c}_k) = (\mathbf{u}_1 \cdots \mathbf{u}_k)$, the left singular vectors in LSI/SVD (see [3] for details).

We can also model words as defined by their occurrences in the document space. Here the data are the words, indexed by documents and are represented as row vectors in the word-document matrix X. Consider k (normalized) row vectors $\mathbf{r}^1 \cdots \mathbf{r}^k$ (collectively denoted as R_k) representing k characteristic words. Using the word-word similarity metric, we assume the probability for the occurrence of word $\mathbf{t}^\alpha (\alpha = 1, \cdots, d)$ to be

$$p(\mathbf{t}^\alpha | \mathbf{r}^1 \cdots \mathbf{r}^k) = e^{(\mathbf{t}^\alpha \cdot \mathbf{r}^1)^2} \cdots e^{(\mathbf{t}^\alpha \cdot \mathbf{r}^k)^2} / Z(R_k). \tag{6}$$

Using maximum likelihood estimation, the document - document similarity matrix $X^T X$ arise, and the optimal analytical solution are $(\mathbf{r}^1 \cdots \mathbf{r}^k) = (\mathbf{v}^1 \cdots \mathbf{v}^k)$, the right singular vectors of LSI/SVD.

Eqs.(3,6) are dual probability representations of the LSI. This dual relation is further enhanced by the facts that $X X^T$ and $X^T X$ have the same eigenvalues; left and right LSI vectors are related by $\mathbf{u}_j = (1/\sigma_j) X \mathbf{v}_j, j = 1, \cdots, k$. Both probability representations have the same maximal log-likelihood

$$\ell_k = \sigma_1^2 + \cdots + \sigma_k^2 - n\log Z_k. \tag{7}$$

This also suggests that the contribution of (or the statistical significance) of each LSI index vector is approximately the square of its singular value. This quadratic dependence indicates that LSI index vectors with small singular values are much more insignificant than they were perceived earlier: we previously thought contributions of LSI index vector are proportional to singular values linearly, since their singular values appear directly in SVD.

4 Optimal Semantic Subspace

From a statistical point of view, LSI amounts to an effective dimensionality reduction. Dimensions with small singular values are often viewed as representing semantic noises and thus are ignored. This generic argument, considering its fundamental importance, needs to be clarified and quantified. Our model provides a mechanism to do so by checking the statistical significance of the semantic dimensions - if a few semantic dimensions can effectively characterize the data statistically, as indicated by the likelihood of the model, we believe they also effectively represent the semantic meanings/relationships as defined by the cosine similarity.

Thus the key is to calculate the log-likelihood for the k-dim latent semantic subspace, Eq.7. The analytically intractable integral Z_k, Eq.4, can be evaluated numerically by generating uniform random numbers in the domain of the integration: on the unit sphere in the positive quadrant. We found this sampling method converges very quickly. It achieves accuracy of 4 decimal places with merely 2000 points for $d = 2000 - 5000$ dimensions.

We calculated the likelihood curves for standard test document collections in IR : CRAN (1398 document abstracts on Aeronautics from Cranfield Institute of Technology), CACM (3204 abstracts of articles in *Communications of ACM*), MED (1033 abstracts from National Library of Medicine), and CISI (1460 abstracts from Institute of Scientific Information). Here we use the standard term frequency-inverse document frequence (tf.idf) weighting. Each document is normalized to 1. Results for the Cranfield collection are shown in Figure 1. Both word-space and document-space likelihoods grow steadily and rapidly as k increases from 1 up to $k_{opt} = 377\text{-}465$, clearly indicating that the probability models provide better and better statistical descriptions of the data. However, starting from $k > k_{opt}$, the likelihood actually decreases, indicating no meaningful statistical information is represented by those LSI index vectors with smaller eigenvalues. Results for the CACM are shown in Figure 2. Likelihood curves for other collections are similar. Thus the existence of optimal semantic subspace is conclusively demonstrated. If we pick the first peak as k_{opt}, then $k_{opt} = 377$ for Cranfield, 629 for Medline, 726 for CACM, and 846 for CISI. k_{opt} value for CACM is close to the experimental result [15], while k_{opt} value for Medline is larger than the experimental result [16].

5 Do LSI Dimensions Have Meaning?

As discussed before, the statistical significance of each LSI dimension relates to its singular value squared. The statistical significance of each LSI dimensions for CRAN and CACM are shown in Figures 1b, 2b. They both follow a Zipf distribution [17]

$$\lambda_i = a \cdot i^b$$

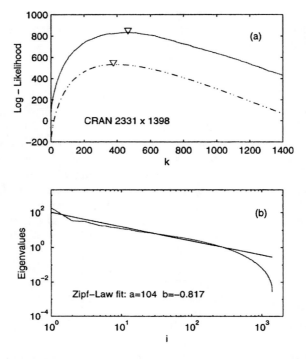

Figure 1. *Results for Cranfield collection. (a) Log-likelihood: solid line for word-space model and dashed line for document-space model. Peak points are indicated. (b) Statistical significance (eigenvalues, σ_i^2) of LSI vectors plotted in log-log scale. The straight line is the Zipf-law fit. The two curves are indistinguishable if plotted in linear scales.*

with the exponent $b = -0.82$, very close to $b = -1$. All other document collections display very similar Zipf distributions.

It is well known that English words ranked by frequency of occurrence, cities ranked by population, webpages ranked by its popularity, etc, all follow Zipf distribution. The clear common theme between these diverse entities is that each of them has a distinct set of characters and identity. Since the statistical significance of LSI indexing vectors in all documents we calculated clearly follow the Zipf distribution, we therefore infer that LSI indexing vectors also have distinct characters and identities in which they represent some latent/hidden concepts.

6   Conclusions

Using similarity measures in information retrieval, we introduced a probabilistic generative model for document occurrence. LSI-type dimension reduction then becomes finding optimal model parameters using maximum likelihood estimation, during which document-document similarity matrix and word co-occurrence matrix

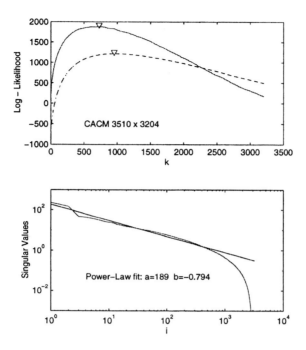

Figure 2. *Log-likelihood and significances of LSI index vectors for CACM collection. Notations are same as in Figure 1.*

arise naturally. LSI are the optimal solutions of the model.

Semantic associations characterized by the LSI dimensions are understood as the statistical significance, and are measured by the likelihood of the model. Calculations on four standard document collections indicate the existence of optimal semantic subspace and the calculated optimal subspace dimensions are close to experimental values. Importance of LSI indices follows a Zipf-like distribution, indicating LSI dimensions represent some hidden concepts or identities. Overall, the model provides a statistical framework for understanding and developments of LSI in IR.

Besides automatic information retrieval and filtering, LSI has also been used in other areas, such as automatic word sense disambiguation (the word *capital* could mean *capital goods, city where government seats,* etc.) in context space [17], etc. Our model applies there too, as long as the semantic structures as defined by the dot-product similarity remain the essential relationship.

Acknowledgement. I thank H. Zha, P. Husbands, Z. Zhang, O. Marques and H. Simon for help and valuable discussions; M. Berry and I. Dhillon for giving illuminating seminars at NERSC/LBL. This work is supported by U.S. Department of Energy under contract DE-AC03-76SF00098 through a LDRD fund at Lawrence Berkeley National Laboratory.

Bibliography

[1] B.T. BARTELL, G.W. COTTRELL, AND R.K. BELEW, *Representing Documents Using an Explicit Model of Their Similarities*, J. Amer. Soc. Info. Sci. 46, pp. 251-271, 1995.

[2] M.W. BERRY, S.T. DUMAIS, G.W. O'BRIEN, *Using Linear Algebra for Intelligent Information Retrieval*, SIAM Review 37, pp. 573-595, 1995.

[3] C.H.Q. DING, *A Similarity-based Probability Model for Latent Semantic Indexing*, Proc. of SIGIR'99 (ACM Press, 1999), pp.59-65.

[4] I. DHILLON AND D. MODHA, *Concept Decomposition for Large Sparse Text Data Using Clustering*, To appear in *Machine Learning*.

[5] S. DEERWESTER, S.T. DUMAIS, T.K. LANDAUER, G.W. FURNAS, R.A. HARSHMAN, *Indexing by latent semantic analysis*, J. Amer. Soc. Info. Sci.41, pp:391-407 (1990).

[6] S.T. DUMAIS, *Using LSI for Information Filtering: TREC-3 Experiments*, Third Text REtrieval Conference (TREC3), D. Harman, Ed., National Institute of Standards and Technology Special Publication, 1995.

[7] T. HOFMANN, *Probabilistic Latent Semantic Indexing*, Proc. of SIGIR'99 (ACM Press, 1999), pp.50-57.

[8] N. FUHR, *Probabilistic Models in Information Retrieval*, Computer Journal 35, 243, 1992.

[9] G.W. FURNAS, T.K. LANDAUER, L. GOMEZ, S.T. DUMAIS, *The Vocabulary Problem in Human-System Communications*, Commun. ACM 30, pp. 964-971, 1987.

[10] G. GOLUB AND C.V. LOAN, Matrix Computation, Johns-Hopkins, Baltimore, 2nd ed. 1989.

[11] C.H. PAPADIMITRIOU, P. RAGHAVAN, H. TAMAKI, S. VEMPALA, *Latent Semantic Indexing: A Probabilistic Analysis*, Proc. of Symposium on Principles of Database Systems (PODS), Seattle, Washington, June 1998. ACM Press.

[12] C.J. VAN RIJSBERGEN, Informational Retrieval, 2nd Edition, Butterworths, 1979.

[13] G. SALTON AND M.J. McGILL, Introduction to Modern Information Retrieval, McGraw-Hill, 1983.

[14] H. SCHUTZE, *Dimension of Meaning*, Proc. of Supercomputing'92. (IEEE Press, 1992), pp.787-796.

[15] Y. YANG, *Noise Reduction in a Statistical Approach to Text Categorization*, Proc. of SIGIR'95 (ACM Press, 1995), pp.256-263.

[16] H. ZHA, O. MARQUES AND H. SIMON, *A Subspace-Based Model for Information Retrieval with Applications in Latent Semantic Indexing*, Proc. of Irregular '98, Lecture Notes in Computer Science, **1457**, (Springer-Verlag, 1998), pp. 29-42.

[17] G.K. ZIPF Human Behavior and the Principle of Least Effort, Addison-Wesley, 1949.

Symbolic Preprocessing Techniques for Information Retrieval Using Vector Space Models[*]

Michael W. Berry[†], Padma Raghavan[‡], and Xiaoyan Zhang[§]

1 Introduction

Consider the vector space model of information retrieval [9] in which both terms and documents in a text-collection are encoded as vectors in high dimensional space. More specifically, some initial preprocessing [2] is used to extract n documents and m indexable terms from the text collection to construct an $m \times n$ term-by-document matrix M. The element $M_{i,j}$ is typically represented as the product $L(i,j) \times G(i)$ where $L(i,j)$ is the local weighting for term i in document j and $G(i)$ is global weighting for term i. There are a variety of schemes for determining global and local weightings [2]. Thus, a document vector corresponds to a column of the matrix M with elements representing weighted term frequencies [2]. A user's query is then represented by a vector which is constructed using the terms in the query in a manner consistent with weighting schemes used in constructing M. Retrieving documents corresponding to a query vector amounts to searching the column subspace

[*]This work was supported in part by the National Science Foundation through grants NSF-ACI-97-21361 and NSF-CCR-98-18334.

[†]Department of Computer Science, The University of Tennessee, Knoxville, TN 37996, E-mail: berry@cs.utk.edu.

[‡]Department of Computer Science and Engineering, The Pennsylvania State University, University Park, PA 16802, E-mail: raghavan@cse.psu.edu.

[§]Department of Computer Science, The University of Tennessee, Knoxville, TN 37996, E-mail: zhang@cs.utk.edu.

of M to find document vectors similar to the query vector.

One measure of similarity that is commonly used is the cosine of the angle between the query and a document vectors. Let m_j denote the j-th column of M (and hence the j-th document) and q denote the query vector; $\cos \theta_j$, the cosine of the angle between these vectors given by:

$$\frac{m_j{}^T q}{||m_j||_2 ||q||_2}.$$

The two-norms of the document vectors can be computed once and stored. The dot product in the numerator of the expression is computed for a query vector against all document vectors. Now documents can be ranked in relevance by sorting documents in decreasing order of the cosine values. There are several drawbacks of this basic model of information retrieval and many schemes have been proposed to enhance this basic approach. A popular vector space modeling scheme is Latent Semantic Indexing (LSI) [4] which replaces M by a low-rank approximation; such a low-rank approximation can be computed using either the singular value decomposition(SVD) [1] or the semi-discrete decomposition(SDD) [6].

The basic subspace model requires computing two norms of the document vectors once and reusing them per query; additionally, a multiplication of the query vector with the matrix M is needed (per query) to complete computing cosine values. The LSI model requires extra computation, namely, to compute a low-rank approximation of the original term-document matrix M. Such decompositions are computationally demanding. For example, the cost of computing an SVD using a Lanczos type procedure is directly proportional to the cost of a large number of matrix-vector multiplications by M and M^T.

In this paper, we consider inexpensive preprocessing methods aimed at reducing the cost of query processing using vector space models using a method such as LSI. Our goal is to formulate schemes that extract a small submatrix $\tilde{M}$ from the original term-document matrix M. Then LSI is applied to $\tilde{M}$ to retrieve a set of relevant documents. Such preprocessing can also be used in a dynamic setting, for example, information retrieval based on fast-changing term-document collections on the world wide web. Our preprocessing methods are *symbolic*, i.e., they consider the *graph* counterpart of the matrix M. We show that some natural adaptations of well known graph-theoretic schemes can effectively extract small subsets of M which can be used with LSI to retrieve documents without degrading the quality of retrieval.

The rest of this paper is organized as follows. Section 2 provides some background material. Sections 3 and 4 contain our main contributions. Section 5 contains some concluding remarks.

2 Background

For background information on information retrieval we recommend the textbook by Korfhage [7]. The book by Berry and Browne provides a good overview of mathematical modeling and text retrieval using search engines [2]. The survey paper by Berry, Drmač, and Jessup [1] is a good starting point for understanding the role of matrix decompositions in vector space methods for information retrieval. The rest of this section provides some basic definitions used in this paper.

Quantifying quality of retrieval. Two quantities, *precision* and *recall* are typically used to measure the quality of retrieval. Precision is defined as the ratio of the number of relevant documents retrieved to the total number of documents retrieved. Recall is defined as the ratio of the number of relevant documents retrieved to the total number of relevant documents in the collection.

Vector space methods provide a relevance ranking of all documents in the collection with respect to a given query. The *average precision* is the most common measure used to assess the performance of such methods. If the method returns an ordered list of n documents judged relevant to a query, a recall-precision pair (r_i, p_i) can be computed at each point i in the list as follows. The pseudo-precision at recall level $x \in [0,1]$ is defined as:

$$P(x) = \max\{p_i : r_i \geq (x * r_n), i = 1, \cdots, n\}.$$

The k-point interpolated average precision for a single query is defined as:

$$P = (1/k) \sum_{i=0}^{i=k-1} \{P(i/(k-1))\}.$$

Typically, a 11-point interpolated average precision is computed for each query using $P(x)$ for $x = 0, 0.1, 0.2, \cdots, 1.0$. Results for multiple queries are specified using the mean or the median value of P over all queries; we use the mean in this paper.

Computational cost of LSI. The computational cost of LSI using the SVD is dominated by the cost for computing the matrix decomposition using a Lanczos type procedure. This cost is directly proportional to the cost of a large number of matrix-vector multiplications by M and M^T. In terms of the matrix M, the cost is proportional to the sum of the number of rows and columns and the number of nonzeroes. Our preprocessing techniques are aimed at reducing the cost by replacing M by a smaller submatrix $\tilde{M}$. To measure the effectiveness of our filtering methods we use the number of nonzeroes in $\tilde{M}$ as well as its size, i.e., the number of rows and columns.

The graph of a sparse matrix. A matrix A is symmetric if $A_{ij} = A_{ji}$ and it is sparse if most of its elements are zero. The *undirected* graph of a sparse symmetric matrix A has a vertex for each row/column and an edge between vertices (i,j) iff $A_{i,j} \neq 0$. This graph shows the sparsity structure, i.e., linkages between rows and columns of the matrix. The term document matrix M is typically sparse but it is not symmetric; the same is true of $B = [M|q]$, the query augmented term-by-document matrix. Using an undirected graph model makes associated algorithms simpler. We therefore use G, the graph of the symmetric matrix:

$$\begin{pmatrix} 0 & B \\ B^T & 0 \end{pmatrix}.$$

This matrix is not constructed explicitly, instead, the graph is traversed implicitly using the standard sparse storage scheme for the matrix. For more on graphs of matrices and their use in matrix computations, we refer the reader to the book by George and Liu [5].

3 Symbolic Preprocessing Techniques

Our methods are based on traversing the graph defined above to filter out a smaller relevant subgraph (and hence submatrix). In short, we construct a *query-specific* matrix $\tilde{M}$ which is much smaller than M and we apply LSI on $\tilde{M}$. The preprocessing cost is typically negligible and is no more than the cost of accessing elements in $\tilde{M}$ a few times.

We first considered a simple *level search* (or breadth first search) of the graph [8]. We start the search with the vertex in the graph corresponding to the query. The initial level, level 0, consists of the query itself. The next level (level 1) consists of the terms of the query. Level 2 contains all documents that contain a term in level 1. Level 3 contains terms (not in previous levels) that are in documents at level 2 and so on (even numbered levels contain documents and odd numbered levels contain terms). The level search could be arbitrarily terminated at a given level; alternatively it will terminate when the collection of terms and documents is exhausted.

Simple level search does not result in many levels on typical term-document matrices. A significant fraction of the total number of documents are encountered in the first few levels. Generating a submatrix $\tilde{M}$ that corresponds to the first few levels for a query results in relatively small savings in size. We therefore concluded that filtering using simple level search is not useful.

Weighted level search. We next considered level search schemes that can take into account the values of nonzero elements in the matrix M. Recall that the element $M_{i,j}$ is represented as the product $L(i,j) \times G(i)$ where $L(i,j)$ is the local weighting for term i in document j and $G(i)$ is global weighting for term i. In our weighted level search, we start with the query in level 0 and its terms in level 1. We assign weight $L(i,j) \times G(i)$ to an edge leading to document j from term i. The weight of document in the level search is set to the two norm of the weights over all edges leading into the document. Only documents with weights greater than a certain threshold are *retained* in the level search; those with lesser weights are *discarded*. This weighting process typically leads to fewer documents at an even numbered level and has the effect of increasing the maximum number of levels for a given query. Figure 1 illustrates weighted level search.

Weighted level search with different threshold conditions, such as the mean or median performed significantly better than simple level search. Consider using such a level search as a retrieval method:

- the document collection returned was a small fraction of the original size, in the range 7% − 25% of the original,

- the average recall over all queries was high, in the range 56% − 75%, but

- the precision was very poor.

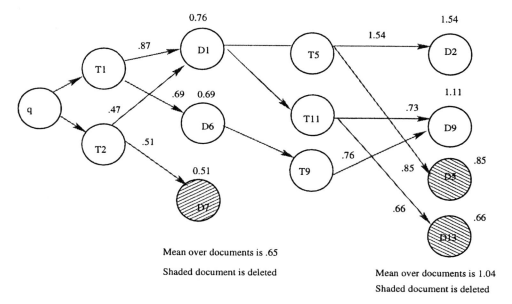

Figure 1. *Example illustrating weighted level search.*

These results indicate that such a scheme is not an adequate retrieval method but that it can be an effective filter; the precision can be improved using LSI on the filtered subset.

Pruned weighted level search. We next considered ways to further refine our weighted level search. We observed that the subset returned by weighted level search contained many terms that occurred in a very small number of documents in the subset. We modified the subset by pruning such terms; we call this pruned weighted level search. Once again the pruning can be implemented using a threshold, i.e., a condition of the form prune terms connected to less than 3 documents.

Merging documents or terms. A successful scheme in sparse matrix/graph applications is that of merging vertices that are nearly *indistinguishable*, i.e., they have similar connectivities. We add a document merging step to further reduce the filtered submatrix size. We use a greedy heuristic with the following basic selection step. Pick a document d_i of maximal degree (containing many terms); next pick document d_j of maximal degree containing terms in d_i (d_j it is a neighbor of a term in d_i). If the number of terms common to d_i and d_j exceeds a threshold, merge them into a new document and remove d_i and d_j from the original set. This step is repeated until all documents have been selected. The same merging process can also be applied to terms.

A natural question is whether the merge should be performed before or after level search. We show in the next section that merging after level search is better. For merged documents returned by LSI, we select members that pass the cosine test.

	MEDLINE	CISI	TIME	FBIS	LATIMES
# of docs	1,033	1,460	425	4,625	1,086
# of terms	5,831	5,609	10,804	42,500	17,903
Nonzeroes	52.0 K	68.2 K	83.6 K	1,573 K	250 K
# of queries	30	112	82	43	48
Mean terms/docs	50.35	46.74	196.71	316.31	230.42
Mean terms/query	10.2	21.8	7.8	39	28.8

Table 1. *Characteristics of term-document matrices in test collection.*

4 Empirical Results

We now provide some empirical results demonstrating the effectiveness of our filtering techniques. More detailed empirical results related to our level search methods can be found in our earlier paper [10]. We use a well known collection of term-document matrices shown in Table 1. Each matrix has an associated set of queries with a specified set of relevant documents per query. This information is used to compute precision recall curves for reporting the retrieval quality of our methods.

We compare the performance of LSI with and without filtering techniques. We begin with Figure 2 which shows the performance of LSI on the original term document matrices and on the submatrices obtained using filtering by means of weighted level search (WLS). The precision recall curves are the mean of 11-point precision recall curves over all queries for a given term-document collection. For the same level of recall, LSI is slightly better than LSI-WLS for MEDLINE, CISI, and LATIMES. However, for the TIME and FBIS collection, filtering with weighted level search actually improves the precision for the same level of recall.

Figure 3 shows the performance of LSI on the original term document matrices and on the submatrices obtained after pruned weighted level search (PWLS; results reported correspond to pruning away terms connected to only one document in the subset. The precision-recall curves are practically unchanged from those in Figure 2 indicating that pruning away poorly connected terms does not affect the quality of retrieval.

Figure 4 shows the mean over all 5 data collections of the plots in Figure 2 and 3. This figure shows that on average, weighted level search filtering improves precision at less than 50% recall. On the other hand, the precision degrades for larger levels of recall. The performance of pruned weighted level search is somewhat worse for all levels of recall. The lowest plot in Figure 4 shows the gain or loss in precision at all levels of recall. It is interesting to observe that despite filtering out on average more than 70% of the nonzeroes, precision degrades by less than 5.94% and can be improved by as much as 3.27%.

Figure 5 shows the effect of merging documents. We found that it is important to merge documents after filtering out the subset using weighted level search. If the merging is applied to the original term document matrix before level search,

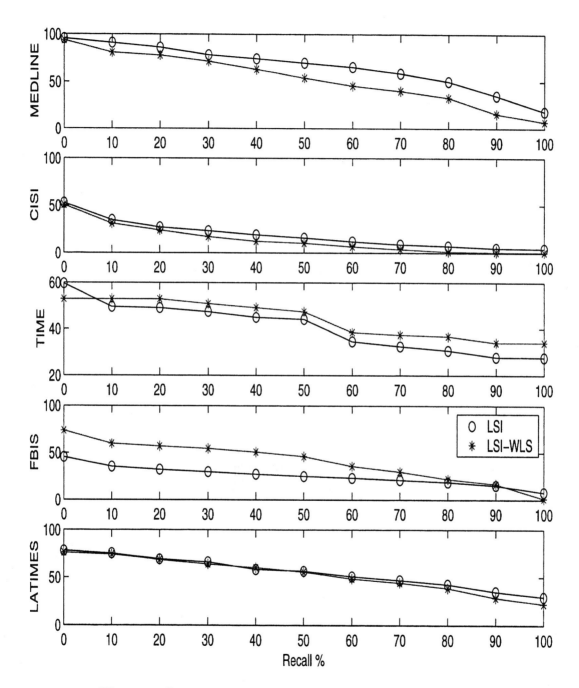

Figure 2. *Precision-recall curves for LSI and LSI-WLS; precision is shown along the Y-axis.*

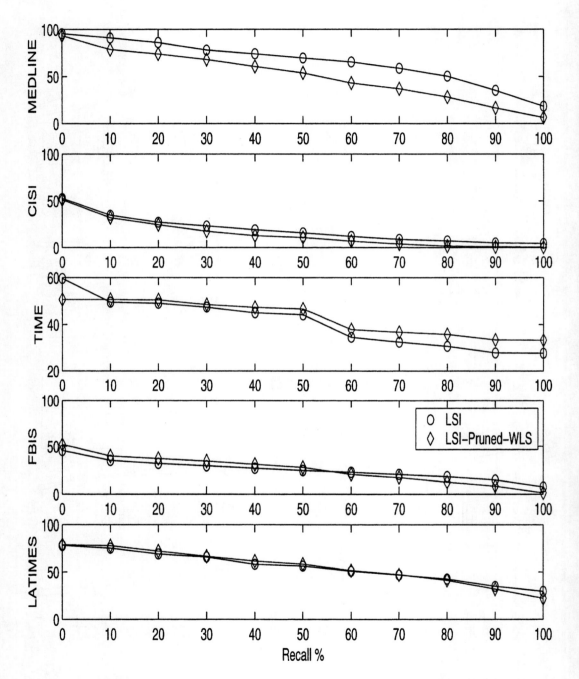

Figure 3. *Precision-recall curves for LSI and LSI-Pruned-WLS; precision is shown along the Y-axis.*

there is an additional problem of computing the weights of the merged documents. A simple method such as using the average weight per term over both documents is not very effective. We show the performance for the FBIS collection in Figure 5; note the dramatic degradation in performance when the merge is applied first.

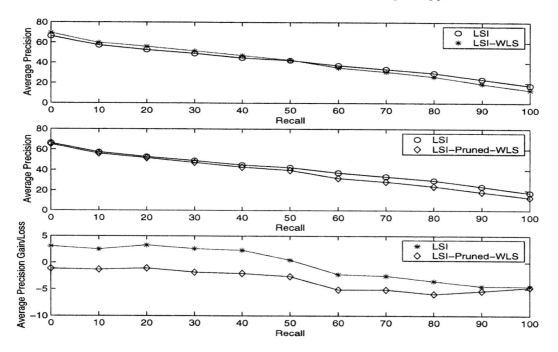

Figure 4. *Mean precision-recall curves for LSI, LSI-WLS, and LSI-Pruned-WLS over all 5 data collections.*

We next consider the effect of weighted level search and pruned weighted level search on the size of the submatrix. Recall that our goal was to filter out a significantly smaller subset. The size data with and without preprocessing is shown (over all queries per data collection) in Figure 6. On average, LSI with weighted level search reduces the number of nonzeroes to 33.84%, the number of terms to 74.03%, and the number of documents to 22.14%. Pruned weighted level search improved these results further; on average the number of nonzeroes is reduced to 28.33%, and the number of terms is reduced to 35.26% (pruning does not affect the number of documents). Merging of documents on average reduces the number of nonzeroes and documents by an additional 12%.

We were somewhat surprised to see that filtering could improve the retrieval quality in some instances, namely, TIME and FBIS. We conjecture that this a *noise reduction* effect related to the significantly larger number of terms per document (on average) for these two collections; see Figure 7.

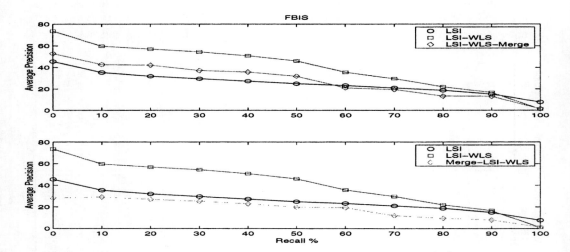

Figure 5. *Precision-Recall Graphs with document merging.*

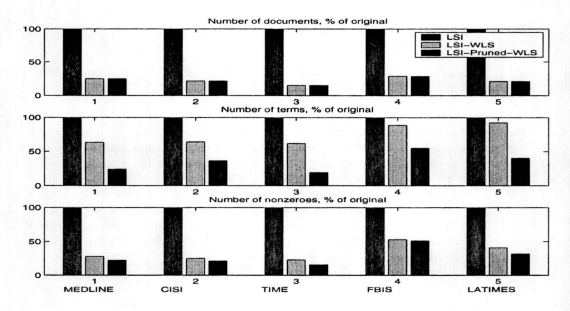

Figure 6. *Bar Graphs of Average Submatrix Size.*

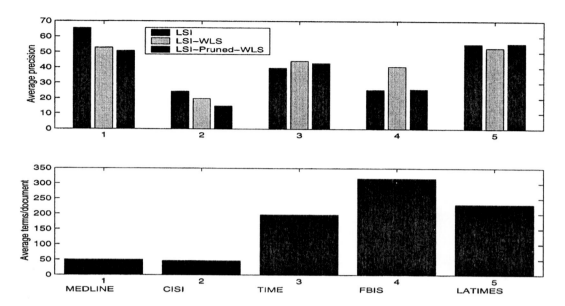

Figure 7. *Association of Performance with Matrix Attribute.*

5 Conclusions

Symbolic filtering using level search followed by document merging appears to be an effective strategy. On average the number of nonzeroes is reduced by 72% and precision-recall curves are comparable to those for LSI on the original matrix. For term-document collections with a large ratio of terms to documents, such filtering appears to improve precision by $10\% - 60\%$.

Bibliography

[1] M. BERRY, S. DUMAIS, AND G. O'BRIEN, *Using Linear Alegbra for Intelligent Information Retrieval*, SIAM Review, 37 (1995), pp. 573–595.

[2] M. W. BERRY AND M. BROWNE, Understanding Search Engines: Mathematical Modeling and Text Retrieval, SIAM, Philadelphia, 1999.

[3] M. W. BERRY, Z. DRMAČ, AND E. R. JESSUP, *Matrices, Vector Spaces, and Information Retrieval*, SIAM Review, 41 (1999), pp. 335–362.

[4] S. DEERWESTER, S. DUMAIS, G. FURNAS, T. LANDAUER, AND R. HARSHMAN, *Indexing by Latent Semantic Analysis*, Journal of American Society for Information Science, 41 (1990), pp. 391–407.

[5] A. GEORGE AND J. W. H. LIU, *Computer Solution of Large Sparse Positive Definite Systems*, Prentice-Hall, 1981.

[6] T. G. KOLDA AND D. P. O'LEARY, *A Semi-Discrete Matrix Decomposition for Latent Semantic Indexing in Information Retrieval*, ACM Transactions on Information Systems, 16 (1998), pp. 322–346.

[7] R. R. KORFHAGE, Information Storage and Retrieval, John Wiley & Sons Inc., New York, 1997.

[8] K. MEHLHORN, Graph Algorithms and NP-Completeness, Springer-Verlag, Berlin Heidelberg, 1984.

[9] G. SALTON AND M. MCGILL, Introduction to Modern Information Retrieval, McGraw-Hill, New York, 1983.

[10] X. ZHANG, M. W. BERRY, AND P. RAGHAVAN, *Level Search Techniques for Scalable Information Filtering and Retrieval*, Information Processing and Management, (2000). In press.

Part III

Clustering Algorithms and Applications

Detecting Emerging Concepts in Textual Data Mining*

William M. Pottenger[†][‡] *and Ting-Hao Yang*[§]

1   Introduction

Recent advances in computer technology are fueling radical changes in the nature of information management. Increasing computational capacities coupled with the ubiquity of networking have resulted in widespread digitization of information, thereby creating fundamentally new possibilities for managing information. One such opportunity lies in the budding area of textual data mining. With roots in the fields of statistics, machine learning and information theory, data mining is emerging as a field of study in its own right. The marriage of data mining techniques to applications in textual information management has created unprecedented opportunity for the development of automatic approaches to tasks heretofore considered intractable.

This article summarizes our research to date in the automatic identification of emerging trends in textual data. Applications are numerous: the detection of trends in warranty repair claims, for example, is of genuine interest to NCSA industrial partners Caterpillar and Boeing. Technology forecasting is another example with numerous applications of both academic and practical interest. In general, trending analysis of textual data can be performed in any domain that involves written records of human endeavors whether scientific or artistic in nature.

---
*This work was supported by Lehigh University and the Eastman Kodak Company in partnership with the National Center for Supercomputing Applications at the University of Illinois.

[†]Co-author William M. Pottenger expresses his sincere gratitude to his Lord and Savior Jesus Christ for His help in this work.

[‡]Department of Electrical Engineering and Computer Science, Lehigh University, Bethlehem, PA 18015, E-mail: billp@eecs.lehigh.edu.

[§]National Center for Supercomputing Applications, University of Illinois at Urbana-Champaign, Champaign, IL 61801, E-mail: tyang1@uiuc.edu.

Trending of this nature is primarily based on human-expert analysis of sources (e.g., patent, trade, and technical literature) combined with bibliometric techniques that employ both semi and fully automatic methods [1]. Automatic approaches have not focused on the actual content of the literature primarily due to the complexity of dealing with large numbers of words and word relationships. With advances in computer communications, computational capabilities, and storage infrastructure, however, the stage is set to explore complex interrelationships in content as well as links (e.g., citations) in the detection of time-sensitive patterns in distributed textual repositories.

Semantics are, however, difficult to identify unambiguously. Computer algorithms deal with a digital representation of language and we do not have a precise interpretation of the semantics. The challenge thus lies in mapping from this digital domain to the semantic domain in a temporally sensitive environment. In fact, our approach to solving this problem imbues semantics to a statistical abstraction of relationships that change with time in literature databases.

2   An Overview of Our Approach to Detecting Trends in Textual Information

Our research objective is to design, implement, and validate a prototype for the detection of emerging content through the automatic analysis of large repositories of textual data. Trends in warranty repair claims, technology forecasting, and automatic detection of emerging interpretations in case law are just a few examples of the variety of applications in which the techniques can be applied. Technology forecasting, as a specific example, employs collections of trade, technical, and patent literature. Such collections are partitioned into topical domains of knowledge that we refer to as regions of semantic locality [2]. These topical domains of knowledge are traced over time to detect emerging trends in conceptual content.

The process of detecting emerging conceptual content that we envision is analogous to the operation of a radar system. A radar system assists in the differentiation of mobile vs. stationary objects, effectively screening out uninteresting reflections from stationary objects and preserving interesting reflections from moving objects. In the same way, our proposed techniques will identify regions of semantic locality in a set of collections and screen out topic areas that are stationary in a semantic sense with respect to time. As with a radar screen, the user of our proposed prototype must then query the identified hot topic regions of semantic locality and determine their characteristics by studying the underlying literature automatically associated with each such hot topic region.

The following steps are involved in the process: concept identification/extraction; concept co-occurrence matrix formation; knowledge base creation; identification of regions of semantic locality; the detection of emerging conceptual content; and a visualization depicting the flow of topics through time. Each of these steps is outlined in more detail below. Several aspects of this approach reflect our initial intuition on how the problem should be addressed. Each of these six steps will be addressed in the course of our research in order to refine our approach.

3 Technical Details

This section of the article deals with our approach in detail.

3.1 Concept identification/extraction

Our approach to concept identification/extraction includes the following three steps: input item (document) parsing, parts of speech tagging, and concept identification. The parsing stage takes SGML, HTML or generalized XML tagged items as input. We have utilities to convert from a variety of input formats to XML, including proprietary airline safety data and US government patent data. Based on AI techniques outlined in [3] and [4], our parts of speech tagging approach includes the use of both lexical and contextual rules for identifying various parts of speech. After identifying each word's part of speech, we invoke a finite-state machine (pictured in Figure 1) that accepts the language generated by a regular grammar of a subset of the English language [5], [6]. Our enhanced state-machine identifies and extracts concepts consisting of complex noun phrases composed of multiple modifiers, including gerund verb forms. The final result of these three steps is a reformulation of the original collection that includes a summation of the location and number of occurrences of each extracted concept. The next stage of the process receives this reformulated collection.

3.2 Concept co-occurrence matrix formation

Co-occurring defines concepts that occur within the same item. An item can be defined as an intelligently created logical unit of text that is cohesive semantically. Examples include abstracts, titles, web pages, airline safety incident reports, patents, etc. The co-occurrence relation is reflexive and symmetric but not transitive. Given concepts extracted by the above process, we compute concept frequency and co-occurrence matrices. We also compute the frequencies of co-occurrences of concept pairs among all items in the set.

The literature discusses various definitions of co-occurrence [7]. Our approach incorporates metric measures based on proximity as well as measures that dynamically define the extent of sub-items within a given item. Our preliminary results indicate that this latter approach is crucial in dealing with the full text of items. We also reported on research in parallelizing the computation of such semantic relations based on the theory of coalescing loop operators [9].

3.3 Knowledge base creation

Knowledge base creation is a meta-level organizational process. For each concept in each matrix (in each of the time-sensitive collections) we rank co-occurring concepts. This one-to-many mapping associates each concept with a list of related concepts ranked by similarity. Co-occurring concepts are ranked in decreasing order of similarity. More general concepts occur lower in the list. Each concept pair (concept to ranked concept) is weighted, creating asymmetric measures of pairwise similarity

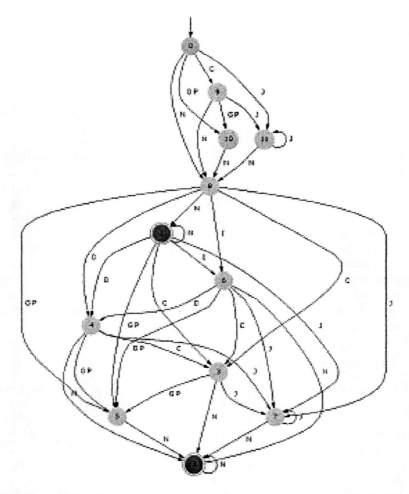

Figure 1. *A Finite State Automaton for Recognizing Complex Noun Phrases*

between concepts. The similarity is a mapping from one concept to another that quantitatively determines how similar they are semantically. We term the resultant mapping a knowledge base[1]. A knowledge base is represented as an asymmetric directed graph in which nodes are concepts and arc weights are similarity measures. The knowledge base can also be visualized as a graph, illustrated by example on the left below, in which vertices represent concepts and edges represent the pair-wise similarity between two concepts.

In [8] the first author implemented techniques that produce a knowledge base using an extension of the statistical model developed in [10] and [11]. Ongoing research at Lehigh University includes enhancement of this cluster function to ac-

---

[1]Note that follow-on work that builds on [10] terms this a *concept space*.

count for several additional factors including, for example, metrics such as the ratio of commonly used to total words in a concept.

3.4 Identification of regions of semantic locality

The resulting weight assignments from knowledge base creation are context-sensitive. We use these weights to determine regions of semantic locality (i.e., conceptual density) within each collection. We thus detect clusters of concepts within a knowledge base [2], [12], [13].

The result is a knowledge base consisting of regions of high-density clusters of concepts, i.e., subtopic regions of semantic locality. These regions consist of clusters of concepts that commonly appear together and collectively create a knowledge neighborhood. Our premise is that we can impute a constrained, contextual transitivity to the co-occurrence relation [2], thereby forming regions of semantic locality. The motivation for the use of the term semantic locality comes from the commonly applied premise that grouping similar concepts together leads to increased effectiveness and efficiency in query search and retrieval [14]. Note however that the similarity relation is by definition not transitive. The theoretical basis for our algorithm, *sLoc*, is the concept we term contextual transitivity in the similarity relation. In essence, this means that depending on the context (structure and distribution of the similarities in the knowledge base), a threshold is decided upon and transitivity is constrained accordingly. Contextual transitivity extends Schütze's conceptualization of second order co-occurrence [17] by using n-order co-occurrence, where n varies with the underlying semantic structure of the model[2].

The computational core of sLoc is based on an algorithm due to Tarjan [13]. Tarjan's algorithm uses a variant of depth-first search to determine the strongly connected components of a directed graph. This was the first algorithm to solve the problem in linear time. This is an important feature due to the fact that graph clustering is a NP-hard problem and the only heuristics we are aware of are not linear. The theory can be found in [18]. Figure 2 depicts the operation of Tarjan's algorithm as it identifies strongly connected regions (R1, R2, R3) in a simple graph.

Before tackling the sLoc algorithm in detail we must first introduce the following notation:

- Let $\mathcal{N}$ be the set of nodes i in the input graph, and let N be the total number of nodes.

- Let $\mathcal{A}$ be the set of arcs in the input graph, A the total number of arcs. An arc $a_{i,j} \in \mathcal{A}$ goes from node i to node j.

- Let $\mathcal{W}$ be the set of arc weights in the graph, $w_{i,j}$ is the weight of the arc going from node i to node j.

Therefore $\mathcal{W} = \{w_{i,j}\}_{(i,j) \in \mathcal{N}^2}$. A knowledge base is an asymmetric graph and thus $w_{i,j}$ may differ from $w_{j,i}$. Moreover, if $a_{i,j} \notin \mathcal{A}$ then $w_{i,j} = 0$; in particular, for all

---

[2]An interesting aside is that the efficacy of LSI can be viewed as the result of an implicit use of constrained, n-order co-occurrence based on contextual transitivity of the co-occurrence relation.

94

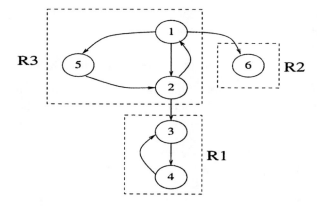

Figure 2. *An Example Application of Tarjan's Algorithm*

i, $w_{i,i} = 0$. Now, let M be the mean of the arc weights:

$$M = \frac{1}{A} \sum_{(i,j) \in N^2} w_{i,j}$$

We term the standard deviation of the distribution of arc weights SD:

$$SD = \sqrt{\frac{1}{A-1} \sum_{(i,j) \in N^2} (w_{i,j} - M)^2}$$

The sLoc Algorithm Step by Step

Figure 3 depicts the three steps of the sLoc process. Prior to the first step, the weights in the knowledge base are normalized (step 0 in Figure 3 below). The first step in sLoc is to statistically prune the input graph. Arcs of weight smaller than a certain threshold τ are virtually pruned. Note that since the similarities are asymmetric, an arc from concept a to concept b can be pruned while the arc back from b to a remains. The second step involves the identification of the clusters within the graph. Tarjan's algorithm is applied to find strongly connected regions. At this stage each strongly connected region is a cluster. The size of a given cluster is the number of nodes (concepts) it contains. During the third and final step, clusters of size smaller than parameter s are discarded (they are assumed to be outliers). We interpret the remaining clusters as regions of semantic locality in the knowledge base.

The greater τ, the more arcs are cut off, and therefore the smaller in size the strongly connected regions. Thus, the greater τ the smaller in size and the more focused will be the regions of semantic locality. Our premise is that the optimum τ can be determined statistically as a function of the mean M, the standard deviation SD and other knowledge base dependent variables (e.g., size, maximum weight,

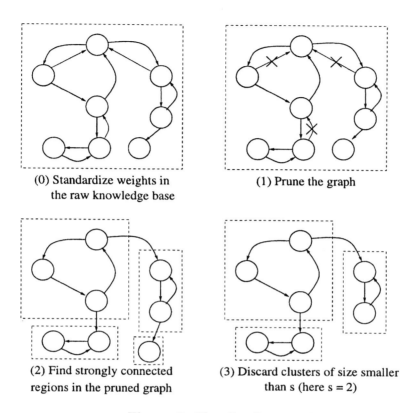

(0) Standardize weights in
the raw knowledge base

(1) Prune the graph

(2) Find strongly connected
regions in the pruned graph

(3) Discard clusters of size smaller
than s (here s = 2)

Figure 3. *The sLoc Process*

etc.). We have conducted some preliminary experiments to study the distribution of weights in various knowledge bases. Our preliminary results indicate that the distribution of weights is quite consistent across both subject domain and collection size. Figure 4 represents one such common distribution. This was computed from the MED gold standard information retrieval collection [16].

It should be stressed that we have yet to compute a knowledge base that does not exhibit a distribution of this nature. Given this fact, we have developed the following heuristic for the threshold τ: $\tau(\alpha) = max(w) - \alpha * SD$. In this equation, τ is the cut-off weight used to prune the graph and α is the number of standard deviations. For example, $\tau(1/2)$ is the threshold corresponding to the maximum weight in the graph minus half of the standard deviation of the distribution of arc weights.

We have also conducted experiments that indicate the optimal range of α lies in the range $[1.5, 2.0]$. Obtaining a scalable definition for the threshold is ongoing research.

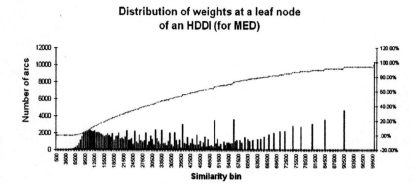

Figure 4. *The Distribution of Weights for the MED Collection*

3.5   Detection of Emerging Conceptual Content

Our fundamental premise is that computer algorithms can automatically detect emerging content by tracing changes over time in concept frequency and association. By taking a snapshot of the statistical state of a collection at multiple points in time, we expect to trace the emergence of hot topics.

We have identified at least two important features that an emerging concept should possess. First, in order to classify a concept as emerging, it should be semantically richer at a later time than it was at an earlier time. Second, an emerging concept should occur more frequently as an increasing number of items (documents) reference it. We can approximate the semantic richness of a concept by the number of other concepts that are in the same region of semantic locality. To be an emerging concept, we maintain that the number of occurrences of a particular concept should exhibit an accelerating occurrence in a large corpus. In addition, if occurrences are artificially high they fall into a class of redundant concepts. Combining these constraints, we have automatically identified emerging content given a statistically significant sample of items from the domain of interest. In preliminary experiments, we have achieved a precision of 34.8% and and a recall of 24.1% [15].

We employ a cluster-based approach in which individual clusters of concepts represent regions of semantic locality that encompass portions of one or more items. Item-based approaches attempt to measure deltas in semantics between items. Based on our research in cluster-based retrieval mechanisms, however, we maintain that clusters more accurately capture the dynamics of the semantics between collections of items being compared across time.

Our approach hinges on developing a machine-learning model (e.g., an artificial neural network) to learn the function that maps from the statistical domain to the semantic domain. The input features we experimented with included the following:

   (i) Number of occurrences of the concept in the trial year
  (ii) Number of occurrences of the concept in the year before the trial year
 (iii) Number of occurrences of the concept in the year two years before the trial

year

(iv) Number of total occurrences of the concept before the trial year

(v) Number of concepts in the cluster containing the concept in the trial year

(vi) Number of concepts in the cluster containing the concept in the year right before the trial year

(vii) Number of words with length at least four in the concept

The first through the fourth features describe the occurrence frequency of concepts. The fifth and sixth features are cluster related features and describe clusters and their change in size over time. The last feature is used to describe concept length and is a heuristic measure of the potential importance of concepts.

Figure 5 depicts a model of our initial approach to classify emerging concepts based on the winner take all strategy [19] employing a $7 \times 10 \times 2$ neural network. When evaluating a test example, we employed a variable threshold between 0 and 1 added to the positive output. This new combined value is compared to the negative output. If the combined value is higher, the concept is identified as an emerging concept (positive), otherwise, it is identified as non-emerging concept (negative). The purpose of this approach is to develop a learning model for achieving better recall (just as a radar system depends on good recall) because domain experts will do the final filtering. By adjusting the threshold, we maintain that the domain expert can achieve a suitable balance of precision and recall.

4 Results

There are four databases we used to acquire the data for this research. These databases are the USPTO patent database, IBM patent database, INSPEC database and Compendex database. The first two databases store patent documents submitted to each repository. The last two databases store research publication abstracts. However, there is some overlap of the information stored in these two research publication databases, and potential overlap in the two patent databases. Four major collections were used in this research. These are the IPP 6999 collection, CPP 6999 collection, BPP 7599 collection and UPP 7698 collection. The first letter in each collection title represents the source database; for example, IPP 6999 collection is the set of papers from the INSPEC Database. The following characters represent the abbreviation of the subject domain, for example, PP stands for Processor and Pipeline. The last four digits represent the time frame over which the documents were extracted, for example, 6999 means the documents in this collection were submitted to the database from 1969 to 1999. Each collection contains only the titles and abstracts from the documents. The CPP 6999 collection contains all the titles and abstracts from the papers from 1969 to 1999 that contain both the noun phrases pipeline and processor. The BPP 7599 collection contains all the titles and abstracts from the patent documents from 1975 to 1999 that contain the same two noun phrases. The UPP 7698 collection contains all the titles and abstracts from the patents from 1976 to 1998 that contain the same two noun phrases. The difference in the input years is due to the fact that each database stores different collections of

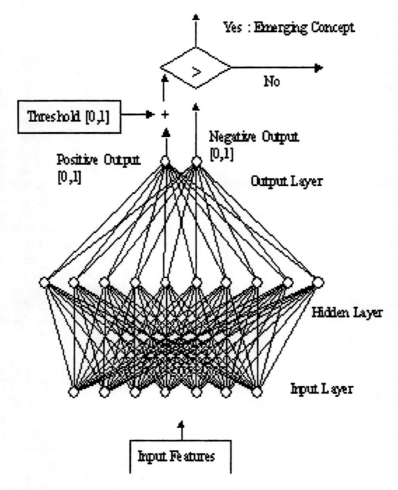

Figure 5. *A* 7 × 10 × 2 *neural network model for learning emerging concepts*

documents. For example, the USPTO database contains patent information from
1976 to 1998; the IBM database contains patent information from 1975 to 1999; the
INSPEC and Compendex databases contain publications from 1969 to 1999.

Our results are depicted in terms of an evaluation metric based on the following
definitions of precision and recall:

$$precision = \frac{pp}{pp + np} \tag{1}$$

$$recall = \frac{pp}{pp + pn} \tag{2}$$

In these formulas, pp is the number of positive examples identified as positive, pn is the number of positive examples identified as negative (false negatives), and np is the number of negative examples identified as positive (false positives).

When the threshold added is one, all concepts are identified as emerging concepts. In this scenario, the precision is the ratio of detected to total concepts and the recall is 100%. There are no false negatives. If the threshold is zero, the network is trained to minimize the total error in the training set, and the error of the testing set is usually not minimal. By changing the threshold, we can improve either the recall or the precision based on our need.

As noted, because the initial focus of our work is to achieve good recall, we have employed another metric termed F_β in the evaluation of performance:

$$F_\beta = \frac{(1 + \beta^2) \times precision \times recall}{\beta^2 \times precision \times recall} \tag{3}$$

This metric is a weighted average of precision and recall and depends on the definition of β as the precision/recall ratio at which a user is prepared to trade a given increment in recall for an equal loss of precision [20].

Figure 6 exemplifies how precision and recall have been computed within this framework where precision, recall, and F_β are:

$$precision = \frac{A}{A + D} = \frac{5}{5 + 3} = 0.625 \tag{4}$$

$$recall = \frac{A}{A + B} = \frac{5}{5 + 5} = 0.5 \tag{5}$$

$$F_{\beta=\sqrt{0.5}} = \frac{(1 + \beta^2) \times precision \times recall}{\beta^2 \times precision \times recall} = \frac{(1 + 0.5) \times 0.625 \times 0.5}{0.5 \times 0.625 \times 0.5} = 0.577 \tag{6}$$

In our examples, three different neural networks were applied for learning emerging concepts. The first one uses 10 hidden neurons and runs 10000 epochs. The second network uses 20 hidden neurons and runs 10000 epochs, and the last network uses 40 hidden neurons and runs 50000 epochs. The reason we chose these three network settings is that these three networks were computationally feasible under current hardware resources. With the SUNW Ultra-Enterprise-10000 processor, it took two hours to train 10 hidden neurons with 10000 epochs, and it takes about 11 hours to train 40 hidden neurons with 50000 epochs. It is possible to use more hidden neurons and more epochs, however, it also takes more computational resources.

Figure 7 shows the precision and recall for the four testing sets using a neural network with 40 hidden neurons and 50000 epochs. The results indicate that the prediction performance of the model ranged from good for CPP 6999 to relatively poor for BPP 7598. The average precision and recall is 0.317 and 0.359, respectively. These results confirm that emerging concepts are learnable under the current framework. Compared with a baseline precision of 0.0686, this is an improvement of a factor of 4.62.

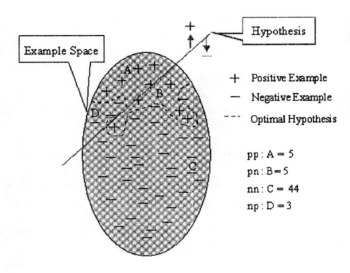

Figure 6. *The concept of positive examples, negative examples and hypothesis*

5 Related Work

Several research projects are exploring solutions to the detection of changes in top-ics. The Topic Detection and Tracking Pilot Study (TDT) project, for example, segments streams of data into distinct stories and identifies new events occurring in news stories [22], [21]. The TDT problem consists of three major tasks: (1) segmenting a stream of data, especially recognized speech, into distinct stories, (2) identifying those stories that are the first to discuss a new event occurring in the news, and (3) finding all stories in the stream given a small number of sample news stories about an event.

Major methods for new event detection in text data mining research comes from work at Carnegie Mellon University (CMU), University of Massachusetts (UMass) and Dragon. The CMU approach clusters stories in a bottom-up fashion based on their lexical similarity and proximity in time. The UMass approach uses a variant of single-link clustering and builds up cluster groups of related stories to present events. The UMass method focuses on rapid changes by monitoring sudden changes in term distribution over time. The Dragon approach, based on observa-tions of term frequencies, uses adaptive language models from speech recognition.

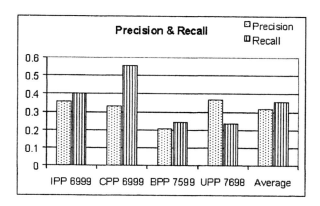

Figure 7. *Precision and Recall for Test Sets*

It hypothesizes a novel event when prediction accuracy of the adapted language models drops relative to the background models. The results show that the CMU incremental approach achieves 62%/67% in precision/recall, the CMU group average clustering top-level approach reaches 83%/43%, the Dragon approach reaches 61%/69%, the UMass 100T approach reaches 34%/53%, and the UMass 10T reaches 33%/16%.

Kumar and other researchers in the IBM Almaden Research Center use a graph-theoretic approach to identify emerging communities in cyberspace [23]. The concept is that competitive websites in the same emerging community do not reference one another. Additionally, they may choose not to reference each other because they do not share the same points of view. Noncompetitive sites and those with similar points of view do link to these non-mutual-referencing sites. Thus, websites in the same community become a strongly connected bipartite graph. [23] proposed an efficient and effective algorithm to find the strongly connected cyberspace bipartite sub-graphs and cores. A core is a complete bipartite graph. An initial crawl found that 56% of the sampled communities were not in Yahoo! while a crawl 18 months later found 29% were not in Yahoo!. [23] interprets this finding as a measure of reliability of the trawling process, namely, that many communities that they identified as emerging 18 months ago did later emerge. The average level of these communities in the Yahoo! hierarchy was 4.5.

The Envision system at Virginia Tech is a digital library of computer science literature. It allows users to explore trends in digital library metadata [24]. Envision visually displays information search results as a matrix of icons with layout semantics that users control. The system gives users access to complete bibliographic information, abstracts, and full content. It graphically presents a variety of document characteristics and supports an extensive range of user tasks. By using the Envision system, users can browse topics and trends graphically to identify emerging concepts.

ThemeRiver is a prototype (mock-up) that visualizes thematic variations over time across a collection of documents [25]. As it flows through time, the river changes width to depict changes in the thematic strength of temporally collocated documents. The river is within the context of a timeline and a corresponding textual representation of external events. This enables users to visualize trends and detect emerging themes. However, the proposed ThemeRiver system and the Envision system rely on human expertise to identify topics – they do not provide a fully automatic approach to identify emerging topics in collections as does our approach.

The goal of many of these research projects is essentially to detect changes in topics – disruptive events exhibiting discontinuities in semantics. Our research [15], [2], focuses on integrative or non-disruptive emergence of topics that build on previously existing topics. There is a subtle but important difference between these two approaches, and based on our research to date, we maintain that an integrative, cluster-based approach is necessary to identify emerging conceptual content with high precision.

6   Conclusion

We have constructed an artificial neural network classification model to classify emerging concepts. Three different networks were used to compare their performance. By changing an output threshold, we provided a method to improve the recall while maintaining an acceptable precision. The results also show that the performance is far better than the baseline precision.

In conclusion, our model has been successfully employed to recognize emerging concepts. There are many reasons we believe this model is well suited for textual data mining. These include such results like (1) cluster space is higher resolution than document space, (2) the features provided by cluster structures reflect the semantic relation well, and (3) the features provide sufficient information for classification. We believe this approach will result in significant advances in the fields of data mining and machine learning based on statistical approaches to semantic analysis.

Bibliography

[1] H. D. WHITE AND K. W. McCAIN, Bibliometrics, Annual Review of Information Science and Technology, Elsevier, 1989.

[2] F. D. BOUSKILA AND W. M. POTTENGER, *The Role of Semantic Locality in Hierarchical Distributed Dynamic Indexing*, Proceedings of the International Conference on Artificial Intelligence (IC-AI'2000), Las Vegas, NV, 2000.

[3] G. COOKE, *SemanTag*, www.rt66.com/gcooke/.

[4] E. BRILL, *A Simple Rule-based Part of Speech Tagger*, Proceedings of the Third Conference on Applied Natural Language Processing, Trento, Italy, 1992.

[5] R. BADER, M. CALLAHAN, D. GRIM, J. KRAUSE, N. MILLER AND W. M. POTTENGER, *The Role of the $HDDI^{TM}$ Collection Builder in Hierarchical Distributed Dynamic Indexing*, www.eecs.lehigh.edu/\~billp/pubs/HDDICB.doc, 2000.

[6] L. KARTTUNEN, *Directed Replacement*, In the Proceedings of the 34th Annual Meeting of the Association for Computational Linguistics, Santa Cruz, California, 1996.

[7] RICARDO BAEZA-YATES AND BERTHIER RIBEIRO-NETO, EDS., Modern Information Retrieval, ACM Press, New York, 1999.

[8] WILLIAM MORTON POTTENGER, *Theory, Techniques, and Experiments in Solving Recurrences in Computer Programs*, Ph.D. thesis, Center for Supercomputing Research and Development in the Department of Computer Science at the University of Illinois at Urbana-Champaign, 1997.

[9] WILLIAM M. POTTENGER, *The Role of Associativity and Commutativity in the Detection and Transformation of Loop-Level Parallelism*, Proceedings of the 12th International Conference on Supercomputing, Melbourne, Australia, 1998.

[10] H. CHEN AND K. J. LYNCH, *Automatic Construction of Networks of Concepts Characterizing Document Databases*, IEEE Transactions on Systems, Man and Cybernetics, 22(5):885-902, 1992.

[11] H. CHEN, J. MARTINEZ, T. NG AND B. R. SCHATZ, *A Concept Space Approach to Addressing the Vocabulary Problem in Scientific Information Retrieval: An Experiment on the Worm Community System*, Journal of the American Society for Information Science, Volume 48, Number 1, 1997.

[12] F. D. BOUSKILA, *The Role of Semantic Locality in Hierarchical Distributed Dynamic Indexing and Information Retrieval*, M.S. Thesis, Department of Electrical and Computer Engineering at the University of Illinois at Urbana-Champaign, 1999.

[13] R. E. TARJAN, *Depth First Search and Linear Graph Algorithms*, SIAM Journal of Computing, 1:146-160, 1972.

[14] K. SPARCK-JONES, Automatic Keyword Classification for Information Retrieval, Butterworths, London, 1971.

[15] T. YANG, *Detecting Emerging Conceptual Contexts in Textual Collections*, M.S. Thesis, Department of Computer Science at the University of Illinois at Urbana-Champaign, 2000.

[16] G. SALTON, Automatic Text Processing, Addison-Wesley Publishing Company, Inc., Reading, MA, 1989.

[17] H. SCHÜTZE, *Automatic Word Sense Discrimination*, Computational Linguistics, vol. 24, no. 1, pp. 97-124, 1998.

[18] V. AHO, J. E. HOPCROFT, AND J. ULLMAN, The Design and Analysis of Computer Algorithms, Addison-Wesley, Reading, MA, 1974.

[19] W. MAASS, *Neural Computation with Winner-Take-All as the Only Nonlinear Operation*, Advances in Neural Information Processing Systems 1999, vol. 12, MIT Press, Cambridge, 2000.

[20] N. JARDINE AND C. J. VAN RIJSBERGEN, *The Use of Hierarchic Clustering in Information Retrieval*, Information Storage and Retrieval, 7, 217-240, 1971.

[21] Y. YANG, J. CARBONELL, R. BROWN, T. PIERCE, B. T. ARCHIBALD, X. LIU, *Learning Approaches for Detecting and Tracking News Events*, IEEE Intelligent Systems: Special Issue on Applications of Intelligent Information Retrieval, vol. 14(4), pp32-43, 1999.

[22] J. ALLAN, J. CARBONELL, G. DODDINGTON, J. YAMRON, AND Y. YANG, *Topic Detection and Tracking Pilot Study: Final Report*, Proceedings of the DARPA Broadcast News Transcription and Understanding Workshop, 1998.

[23] R. KUMAR, P. RAGHAVAN., S. RAJAGOPALAN AND A. TOMKINS, *Trawling Emerging Cyber-Communities Automatically*, Eighth International World-Wide-Web Conference, 1999.

[24] L. T. NOWELL, R.K. FRANCE, D. HIX, L.S. HEATH, AND E.A. FOX, *Visualizing Search Results: Some Alternatives to Query-Document Similarity*, Proceedings of SIGIR '96, Zurich, 1996.

[25] S. HAVRE, B. HETZLER, AND L. NOWELL., *ThemeRiver: In Search of Trends, Patterns, and Relationships*, Presented at IEEE Symposium on Information Visualization, San Francisco, 1999.

Clustering Large Unstructured Document Sets

Jacob Kogan[*]

1 Introduction

Embedding a text collection into a finite dimensional Euclidean space is a standard approach to information retrieval related problems. Given a set of vectors one would like to partition it into clusters, so that vectors in a cluster are more similar to each other, then to vectors in other clusters (see [2]).

In this paper we present a two step clustering algorithm. The first step splits a large set of vectors into convex clusters. The second step is applied to each convex cluster separately. The application generates small high quality convex clusters. The paper is organized as follows: In Section 2 we present the second step of the clustering algorithm. In Section 3 we briefly discuss the first step of the proposed procedure and indicate how the output of step 1 is becoming the input of step 2. Appendix contains technical details concerning Section 2.

2 First Variation Clustering

Most of the clustering methods suffer from the defect that they can never repair what was done in previous steps. Indeed, whatever a divisive algorithm has split up can not be reunited. Once an agglomerative algorithm has joined two objects, they can not be separated in the future (see [7]). The section describes a clustering algorithm that attempts to avoid this drawback.

First we introduce basic notations. For two vectors $\mathbf{x} = (x_1, \ldots, x_m)^T$ and $\mathbf{y} =$

---

[*]Department of Mathematics and Statistics, University of Maryland Baltimore County, Baltimore, MD 21228. Email: kogan@umbc.edu.

$(y_1, \ldots, y_m)^T$ in $\mathbf{R}^m$ we denote their dot product $\sum_{i=1}^{m} x_i y_i$ by $\mathbf{x}^T \mathbf{y}$. For a set of vectors $\mathbf{X} = \{\mathbf{x}_1, \ldots, \mathbf{x}_n\} \in \mathbf{R}^m$ we denote the expectation $\dfrac{1}{n} \sum_{i=1}^{n} \mathbf{x}_i$ by $\mathbf{e}(\mathbf{X})$, and $\mathrm{var}(\mathbf{X})$ stands for $\dfrac{1}{n} \sum_{i=1}^{n} (\mathbf{x}_i - \mathbf{e}(\mathbf{X}))^T (\mathbf{x}_i - \mathbf{e}(\mathbf{X}))$. Cardinality n of the set $\mathbf{X}$ is denoted by $|\mathbf{X}|$.

Let $\mathcal{C} = \{\mathbf{C}_1, \ldots, \mathbf{C}_k\}$ be a disjoint partition of the set $\mathbf{X} = \{\mathbf{x}_1, \ldots, \mathbf{x}_n\} \subset \mathbf{R}^m$. The quality of the partition is given by

$$q(\mathcal{C}) = \sum_{i=1}^{k} |\mathbf{C}_i| \, \mathrm{var}(\mathbf{C}_i) + wk. \tag{1}$$

When $w = 0$ the trivial partition (i.e. $\mathbf{C}_i = \{\mathbf{x}_i\}$, $i = 1, \ldots, n$) minimizes (1). For many reasons this partition is not the optimal one. The weight $w > 0$ imposes penalty on the number of clusters, and prevents the trivial partition from minimizing (1).

Definition 5. *A first variation of a partition* $\mathcal{C} = \{\mathbf{C}_1, \ldots, \mathbf{C}_k\}$ *is a partition* $\mathcal{C}' = \{\mathbf{C}'_1, \ldots, \mathbf{C}'_{k'}\}$ *obtained from* $\mathcal{C}$ *by removing a single point* $\mathbf{x}$ *from a cluster* $\mathbf{C}_i$ *of* $\mathcal{C}$ *and adding this point to a cluster* $\mathbf{C}_j$ *of* $\mathcal{C}$, *or creating a new singleton cluster* $\mathbf{C}'_{k+1} = \{\mathbf{x}\}$.

Note, that $\mathcal{C}$ is a first variation of itself.

The First Variation Clustering algorithm is given next:

1. Pick up an initial partition. (There is a number of candidates for the initial partition. In Section 3 we shall consider an initial partition where all the vectors are placed in one cluster.)

2. Build a new partition next($\mathcal{C}$) that satisfies the following conditions:

   - next($\mathcal{C}$) is a first variation of $\mathcal{C}$,
   - for each first variation $\mathcal{C}'$ one has $q(\text{next}(\mathcal{C})) \le q(\mathcal{C}')$.

3. <u>if</u> ($q(\text{next}(\mathcal{C})) < q(\mathcal{C})$)
         goto 2
   <u>else</u>
         stop

The resulting partition is called the optimal partition. The optimal partition is denoted by opt($\mathcal{C}$).

While the First Variation Clustering is reminiscent of the $k-$means clustering (see [5], [9]), we show by an example that the presented algorithm is more accurate than the $k-$means clustering.

Example 8.1. *Let* $\mathbf{X} = \{\mathbf{x}_1, \mathbf{x}_2, \mathbf{x}_2, \mathbf{x}_4, \mathbf{x}_5\} \subset \mathbf{R}^2$, *where*

$$\mathbf{x}_1 = (-1,1)^T, \ \mathbf{x}_2 = (-1,-1)^T, \ \mathbf{x}_3 = (0,0)^T, \ \mathbf{x}_4 = \left(\frac{\sqrt{3}}{2}, \frac{1}{2}\right)^T, \ \mathbf{x}_5 = \left(\frac{\sqrt{3}}{2}, -\frac{1}{2}\right)^T.$$

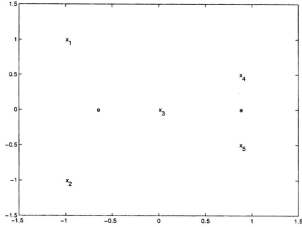

Consider the partition $\mathcal{C} = \{\mathbf{C}_1, \mathbf{C}_2\}$, *where* $\mathbf{C}_1 = \{\mathbf{x}_1, \mathbf{x}_2, \mathbf{x}_3\}$, *and* $\mathbf{C}_2 = \{\mathbf{x}_4, \mathbf{x}_5\}$.

Note that $q(\mathcal{C}) = 3\frac{1}{6} + 2w$, $\mathbf{e}(\mathbf{C}_1) = \left(-\frac{2}{3}, 0\right)^T$, *and* $\mathbf{e}(\mathbf{C}_2) = \left(\frac{\sqrt{3}}{2}, 0\right)^T$.

While an iteration of the $k-$means algorithm does not change the present partition, an iteration of the First Variation Clustering (with any $w > \frac{5}{3}$) generates partition $next(\mathcal{C}) = \{\mathbf{C}_1', \mathbf{C}_2'\}$, *where* $\mathbf{C}_1' = \{\mathbf{x}_1, \mathbf{x}_2\}$, *and* $\mathbf{C}_2' = \{\mathbf{x}_3, \mathbf{x}_4, \mathbf{x}_5\}$.

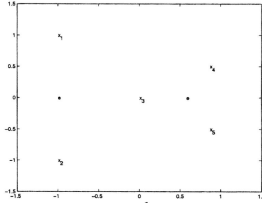

Note that $q(next(\mathcal{C})) = 3 + 2w < q(\mathcal{C}) = 3\frac{1}{6} + 2w.$

While more accurate, the First Variation Clustering is not as fast as the k−means algorithm. The best clustering results are obtained when the two clustering algorithms are combined.

The partition next(C) depends on the weight w. To emphasize the dependence we denote the partition by next(C, w). While large w prevents creation new singleton clusters, small w *encourages* building of new singletons. It is easy to show (for details see Section 3) the existence of two scalars $\underline{w} < \overline{w}$ so that for each partition C of **X** the following holds:

1. if $w' < \underline{w}$ and $w'' < \underline{w}$, then next(C, w') =next(C, w'').

2. if $w' > \overline{w}$ and $w'' > \overline{w}$, then next(C, w') =next(C, w'').

The range of w–values leading to distinct optimal partitions is, therefore, located in the compact interval $[\underline{w}, \overline{w}]$.

We remark that the First Variation Clustering requires storage of the distance matrix in the fast memory. The fast memory limitations prevent clustering large data sets. In the next section we present a combination of the First Variation Clustering and the Principal Directions Divisive Partitioning introduced by Boley [4]. The combination of the algorithms is capable of handling large vector collections.

3 Clustering Large Data Sets

The Principal Directions Divisive Partitioning (PDDP) clustering is based on the computation of the leading principal direction of the covariance matrix at each stage of the partitioning. The relevant vectors are projected on the leading principal direction, and the projections are split into two clusters. The partition of the vectors is based on the partition of the projections. The algorithm does not use any distance, or similarity measure, and, therefore, is capable of clustering large data sets. Since projection does not increase the distance between vectors, neighboring vectors will remain in the same cluster. On the other hand unrelated vectors may be assigned to the same cluster just because the distance between their projections is small. In order to avoid this phenomenon we employ the two step procedure:

1. Apply the PDDP algorithm to the entire collection to split it into large convex clusters (up to 5,000 vectors per cluster).

2. Apply the First Variation Clustering to each convex cluster generated in Step 1.

While, in some cases, the PDDP may generate large *coarse* clusters the First Variation Clustering partitions large *coarse* clusters into small *fine* clusters.

Acknowledgement. The author thanks Jonathan Bell for valuable suggestions that improved exposition of the results.

Bibliography

[1] K. ALSABTI, S. RANKA, AND V. SINGH, <u>An Efficient Space-Partitioning Based Algorithm for the k-Means Clustering</u>, PAKDD 1999, pp. 355-359.

[2] M. BERRY AND M. BROWNE, <u>Understanding Search Engines: Mathematical Modeling and Text Retrieval</u>, SIAM, Philadelphia, 1999.

[3] M.W. BERRY, Z. DRMAČ, AND E.R. JESSUP, <u>Matrices, Vector Spaces, and Information Retrieval</u>, SIAM Review 41(2):335-362, 1999.

[4] D. BOLEY, <u>Principal Directions Divisive Partitioning</u>, Data Mining and Knowledge Discovery 2(4):325-344, 1998.

[5] L. BOTTOU AND Y. BENGIO, <u>Convergence Properties of the k-Means Algorithms</u>, In Advances in Neutral Information Processing Systems 7, Tesario G., Touretzky D. (eds.), The MIT Press, pp. 585-592, 1995.

[6] I.S. DHILLON AND D.S. MODHA, <u>A Data-Clustering Algorithm on Distributed Memory Multiprocessors</u>, KDD, 1999.

[7] L. KAUFMAN AND P.J. ROUSSEEUW, <u>Finding Groups in Data</u>. Wiley, New-York, 1990.

[8] J. KLEINBERG AND A. TOMKINS, <u>Applications of Linear Algebra in Information Retrieval and Hypertext Analysis</u>, In Proceedings of the eighteenth ACM SIGMOD-SIGACT-SIGART symposium on Principles of database systems, pp. 185-193, 1999.

[9] S.Z. SELIM AND M.A. ISMAIL, <u>K-means-type Algorithms: a Generalized Convergence Theorem and Characterization of Local Optimality</u>, IEEE Transactions on Pattern Analysis and Machine Intelligence 6(1):81-87, 1984.

[10] T. ZHANG, R. RAMAKRISHNAN, AND M. LIVNY, <u>BIRCH: an Efficient Data Clustering Method for Very Large Databases</u>, In Proceedings of the 1996 ACM SIGMOD International Conference on Management of Data, pp. 103-114, 1996.

Appendix

For a given partitions $\mathcal{C}$ the partitions next$(\mathcal{C})$ and opt$(\mathcal{C})$ depend on the weight w. To emphasize the dependence throughout the section we shall denote the partitions by next$(\mathcal{C}, w)$ and opt$(\mathcal{C}, w)$. We next show the existence of an interval $[\underline{w}, \overline{w}]$ with the following properties that hold for each partition $\mathcal{C}$:

1. if $w' < \underline{w}$ and $w'' < \underline{w}$, then next$(\mathcal{C}, w') =$ next$(\mathcal{C}, w'')$.

2. if $w' > \overline{w}$ and $w'' > \overline{w}$, then next$(\mathcal{C}, w') =$ next$(\mathcal{C}, w'')$.

The existence of $\underline{w}$ and $\overline{w}$ shows that in order to obtain all conceivable partitions opt$(\mathcal{C}, w)$ one has to use $w \in [\underline{w}, \overline{w}]$ only.

We start with auxiliary definitions and results.

Definition 6. *For two sets* $\mathbf{Y}$, $\mathbf{Z} \subset \mathbf{R}^m$ *we denote* $\displaystyle\sum_{y \in \mathbf{Y},\ z \in \mathbf{Z}} |\mathbf{y} - \mathbf{z}|^2$ *by* $d^2(\mathbf{Y}, \mathbf{Z})$. *When* $\mathbf{Y} = \mathbf{Z}$ *we denote* $d^2(\mathbf{Y}, \mathbf{Y})$ *just by* $d^2(\mathbf{Y})$.

A straightforward computation shows that for each set $\mathbf{Y}$ one has

$$d^2(\mathbf{Y}) = 2|\mathbf{Y}|^2 \operatorname{var}(\mathbf{Y}). \tag{2}$$

Definition 7. *Let* $\mathbf{Y} \in \mathbf{R}^m$. *For* $\mathbf{z} \in \mathbf{R}^m$ *(that may, or may not belong to* $\mathbf{Y}$*) we denote by*

1. $\mathbf{Y}_{\mathbf{z}}^-$ *the set obtained from* $\mathbf{Y}$ *by removing* $\mathbf{z}$ *from* $\mathbf{Y}$.

2. $\mathbf{Y}_{\mathbf{z}}^+$ *the set obtained by merging* $\mathbf{z}$ *with* $\mathbf{Y}$.

When it does not lead to ambiguity we shall drop the subscript $\mathbf{z}$ *and denote the sets by* $\mathbf{Y}^-$, *and* $\mathbf{Y}^+$.

The following result is straightforward.

Lemma 8. *Let* $\mathbf{Z} = \{\mathbf{z}_1, \ldots, \mathbf{z}_k\}$, *and* $\mathbf{Y} = \{\mathbf{y}_1, \ldots, \mathbf{y}_l\}$. *If*

1. $\mathbf{z} \in \mathbf{Z}$,

2. $k \geq 2$,

3. *the set* $\mathbf{Z}^-$ *is obtained by removing the vector* $\mathbf{z}$ *from* $\mathbf{Z}$,

4. *the set* $\mathbf{Y}^+ = \mathbf{Y} \bigcup \{\mathbf{z}\}$,

then

$$|\mathbf{Z}^-| \operatorname{var}(\mathbf{Z}^-) + |\mathbf{Y}^+| \operatorname{var}(\mathbf{Y}^+) = |\mathbf{Z}| \operatorname{var}(\mathbf{Z}) + |\mathbf{Y}| \operatorname{var}(\mathbf{Y})$$
$$- \frac{k}{k-1} |\mathbf{z} - \mathbf{e}(\mathbf{Z})|^2 + \frac{l}{l+1} |\mathbf{z} - \mathbf{e}(\mathbf{Y})|^2.$$

Definition 9. *For* $\mathbf{Y} \subseteq \mathbf{R}^m$ *a vector* $\mathbf{x_Y}$ *is an element of* $\mathbf{Y}$ *that maximizes* $d^2(\mathbf{y}, \mathbf{Y})$, *i.e.*

$$d^2(\mathbf{x_Y}, \mathbf{Y}) = \max\{d^2(\mathbf{y}, \mathbf{Y}) : \mathbf{y} \in \mathbf{Y}\}.$$

We denote by $m(\mathbf{Y})$ *($M(\mathbf{Y})$ respectively) the minimal (maximal) squared distances between vectors in* $\mathbf{Y}$, *that is:*

$$m(\mathbf{Y}) = \min_{\mathbf{y'} \neq \mathbf{y''} \in \mathbf{Y}} |\mathbf{y'} - \mathbf{y''}|^2, \text{ and } M(\mathbf{Y}) = \max_{\mathbf{y'}, \mathbf{y''} \in \mathbf{Y}} |\mathbf{y'} - \mathbf{y''}|^2.$$

We remark that for each $\mathbf{Y} \subseteq \mathbf{X}$ with $|\mathbf{Y}| > 1$ and $\mathbf{y} \in \mathbf{Y}$ one has

$$m(\mathbf{X}) \leq m(\mathbf{Y}) \leq \frac{1}{|\mathbf{Y}| - 1} d^2(\mathbf{y}, \mathbf{Y}) \leq \frac{1}{|\mathbf{Y}| - 1} d^2(\mathbf{x_Y}, \mathbf{Y}). \tag{3}$$

Universal Bounds $\underline{w}$ and $\overline{w}$

Let $\mathcal{C} = \{\mathbf{C}_1, \ldots, \mathbf{C}_k\}$ be a partition of $\mathbf{X}$. In what follows, we focus on the three types of first variation $\mathcal{C}'$ of $\mathcal{C}$:

1. $\mathcal{C}' = \{\mathbf{C}'_1, \ldots, \mathbf{C}'_k, \mathbf{C}'_{k+1}\}$ obtained from $\mathcal{C}$ by removing $\mathbf{x}$ from a nonsingular cluster $\mathbf{C}_i$ and creating a new singleton cluster $\mathbf{C}'_{k+1} = \{\mathbf{x}\}$.

2. Assume that $\mathbf{C}_k = \{\mathbf{x}\}$ is a singleton, and consider $\mathcal{C}' = \{\mathbf{C}'_1, \ldots, \mathbf{C}'_{k-1}\}$ obtained by merging $\mathbf{C}_k$ with another cluster $\mathbf{C}_i$.

3. $\mathcal{C}' = \{\mathbf{C}'_1, \ldots, \mathbf{C}'_k\}$ is obtained from $\mathcal{C}$ by moving a vector $\mathbf{x}_i$ from a nonsingleton cluster $\mathbf{C}_i$ to a cluster $\mathbf{C}_j$.

We next consider each case in details.

1. $\mathcal{C}' = \{\mathbf{C}'_1, \ldots, \mathbf{C}'_k, \mathbf{C}'_{k+1}\}$ obtained from $\mathcal{C}$ by removing $\mathbf{x}$ from a nonsingular cluster $\mathbf{C}_i$ and creating a new singleton cluster $\mathbf{C}'_{k+1} = \{\mathbf{x}\}$. Note that due to (2)

$$q(\mathcal{C}') - q(\mathcal{C}) = \frac{1}{|\mathbf{C}_i| - 1}\left[\frac{d^2(\mathbf{C}_i)}{2|\mathbf{C}_i|} - d^2(\mathbf{x}, \mathbf{C}_i)\right] + w. \tag{4}$$

Moreover, since

$$\frac{1}{|\mathbf{C}_i| - 1}\left[\frac{d^2(\mathbf{C}_i)}{2|\mathbf{C}_i|} - d^2(\mathbf{x}, \mathbf{C}_i)\right] \geq -\frac{1}{|\mathbf{C}_i| - 1}d^2(\mathbf{x}, \mathbf{C}_i) \geq -M(\mathbf{C}_i) \geq -M(\mathbf{X}),$$

one has

$$q(\mathcal{C}') - q(\mathcal{C}) \geq w - M(\mathbf{X}). \tag{5}$$

In particular,

$$\text{when } w \geq M(\mathbf{X}) \text{ one has } q(\mathcal{C}') - q(\mathcal{C}) \geq 0. \tag{6}$$

At the same time, by removing $\mathbf{x}_{\mathbf{C}_i}$ from $\mathbf{C}_i$ one has

$$q(\mathcal{C}') - q(\mathcal{C}) = \frac{1}{|\mathbf{C}_i| - 1} \left[\frac{d^2(\mathbf{C}_i)}{2|\mathbf{C}_i|} - d^2(\mathbf{x}_{\mathbf{C}_i}, \mathbf{C}_i) \right] + w$$

$$= \frac{1}{|\mathbf{C}_i| - 1} \left[\frac{\displaystyle\sum_{\mathbf{x} \in \mathbf{C}_i} d^2(\mathbf{x}, \mathbf{C}_i)}{2|\mathbf{C}_i|} - d^2(\mathbf{x}_{\mathbf{C}_i}, \mathbf{C}_i) \right] + w$$

$$\leq \frac{1}{|\mathbf{C}_i| - 1} \left[\frac{|\mathbf{C}_i| d^2(\mathbf{x}_{\mathbf{C}_i}, \mathbf{C}_i)}{2|\mathbf{C}_i|} - d^2(\mathbf{x}_{\mathbf{C}_i}, \mathbf{C}_i) \right] + w$$

$$= -\frac{1}{2} \frac{1}{|\mathbf{C}_i| - 1} d^2(\mathbf{x}_{\mathbf{C}_i}, \mathbf{C}_i) + w \text{ (and due to 3)}$$

$$\leq m(\mathbf{X}) + w.$$

Finally one has

$$q(\mathcal{C}') - q(\mathcal{C}) \leq -\frac{1}{2} m(\mathbf{X}) + w. \tag{7}$$

2. Assume that $\mathbf{C}_k$ is a singleton, and consider $\mathcal{C}' = \{\mathbf{C}'_1, \ldots, \mathbf{C}'_{k-1}\}$ obtained by merging $\mathbf{C}_k = \{\mathbf{x}\}$ with another cluster, say $\mathbf{C}_i$. Then, due to (2),

$$q(\mathcal{C}') - q(\mathcal{C}) = \frac{2d^2(\mathbf{x}, \mathbf{C}_i) + d^2(\mathbf{C}_i)}{2(|\mathbf{C}_i| + 1)} - \frac{d^2(\mathbf{C}_i)}{2|\mathbf{C}_i|} - w$$

$$= \frac{d^2(\mathbf{x}, \mathbf{C}_i)}{|\mathbf{C}_i| + 1} + \frac{d^2(\mathbf{C}_i)}{2} \left[\frac{1}{|\mathbf{C}_i| + 1} - \frac{1}{|\mathbf{C}_i|} \right] - w$$

$$= \frac{1}{|\mathbf{C}_i| + 1} \left[d^2(\mathbf{x}, \mathbf{C}_i) - \frac{1}{2|\mathbf{C}_i|} d^2(\mathbf{C}_i) \right] - w.$$

Since

$$\frac{1}{|\mathbf{C}_i| + 1} \left[d^2(\mathbf{x}, \mathbf{C}_i) - \frac{1}{2|\mathbf{C}_i|} d^2(\mathbf{C}_i) \right] \leq \frac{d^2(\mathbf{x}, \mathbf{C}_i)}{|\mathbf{C}_i| + 1} \leq \frac{d^2(\mathbf{x}, \mathbf{C}_i)}{|\mathbf{C}_i|} \leq M(\mathbf{X}),$$

one has

$$q(\mathcal{C}') - q(\mathcal{C}) \leq -w + M(\mathbf{X}). \tag{8}$$

On the other hand,

$$q(\mathcal{C}') - q(\mathcal{C}) = \frac{1}{|\mathbf{C}_i| + 1} \left[d^2(\mathbf{x}, \mathbf{C}_i) - \frac{1}{2|\mathbf{C}_i|} d^2(\mathbf{C}_i) \right] - w$$

$$\geq -\frac{1}{|\mathbf{C}_i| + 1} \cdot \frac{1}{2|\mathbf{C}_i|} \sum_{\mathbf{x} \in \mathbf{C}_i} d^2(\mathbf{x}, \mathbf{C}_i) - w$$

$$\geq -\frac{1}{|\mathbf{C}_i| + 1} \cdot \frac{1}{2|\mathbf{C}_i|} |\mathbf{C}_i| \cdot (|\mathbf{C}_i| - 1) \cdot m(\mathbf{X}) - w$$

$$\geq -\frac{1}{2} m(\mathbf{X}) - w,$$

and

$$q(\mathcal{C}') - q(\mathcal{C}) \geq -\frac{1}{2} m\left(\mathbf{X}\right) - w. \tag{9}$$

3. $\mathcal{C}' = \{\mathbf{C}'_1, \ldots, \mathbf{C}'_k\}$ is obtained from $\mathcal{C}$ by moving a vector $\mathbf{x}_i$ from a nonsingleton cluster $\mathbf{C}_i$ to a cluster $\mathbf{C}_j$. Due to Lemma 8

$$\begin{aligned}
q(\mathcal{C}') - q(\mathcal{C}) &= -\frac{|\mathbf{C}_i|}{|\mathbf{C}_i| - 1} \left|\mathbf{x}_i - \mathbf{e}(\mathbf{C}_i)\right|^2 + \frac{|\mathbf{C}_j|}{|\mathbf{C}_j| + 1} \left|\mathbf{x}_i - \mathbf{e}(\mathbf{C}_j)\right|^2 \\
&\geq -\frac{|\mathbf{C}_i|}{|\mathbf{C}_i| - 1} \left|\mathbf{x}_i - \mathbf{e}(\mathbf{C}_i)\right|^2 \geq -2\left|\mathbf{x}_i - \mathbf{e}(\mathbf{C}_i)\right|^2.
\end{aligned}$$

Since $\mathbf{e}(\mathbf{C}_i) \in \text{conv } \mathbf{C}_i$, one has

$$\left|\mathbf{x}_i - \mathbf{e}(\mathbf{C}_i)\right|^2 \leq M\left(\mathbf{C}_i\right) \leq M\left(\mathbf{X}\right).$$

This yields

$$q(\mathcal{C}') - q(\mathcal{C}) \geq -2M\left(\mathbf{X}\right). \tag{10}$$

Lemma 10. *Let* $\overline{w} = 3M\left(\mathbf{X}\right)$. *For a partition* $\mathcal{C} = \{\mathbf{C}_1, \ldots, \mathbf{C}_k\}$ *of* $\mathbf{X}$ *and* w_1, $w_2 > \overline{w}$ *one has* $\text{next}(\mathcal{C}, w_1) = \text{next}(\mathcal{C}, w_2)$.

Proof. Due to (6) the partition $\text{next}(\mathcal{C}, w)$ may not be obtained by creating a new singleton cluster when $w > \overline{w}$. If $\mathcal{C}$ contains singletons, then the expression given by (10) exceeds the one given by (8), and $\text{next}(\mathcal{C}, w)$ is obtained from $\mathcal{C}$ by merging the singleton $\mathbf{x}$ and the cluster $\mathbf{C}_i$ so that the expression

$$\frac{2d^2(\mathbf{x}, \mathbf{C}_i) + d^2(\mathbf{C}_i)}{2(|\mathbf{C}_i| + 1)} - \frac{d^2(\mathbf{C}_i)}{2|\mathbf{C}_i|}$$

is minimized with respect to all possible choices of singleton clusters $\mathbf{C}_j = \{\mathbf{x}\}$ and $\mathbf{C}_i$ with $j \neq i$. Since the expression does not depend on w $\text{next}(\mathcal{C}, w_1) = \text{next}(\mathcal{C}, w_2)$ in this case. Finally, if $\mathcal{C}$ contains no singletons, then both $\text{next}(\mathcal{C}, w_1)$ and $\text{next}(\mathcal{C}, w_2)$ are created with no change in the number of clusters, hence independent of w. $\quad\square$

Lemma 11. *Let* $\underline{w} = \frac{1}{2} m\left(\mathbf{X}\right) - 2M\left(\mathbf{X}\right)$. *For a partition* $\mathcal{C} = \{\mathbf{C}_1, \ldots, \mathbf{C}_k\}$ *of* $\mathbf{X}$ *and* w_1, $w_2 < \underline{w}$ *one has* $\text{next}(\mathcal{C}, w_1) = \text{next}(\mathcal{C}, w_2)$.

Proof. Due to (7) for a partition of type 1 one has

$$q(\mathcal{C}') - q(\mathcal{C}) \leq -\frac{1}{2} m\left(\mathbf{X}\right) + w. \tag{11}$$

Due to (9) for a partition of type 2 one has

$$q(\mathcal{C}') - q(\mathcal{C}) \geq -\frac{1}{2}m\left(\mathbf{X}\right) - w. \tag{12}$$

Due to (10) for a partition of type 3 one has

$$q(\mathcal{C}') - q(\mathcal{C}) \geq -2M\left(\mathbf{X}\right). \tag{13}$$

When $w < \underline{w} = \frac{1}{2}m\left(\mathbf{X}\right) - 2M\left(\mathbf{X}\right)$ one has

$$-\frac{1}{2}m\left(\mathbf{X}\right) + w < \min\left\{-\frac{1}{2}m\left(\mathbf{X}\right) - w, \ -2M\left(\mathbf{X}\right)\right\}.$$

This implies that $\text{next}(\mathcal{C}, w)$ is obtained from $\mathcal{C}$ by removing a vector $\mathbf{x}$ from a nonsingleton cluster $\mathbf{C}$ of $\mathcal{C}$ and forming a new singleton cluster $\{\mathbf{x}\}$ so that the vector $\{\mathbf{x}\}$ and the cluster $\mathbf{C}$ satisfy

$$\frac{1}{|\mathbf{C}| - 1}\left[\frac{d^2(\mathbf{C})}{2|\mathbf{C}|} - d^2(\mathbf{x}, \mathbf{C})\right] = \min_{\mathbf{x}_i \in \mathbf{C}_i, \ i=1,\ldots,k} \frac{1}{|\mathbf{C}_i| - 1}\left[\frac{d^2(\mathbf{C}_i)}{2|\mathbf{C}_i|} - d^2(\mathbf{x}_i, \mathbf{C}_i)\right] \tag{14}$$

Since (14) is independent of w, one has $\text{next}(\mathcal{C}, w_1) = \text{next}(\mathcal{C}, w_2)$. This completes the proof. $\square$

Finally we remark that Lemma 10 and Lemma 11 provide conservative estimates for $\underline{w}$ and $\overline{w}$. Indeed, when

$$w < w_- = \frac{1}{2}m\left(\mathbf{X}\right) \tag{15}$$

removing a vector from a nonsingleton cluster and forming a new singleton cluster reduces the quality of partition (see (7)). Hence the optimal partition $\text{opt}(\mathcal{C}, w)$ contains singletons only. We formally summarize the remark as follows.

Lemma 12. *If $w < w_-$, then for each initial partition $\mathcal{C}$ the partition $\text{opt}(\mathcal{C}, w) = \{\{\mathbf{x}_1\}, \ldots, \{\mathbf{x}_n\}\}$.*

Partition Dependent Bound w^+

While considering a specific initial partition, the upper bound for w can be considerably sharpened. In this subsection, we shall focus on the initial partition $\mathcal{C} = \{\mathbf{X}\}$. The quality of the partition is

$$q(\mathcal{C}) = |\mathbf{X}| \operatorname{var}\left(\mathbf{X}\right) + w.$$

The partition $\text{next}(\mathcal{C}, w)$, if different from $\mathcal{C}$, consists of two clusters: a singleton $\mathbf{C}'_1 = \{\mathbf{x}\}$, and $\mathbf{C}'_2 = \mathbf{X}^-$, and $q\left(\text{next}\left(\mathcal{C}, w\right)\right) = |\mathbf{X}^-| \operatorname{var}\left(\mathbf{X}^-\right) + 2w$. Since

$q\left(\text{next}\left(\mathcal{C}, w\right)\right) < q(\mathcal{C})$ one has

$$
\begin{aligned}
w &< |\mathbf{X}| \operatorname{var}\left(\mathbf{X}\right) - \left|\mathbf{X}^{-}\right| \operatorname{var}\left(\mathbf{X}^{-}\right) \\
&= \frac{d^2(\mathbf{X})}{2|\mathbf{X}|} - \frac{d^2(\mathbf{X})}{2(|\mathbf{X}| - 1)} + \frac{d^2(\mathbf{x}, \mathbf{X})}{|\mathbf{X}| - 1} \\
&= \frac{d^2(\mathbf{X})}{2}\left[\frac{1}{|\mathbf{X}|} - \frac{1}{|\mathbf{X}| - 1}\right] + \frac{1}{|\mathbf{X}| - 1}d^2(\mathbf{x}, \mathbf{X}) \\
&= \frac{1}{|\mathbf{X}| - 1}\left[d^2(\mathbf{x}, \mathbf{X}) - \frac{d^2(\mathbf{X})}{2|\mathbf{X}|}\right] \\
&= \frac{1}{|\mathbf{X}| - 1}\left[d^2(\mathbf{x}, \mathbf{X}) - |\mathbf{X}| \operatorname{var}\left(\mathbf{X}\right)\right].
\end{aligned}
$$

The right hand side is maximized when $\mathbf{x} = \mathbf{x_X}$. Hence, if $\mathcal{C}$ is a single cluster and

$$
w > w^{+} = \frac{1}{|\mathbf{X}| - 1}\left[d^2(\mathbf{x_X}, \mathbf{X}) - |\mathbf{X}| \operatorname{var}\left(\mathbf{X}\right)\right] \tag{16}
$$

the partition $\text{next}(\mathcal{C}, w) = \mathcal{C}$.

Lemma 13. *If the initial partition $\mathcal{C}$ is a single cluster that contains the entire set $\mathbf{X}$, then for each $w > w^{+}$ one has $\text{opt}(\mathcal{C}, w) = \mathcal{C}$.*

Lemma 12 and Lemma 13 show that in order to generate an optimal partition $\text{opt}(\mathcal{C}, w)$ different from both the original partition $\mathcal{C} = \{\mathbf{X}\}$ and the trivial partition $\{\{\mathbf{x}_1\}, \ldots, \{\mathbf{x}_n\}\}$ the weight w should belong to the finite interval $[w_{-}, w^{+}]$.

Part IV

Case Studies of Latent Semantic Analysis

Taking a New Look at the Latent Semantic Analysis Approach to Information Retrieval

E.R. Jessup and J.H. Martin[*]

1   Introduction

Latent Semantic Analysis (LSA) [4] is a mathematical approach to the discovery of similarity relationships among documents, fragments of documents, and the words that occur within collections of documents. Although LSA was originally applied in the context of information retrieval [4], it has since been successfully applied to a wide variety of text-based tasks [16].

LSA is a variant of the vector space model for information retrieval that uses a reduced-rank approximation to the term-document matrix. In the information retrieval domain, rank reduction is applied in an effort to remove the *noise* that obscures the semantic content of the data [4]. In this context, two claims are typically made for LSA: that it provides a substantial improvement in retrieval performance over the standard vector space model, AND THAT THIS IMPROVEMent results from LSA's ability to solve what is known as the *synonymy* problem.

Despite the many successful applications of LSA, there are a large number of unanswered questions that bear on where, and in what manner, LSA should be applied. The purpose of this paper is to begin to investigate these issues in LSA's original context of information retrieval and to pose new directions for future work. Among the more critical questions that we address in this paper are the following:

- Does LSA reliably improve retrieval performance as compared to the vector space model?

---

[*]Department of Computer Science, University of Colorado, Boulder, CO 80309-0430. Email: {jessup,martin@cs.colorado.edu}.

- Does LSA improve retrieval performance by addressing the synonymy problem?

- How can the optimal rank be chosen?

- How can relevant and irrelevant documents be distinguished?

- And are there alternative matrix techniques that can be used to discover reduced representations?

This paper is organized as follows: In Sections 2–3, we review the details of the vector space model and LSA. In Section 4, we outline our empirical methods. In Section 5, we compare the retrieval performances of LSA and the full-rank vector space model. In Section 6, we evaluate how the performance of LSA depends on its ability to handle synonyms. In Sections 7–8, we consider the choice of rank and how best to identify relevant documents. In Section 9, we examine the use of other orthogonal decompositions for rank reduction. Finally, in Section 10, we summarize our results.

2 The Vector Space Model

In the vector space model, a collection of documents is encoded as a term-document matrix A, where each column of that matrix represents a single document in the collection. The ith element of the jth column is a function of the frequency of term i in document j. When a collection of d documents is indexed by t terms, the term-document matrix is $t \times d$. A user's query is translated into a t-dimensional column vector q in the same way with the ith element giving the weighted frequency of term i in the query.

In the vector space model, a document is deemed similar to a query if the vector representing it is similar to the vector representing the query according to some measure, typically the cosine of the angle between the two vectors. The full set of cosines is defined by

$$\cos\theta_j = \frac{q^T(Ae_j)}{\|q\|\|Ae_j\|}, \quad j = 1, \dots, d,$$

where d is the number of documents, q is the query vector, and e_j is the jth canonical vector.

3 Reduced-Rank Vector Space Model

LSA is a variant of the vector space model that uses a reduced-rank approximation to the term-document matrix. That approximation A_k is derived from the SVD by retaining only the largest k singular values and corresponding left and right singular vectors. That is,

$$A_k = U_k \Sigma_k V_k^T,$$

where Σ_k is the $k \times k$ diagonal matrix with the largest k singular values on its diagonal, U_k is the $t \times k$ matrix with the corresponding left singular vectors as columns, and V_k is the $d \times k$ matrix with the corresponding right singular vectors as columns. The matrix $A_k = U_k \Sigma_k V_k^T$ is the optimal rank-k approximation of A in that it minimizes the Frobenius norm distance between A and its rank-k approximations [11, 20].

In LSA, the query-document comparison is carried out by computing the cosines of the angles between the query vector and the columns of A_k:

$$\cos\theta_j = \frac{(A_k e_j)^T q}{\|A_k e_j\| \, \|q\|} = \frac{e_j^T V_k \Sigma_k (U_k^T q)}{\|\Sigma_k V_k^T e_j\| \, \|q\|}, \tag{1}$$

for $j = 1, \ldots, d$.

Rank reduction is touted as a mechanism for dealing with imprecision in the term-document matrix. This uncertainty arises primarily from the wide array of lexical choices available to writers. In particular, synonymy permits writers to refer to the same concept with any number of distinct terms, and polysemy permits the same term to refer to an array of distinct concepts. Furnas et al. [12] demonstrate the pervasive nature of these linguistic problems experimentally. Note that this uncertainty is not overcome by expert intervention: there is an average 20% disparity in decisions made by professional indexers [13]. Imprecision also results from artifacts of data collections: a database can be repetitive, containing multiple copies of the same document. For these reasons, no single term-document matrix can be considered an exact representation of a given document collection. Rank reduction is applied in LSA in an effort to find an approximation A_k that actually better represents the semantic content of a collection than does the original term-document matrix A.

Another advantage of rank reduction is that, when k is much less than d, the reduced-rank representation of the database (saved as U_k, Σ_k, and V_k) requires much less storage than does the full term-document matrix A. Changes to the database are accommodated by updating or downdating the factors. See [23] for details of those procedures.

4 Testing the Methods

We set out to answer questions about the performance of LSA by means of a series of empirical tests. In this section, we describe our experimental methodology by introducing the test collections and presenting our mechanisms for judging retrieval quality. We also describe our testing programs.

4.1 The Test Collections

To test our methods and hypotheses, we make use of three widely available standard information retrieval test collections: a collection of articles from TIME magazine (TIME) from 1963 [25], a collection of a set of Medline (MED) [19] articles on various medical topics, and the Cystic Fibrosis collection (CF) [22] which consists

Collection	Number of Terms	Number of Documents	Number of Queries
CF	9529	1238	100
TIME	20853	424	83
MED	12672	1033	30

Table 1. *Numbers of terms, documents, and queries in the test collections.*

of a set of Medline articles containing the phrase *Cystic Fibrosis*. Each of these test collections consists of a set of short articles, a set of queries, and a set of query-document pairs indicating which documents are relevant to which queries. Table 1 provides more of the details of these collections.

Various methods can be used to create the entries of a term-document matrix from a test collection. For the purposes of these experiments, we elected to use the simplest, most widely employed methods of creating the matrix. Namely,

- No stop lists were used (although numbers were removed).

- No stemming was performed.

- Term weighting consists of the standard term frequency times inverse document frequency (TFxIDF) method, for both documents and queries.

We should note that TFxIDF weighting describes a family of related methods. We define the i, j element of the $t \times d$ term-document matrix A as

$$a_{i,j} = tf_{i,j} * idf_i$$

with

$$idf_i = \log \frac{d}{n_i},$$

where $tf_{i,j}$ is the raw term frequency of term i in document j, and n_i is the number of documents in the collection that contain term i. This method balances the importance of a term to a document, evidenced by its frequency in that document, against a term's overall discriminative ability, based on its distribution across the collection as a whole.

4.2   Our Metrics

We evaluate the methods by means of two standard metrics: recall and precision. Recall, which is the fraction of the total number of relevant documents in the collection that are returned, is a measure of completeness. Precision, which is the fraction of the total number of documents returned that are relevant, is a measure of accuracy.

Note that these metrics are based on the notion of a return set of fixed size, and make no use of the notion of the total ranking that is central to the vector space model. To adapt these recall and precision measures to systems that rank an entire collection, it is traditional to present results as a plot of average precision measured at various levels of recall. More specifically, given a query, a ranking, and a set of relevance judgments, we collect the precision values when each of a fixed set of recall levels is achieved. These results are then averaged over the results for all the queries in the collection and plotted.

There is an inherent tension between recall and precision. The simplest way to achieve 100% recall (i.e., to find all the relevant documents) is to return all of the documents in the collection. Of course, doing so normally results in an abysmal precision score. On the other hand, any attempt to be careful and return *only* relevant documents results in a low recall score. As a result, recall-precision curves tend to display high levels of precision at low levels of recall, accompanied by a drop off in precision at higher levels of recall.

Any two systems that provide a ranking of documents with respect to a query can be compared by plotting their respective recall-precision curves on the same plot. In general, systems with higher precision values across a wide range of recall values are superior. That is, the higher the curve on the plot, the better.

4.3 Our Methodology

For ease of code development and data manipulation, we ran our experiments using prototype Matlab codes based on dense matrix representations and operations. Sparse implementations will be necessary for our future studies of complexity issues.

5 How well does LSA work?

The results of our retrieval experiments are summarized in Figures 1, 2, 3 and 4. In each of these figures is plotted average precision at ten levels of recall, where the averages are computed over the complete set of queries for each collection. Figure 1 shows the performance of our baseline vector space model for each of the three collections. Each of the remaining figures shows the performance of the LSA model across a range of reduced ranks for one of the collections.

Before discussing our results with the LSA models, a few words about the basic vector space model results given in Figure 1 are warranted. The curves for the CF and the TIME collections display a fairly typical pattern that illustrates the well-known tradeoff between precision and recall: high precision at low levels of recall with a relatively rapid drop in precision as recall is increased. The curves for the MED collection illustrate an abnormally high level of performance, with relatively high levels of precision maintained across an unusually wide-range of recall levels. As discussed by Deerwester et al. [4], this appearance is likely a result of the way that the document set was created, MED itself being a collection of the results of

126

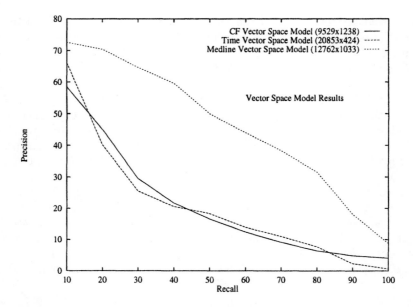

Figure 1. *Precision vs. recall results for the A vector space model for all three collections.*

document searches using the provided query set.

The LSA results for the CF collection shown in Figure 2 demonstrate that the models at and above rank 300 match the vector space model at low levels of recall and outperform the vector space model at recall levels above 30%. The best overall performance is given by the rank 300 model. Note also that, although the 100 and 50 rank models show degraded performance at the lowest levels of recall, they outperform the vector space model at recall levels above 40%.

The LSA results for the TIME collection are not as encouraging. The best rank choice matches the performance of the vector space model, but the performance of LSA steadily degrades as the rank is reduced.

Yet another pattern of results emerges with the MED collection. As can be seen in Figure 4, every LSA model, except the lowest rank model, outperforms the original vector space model. Moreover, the observed improvements in precision are substantial and hold across the entire range of recall levels. These results are particularly impressive given the already high level of performance in the vector space model. Note that although these experiments were not performed in precisely the same fashion as those described in [4], the pattern of results reported here substantially mirrors the results reported there. Again, these exceptional results are likely explained by the method of construction of the MED document collection.

Except for the MED collection, the results from our LSA models do not meet the levels of performance that are anecdotally cited for LSA. It is often stated that LSA models outperform standard vector space models by an average of 30% (see, for example, [17, 24]), but there is no evidence in our results or in the published

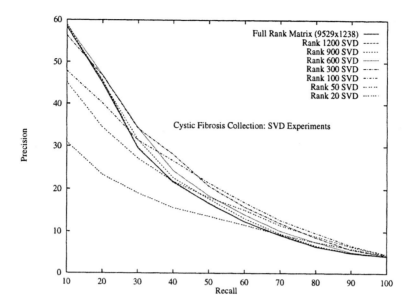

Figure 2. *Precision vs. recall results for the vector space model and 7 LSA models for the CF collection.*

literature indicating that LSA can reliably be expected to deliver such performance on any given collection [4, 6, 7, 8, 9, 10]. Rather an LSA model can almost always be found that can *match*, or slightly outperform, the performance of an unadorned vector space model across a wide range of collections. As we discuss in Section 7, the best level of performance is often obtained using a significantly reduced rank. The published literature does, however, mirror our finding that LSA clearly outperforms the vector space model by a wide margin on the MED collection for most rank choices.

Note that our primary interest here is in gaining a better understanding of the details of the LSA model, its relation to the vector space model, and other methods of rank reduction. We have made no attempts to optimize the performance of either the vector space model or the LSA models with any of the standard information retrieval methods that almost always improve the performance of models such as these. In particular, we did not attempt to assess the impact of stemming, alternative term weighting schemes, or relevance feedback.

6 What about synonymy?

One of the most interesting claims made about LSA is that it addresses the phenomenon of *synonymy*. Although synonymy is a complex issue that has long resisted simple definitions, the core of the issue is the notion that different words can be used to refer to the same, or at least highly similar, concepts. A traditional linguistic test for the synonymy of two words is *substitutability*: two words are said to be

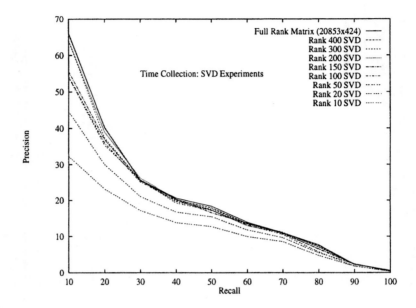

Figure 3. *Precision vs. recall results for the vector space model and 8 LSA models with the TIME collection.*

synonyms if they can be substituted in some context with no effect on the resulting meanings.

This phenomenon is relevant in the context of information retrieval because synonymy-based mismatches between the words used in a query and the words used in a document inevitably lead to decreased retrieval performance. Consider the following example queries:

Tell me about Ford car sales last month.
Tell me about Ford automobile sales last month.

In the first example, the use of *car* may fail to rank highly documents that use the word *automobile*, while the second example may fail to rank highly documents that use the word *car*.

The claim made for LSA is that the representations of documents that make of use different synonyms, but which are otherwise similar, are quite similar to one another in their reduced-rank representations. Returning to our examples, the claim is that documents that make use of either *car* or *automobile* and which are otherwise similar are given similar document vectors by LSA. Correspondingly, query vectors using either of the terms are similar to the reduced-rank representations of documents using either of the terms.

Note that synonymy is just one example of a large class of lexical phenomena that can lead to term mismatches in information retrieval settings. For example, queries such as **Ford vehicle sales** or **Ford SUV sales**, which do not involve the use of synonyms, run into the same mismatch problems as the ones given above. In these cases, the mismatch arises from the use of terms that denote different levels

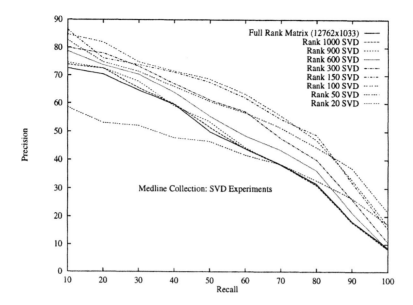

Figure 4. *Precision vs. recall results for the vector space model and 8 LSA models with the MED collection.*

of specificity. See [14] for a longer discussion of various lexical relations that can cause problems for information retrieval systems.

Deerwester et al. [4] claim that overcoming these lexical mismatch problems is the main benefit that LSA provides. More specifically, they claim that the primary benefit that LSA provides is to increase precision at higher levels of recall. The logic of this claim is that query/relevant-document pairs with a high degree of term overlap are already handled well by the normal vector space model, leaving little room for LSA to improve things by increasing the ranking of such documents. On the other hand, query/relevant-document pairs that have little or no term overlap can be improved by LSA since the vector space model has no hope of giving these relevant documents high rankings. Although the logic of this claim seems clear, it has never been directly verified.

A direct approach to assessing this claim would involve identifying naturally occurring synonym sets as they are used in both queries and documents in standard test collections. An assessment could then be made for how well these documents and queries fare in both the vector space and LSA models. Unfortunately, the rather technical nature of the vocabularies in the CF and MED collections make this set rather difficult to identify, and the TIME collection is far too small to yield a reasonable sample of queries and relevant documents making use of such synonym sets.

Because of these issues, we decided to explore a simpler approach that directly addresses the broader term mismatch issue mentioned earlier. The basic idea is to identify all those query/relevant-document pairs that have no terms in common.

In the ordinary vector space model, these pairs produce a cosine of zero, and a correspondingly low ranking. If the synonymy claims for LSA are correct, then these pairs should produce higher cosines and improved rankings in the better LSA models.

We tested this hypothesis using the MED collection. An examination of this collection revealed that only two of the original 33 MED queries have relevant documents containing no terms in common with the query. However, a considerable amount of the term overlap among the remaining queries is due to the presence of high frequency, low content, function words. We therefore relaxed our criteria and considered all query/relevant-document pairs that had no *content words* in common. Following this strategy, we found that of the total 696 query/document relevance judgments in the MED collection, 100 have no content word overlap between the query and the relevant document.

Using the rank 100 SVD MED matrix as a comparison, these documents were observed to improve their rankings by an average of 188 positions for an average 11% improvement in rank over the normal vector space model. By comparison, relevant documents with term overlap improve their positions on average by less than one position. This observation is consistent with the notion that, when it works, the primary benefit conveyed by LSA is on relevant documents with little term overlap with their queries.

Of course, it is possible that LSA is achieving this benefit in a way that would have little impact in realistic settings. For example, an improvement of 100 places from position 1110 to 1010 is of far less benefit in this collection than is an improvement from position 110 to 10. We, therefore, employed a metric designed to assess the nature of the improvement that LSA is providing. This metric is based on the notion of the gap to be closed from a relevant document's position in the vector space model to the top position in the ranking. Consider, for example, a document ranked 100 in the original model and 80 in an LSA model. In terms of position, it has improved by 20 places, but it can also be said to have closed 20% of the distance to the top of the ranking. On the other hand, a move of 20 from position 1000 to 980 has closed a much less impressive 2% of that gap. More formally, we employed the metric Δ/p, where Δ is the difference between the start and end positions of the document and p is the lower of these two positions. In the case where the document has improved its rank this metric is positive; in the case where a document moves down, it reflects a negative score of the same magnitude as an equivalent upward move.

Using this measure, we observe that the zero-overlap relevant documents close on average 20% of their gap in the LSA model, while relevant documents with term overlap on average close only 3% of their gap.

In sum, these results indicate that a considerable amount of the benefit conveyed by LSA results from the upward re-ranking of relevant documents that lack terms in common with their queries. Moreover, it appears to be the case that this benefit is significant because relevant documents are moved a considerable distance towards the top of the ranking. Note, that these results do not show that LSA solves the synonymy problem, nor that synonymy is even a problem in this domain. Nevertheless, they do show that LSA can overcome the broader problem of term mismatch between queries and their relevant documents.

7 What is the right choice of rank?

Rank reduction was first promoted by Deerwester et al. [4] as a mechanism for removing the *noise* that obscures the latent semantic structure of the document collection. Which singular values to retain to best capture that structure remains an unanswered question, but, roughly 100-300 singular values are typically retained regardless of the matrix size (see [2, 6, 18], for example.) In an effort to better quantify that choice, we now take a closer look at the effect of the rank on the performance of LSA.

Collection	Dimensions of Matrix	Rank	Minimum Singular Value	Maximum Singular Value
CF	9529×1238	1238	8.40	290.05
TIME	20853×424	424	2.45	523.09
MED	12672×1033	1033	8.84	283.45

Table 2. *The ranges of singular values for tested term-document matrices.*

We begin our search for a natural choice of rank by examining the singular values of the term-document matrices. Anecdotally, removing noise has become associated with removing *small* singular values. Yet, as Table 2 shows, the term-document matrices we tested are all of full rank, and the range of singular values is not large. No singular value can immediately be considered negligible. A plot of the singular values gives no more clues. Figure 5 shows the singular values of the term-document matrix for the MED collection. This plot has the form typical for the matrices we examined. The singular values decrease smoothly, with no significant gaps or steps to identify natural breaks.

Moving away from the individual singular values, we turn instead to the testing of various ranks. Tables 3 shows the precision at 20% and 50% recall at all tested ranks for the three test collections. Also shown is the percent relative error in the low-rank approximation A_k to the full-rank term-document matrix A in each case. The error reported is $100(1 - \frac{\|A_k\|_F}{\|A\|_F})$, a measure computed conveniently from the recorded singular values.

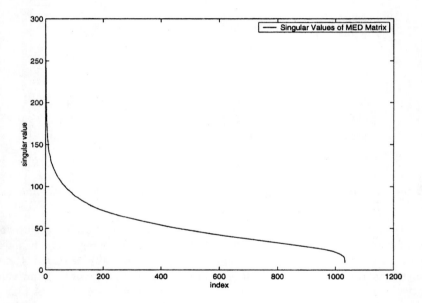

Figure 5. *A plot of the singular values of the MED collection.*

CF:

Rank	% Relative Error in A_k	Precision at 20% Recall	Precision at 50% Recall
1238	0.0	45.02	16.60
1200	0.1	45.62	16.70
900	2.5	45.26	17.69
600	8.0	46.91	18.45
300	19.8	46.76	20.68
100	38.8	40.18	21.44
50	49.4	34.41	18.05
20	61.1	23.34	13.60

TIME:

Rank	% Relative Error in A_k	Precision at 20% Recall	Precision at 50% Recall
424	0.0	40.15	18.36
400	0.3	40.28	17.91
300	3.3	37.34	17.53
200	8.8	38.95	17.24
150	13.1	36.89	16.54
100	19.3	35.99	17.18
50	29.4	35.37	17.21
20	40.8	29.97	15.43
10	47.6	23.12	12.70

MED:

Rank	% Relative Error in A_k	Precision at 20% Recall	Precision at 50% Recall
1033	0.0	70.39	49.98
1000	0.1	72.53	51.52
900	1.0	72.56	53.42
600	6.2	73.72	55.39
300	18.3	77.95	61.19
150	31.1	76.18	67.61
100	38.4	81.95	68.75
50	49.9	74.81	60.66
20	62.4	53.03	46.49

Table 3. *Relative error in A_k and retrieval performance.*

As noted in Section 3, an uncertainty of roughly 20% might naturally be expected in the matrix representation of any collection. For both the CF and MED collections, the LSA rank (300) that results in an error near 20% does in fact provide an improvement in retrieval performance over the full-rank vector space model. More surprising is the fact that the best performance for the MED collection is recorded when the low-rank approximation imposes a nearly 40% error. The LSA results are still better than those for the vector space model when the error is almost 50%. The results for the CF collection are similar. The best precision at 20% recall is found at an error of 8.0%, but a nearly identical precision is recorded at an error of 19.8%. At errors near 40 and 50%, respective precisions of 86% and 73% of optimal are noted. At 50% recall, the results more closely resemble those for the MED collection: best performance is seen at a nearly 40% error, and there is still an improvement over the vector space model at an almost 50% error.

What these numbers tell us is that the pro forma rank range of 100-300 is a reasonable one for the rank 1238 CF and rank 1033 MED collections, but that reasonable performance is also realized for ranks as small as 50.

The TIME collection provides a slightly different scenario. In this case, the best results are seen for full or nearly full rank matrices, but there is actually little difference between the results over a range of relative errors from 3.3 to 29.4% (ranks 300 through 50). When the error grows to 40.8%, the precisions are 75 and 84% of the full rank values for 20 and 50% recall, respectively. Only when the error reaches 47.6% does the performance degrade markedly. Thus, again, a rank range of 50-300 provides acceptable performance although, for this collection, any sizable rank reduction is something of a detriment.

Our results indicate that LSA is doing quite a bit more than merely removing *noise* from the original representation of the term-document matrix: far too much error is present in the models with the best retrieval performance to be consistent with that notion. These results are consistent with those reported by Ding [5]. He presents a probablistic mechanism for selecting the optimal rank based on an analysis of the sizes of the singular values. This result relies on the observed Zipf-like distribution among the singular values found in these models.

For MED, the one dataset that we have in common, Ding's model predicts an optimal rank of 184. This is quite close to the rank of 150 which represents the best MED model we found (note that we did not do a fine-grained search in this range and hence did not examine the performance of a model at rank 184). Clearly, further work is warranted into the relationship between the degree of error introduced by rank reduction and the empirical distribution of singular values observed in these test collections.

8 Which documents are relevant?

In the literature [2, 10, 21], cosine cutoffs as large as 0.9 are recommended. That is, a document is judged relevant to a query only if the cosine defined in equation (1) is at least 0.9 in magnitude. Our tests show that 0.9 is not a good choice.

We examined the cosines computed for the 1,396,056 query-document pairs

Interval	Number of Query/Doc Pairs	Percentage of All Pairs
$[0.7, 1.0]$	0	0%
$[0.6, 0.7)$	28	0%
$[0.5, 0.6)$	95	0.01%
$[0.4, 0.5)$	422	0.03%
$[0.3, 0.4)$	1397	0.10%
$[0.2, 0.3)$	4423	0.32%
$[0.1, 0.2)$	45784	3.27%
$[0.0, 0.1)$	1343907	96.26%

Table 4. *The cosine magnitudes for 1,396,056 query-document pairs.*

from the three databases. Table 4 shows the magnitudes of those cosines. The largest recorded cosine is 0.6781, and over 96% of the cosines are less than 0.1. These results are consistent for all of the contrived and real term-document matrices we tested, and are also typical for other large-order applications [15].

The failure of the 0.9 cutoff does not, however, signal a failure of the method. Figures 2–4 show that LSA does deliver high precision at low recall levels. That is, LSA does produce a reasonable ordering of the first few documents returned. Thus, in applications where only a few of the relevant documents are needed, LSA can indeed be expected to return them early in the retrieval process. Table 5 shows the retrieval results for two sample queries from the MED database. There are 28 documents relevant to query 9, and the first five documents returned by LSA are among them. Nonetheless, the cosines corresponding to those relevant documents are quite small, the maximum being 0.1727. Query 10 provides even more extreme results. There are 24 documents relevant to that query, and four of them are among the first five returned. A fifth relevant document is returned ninth. In this case, the largest cosine is only 0.0190. Note that these queries were chosen to illustrate some sample cosines with relevant documents. The precision values averaged across the entire range of queries is, of course, lower.

These results suggest two alternatives to a fixed cutoff value like 0.9. If recall is not an issue, a small, fixed number of documents can be returned. This solution might be appropriate for a search engine for which the volume of data returned should be limited. When users are interested in a larger number of relevant documents, we suggest the use of a relative cosine cutoff. That is, the computed cosines are all divided by the cosine of largest magnitude, and a fixed cutoff is applied to the results.

Table 6 shows the average recall and precision values for various fixed relative cutoffs. The results for TIME and MED are similar. At a relative cutoff of 0.7,

QUERY 9				
Position	Document Number	Cosine	Recall	Precision
1	409	0.1727	3.57	100.00
2	422	0.1643	7.14	100.00
3	56	0.1570	10.71	100.00
4	30	0.1569	14.29	100.00
5	268	0.1547	17.86	100.00

QUERY 10				
Position	Document Number	Cosine	Recall	Precision
1	543	0.0190	4.17	100.00
2	532	0.0159	8.33	100.00
3	58	0.0125	12.50	100.00
4	540	0.0107	16.67	100.00
9	542	0.0095	20.83	55.56

Table 5. *Retrieval performance in terms of cosine value, recall, and precision for two MED queries. Values are listed for the first five relevant documents retrieved. The position of each document in the retrieved set is also given.*

means that of all the documents with cosines of at least 70% of the maximum cosine that are returned, about half of the relevant documents are found. For the TIME collection, on average roughly half of the documents returned are relevant (56% precision) while, for the MED collection, almost three quarters are relevant (72% precision). These results suggest that a relative cutoff of 0.7 is a reasonable choice.

CF:	Relative Cutoff	Recall	Precision	Number of Documents Returned
	0.90	5.88	73.84	2
	0.80	9.07	72.77	4
	0.70	13.30	63.53	7
	0.60	19.26	53.03	15
	0.50	25.37	45.59	27
	0.40	34.44	37.49	54
	0.30	46.11	28.09	106
	0.20	59.42	19.42	211
	0.10	78.47	10.04	453

TIME:	Relative Cutoff	Recall	Precision	Number of Documents Returned
	0.90	35.65	57.73	1
	0.80	46.44	57.14	2
	0.70	55.96	56.00	3
	0.60	65.81	55.08	5
	0.50	69.56	53.61	6
	0.40	75.25	51.95	8
	0.30	79.15	51.00	10
	0.20	82.50	47.69	14
	0.10	89.98	43.33	26

MED:	Relative Cutoff	Recall	Precision	Number of Documents Returned
	0.90	16.54	84.82	4
	0.80	31.52	76.82	9
	0.70	46.30	72.00	16
	0.60	62.59	63.36	25
	0.50	71.98	56.65	32
	0.40	81.71	47.43	49
	0.30	90.20	38.98	77
	0.20	94.14	32.06	126
	0.10	97.40	22.55	193

Table 6. *Average precision, recall, and total numbers of documents returned for various relative cutoff values.*

The CF collection, however, puts this selection in question. At a relative cutoff of 0.7, the precision is high (64%), but the recall is very low (13%). To find about half of the relevant documents, we need instead to use a relative cutoff in the range 0.2–0.3. Note, that there is a substantial penalty involved in going below this to a cutoff into the range of 0.1 even though it boosts recall to around 78%. At this level of recall, the number of documents that need to be examined is quite large (453), representing nearly one third of the entire collection.

As with many of our other findings, the lesson to take away from this section is somewhat application dependent. However, there are some general guidelines that appear to hold across collections:

- Absolute cosine cutoffs are unlikely to give reasonable performance.

- Applications where precision is critical can use relative cosine cutoffs as high as 90%.

- In settings where recall is critical, cutoffs as low as 20% should give high levels of recall with manageably sized return sets.

9   Are other factorizations good?

The inherent imprecision of the term-document matrix leads to the question of whether an optimal matrix decomposition is actually necessary for rank reduction. In [3], a variant of LSA based on the ULV decomposition is introduced. In this section, we briefly examine another variant, first described in [1], that is based on the QR decomposition. In the latter case, the term-document matrix is factored as $A = QR$ with orthogonal Q and upper triangular R, and its low rank approximation is constructed from reduced-rank forms of these factors. Query-document comparison again requires computation of the cosines between the query vector q and the columns of A. Those cosines are determined from $q^T A$ or, in terms of the QR factors, $q^T QR$.

The ULV decomposition is computed directly from the QR decomposition. That is, if $A = QR$, we can compute the QR decomposition of $R^T = V^T L^T$ so that $A = QLV$. Setting $Q = U$ completes the ULV decomposition $A = ULV$ (ignoring column pivoting). For the term-document matrix with normalized columns, the cosines are now $q^T ULV = q^T QLV = q^T QR$. That is, for query-document comparison, the QR-based variant of LSA gives the same results as the ULV-based variant, but at half the computational cost. Note, however, that, unlike the ULV- and SVD-based methods, QR-based LSA does not provide an orthogonal basis for the term space and so may not lend itself to some functions involving term-term comparison.

In the remainder of this section, we first give the details of the QR-based method then compare it to SVD-based LSA in terms of precision vs. recall. No such comparison is provided in [3], so these results provide the first validation of the use of alternative decompositions.

The QR-based method begins with the QR decomposition of the term-document matrix A using column pivoting, so that $A\Pi = QR$ or $A = QR\Pi^T$, where Q is a $t \times t$ orthogonal matrix, R is a $t \times d$ upper triangular matrix, and Π is a $d \times d$

permutation matrix. QR decomposition with column pivoting tends to push the smaller elements of R to the bottom rows; thus rank reduction is carried out by setting those rows to zero. We denote as R_k the $k \times d$ matrix whose rows equal the first k rows of R and as Q_k the $t \times k$ matrix whose columns equal the first k columns of Q. Then the rank-k approximation to A is

$$A_k^{(QR)} = Q_k R_k \Pi^T.$$

A document is judged relevant to a query if the angle between the vectors representing the document and query are sufficiently small. Recalling equation (1), we compute the cosines

$$\cos \theta_j = \frac{(A_k^{(QR)} e_j)^T q}{\|A_k e_j\| \, \|q\|} = \frac{e_j^T (\Pi R_k^T Q_k^T q)}{\|R_k^T Q_k^T e_j\| \, \|q\|}, \tag{2}$$

for $j = 1, \ldots, d$.

Figures 6-7 compare the precision vs. recall curves for the best choices of ranks for the QR- and SVD-based methods. On all of these plots, the solid line shows the precision vs. recall for the full-rank vector space model. These QR results follow the same problem dependent pattern as observed in Figures 2-4 for SVD-based LSA. Moderate improvement over the vector space model is seen for the CF collection; little or no improvement is seen for the TIME collection; and extraordinary improvement is noted for the MED collection.

For the CF collection, rank 300 is the best choice for both methods. Both provide improvements over the vector space model for recall levels over about 20% with standard SVD-based LSA giving slightly better performance than the QR version. For the TIME collection, 200 is the best rank for both methods, but neither technique provides significant gain over the vector space model.

The situation is a little different for the MED collection. Figure 8 shows the precision vs. recall curves for ranks 100 and 600 for both methods for that collection. In this case, the best rank choice for the SVD is 100 while the best rank choice for QR is 600. Despite the large difference,the SVD performs notably better than does QR for the best ranks, although both provide an improvement over the vector space model. More interesting is the fact that the rank 100 performance is substantially better than the rank 600 performance for the SVD-based method, while the behavior is the opposite for the QR-based method. Indeed, the 100-rank QR version actually performs worse than the vector space model.

These preliminary results suggest that the best choice of rank may be even more strongly problem dependent for the QR-based method than for standard LSA. And how best to choose that rank is not easy to say. Because the SVD provides the optimal low-rank approximation to the term-document matrix, we can expect that the relative error in the approximation derived from the QR decomposition is worse than that derived from the SVD, but we did not compute those errors in this preliminary study.

From these results, we see that for a good choice of rank, the QR-based and ULV-based methods work similarly to the standard SVD-based LSA. Whether it makes sense to consider these alternatives depends on their costs. In the case of

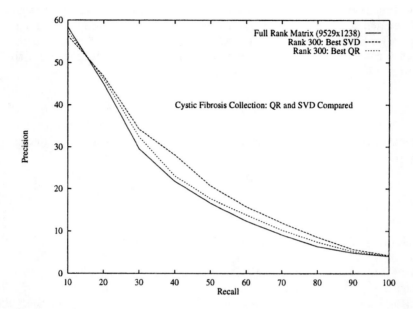

Figure 6. *Maximum precision vs. recall curves for QR and SVD for the CF collection.*

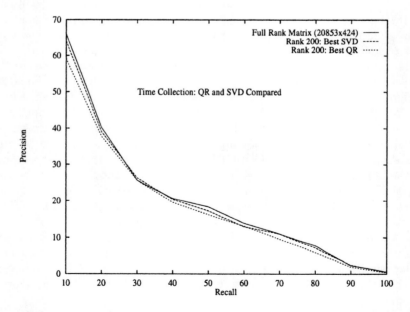

Figure 7. *Maximum precision vs. recall curves for QR and SVD for the TIME collection.*

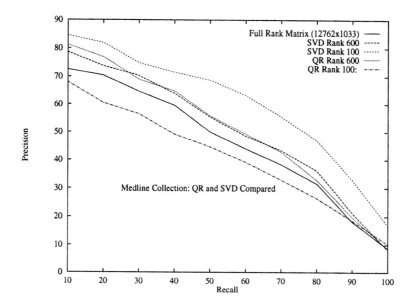

Figure 8. *Maximum precision vs. recall curves for QR and SVD for the MED collection. Curves for rank 100 and 600 are also provided for both methods.*

dense matrices, the rank-k QR-based and SVD-based methods have similar storage requirements ($O(\frac{tk+dk-1}{2k^2})$ and $O(tk+dk)$, respectively), while the ULV-based method requires slightly more space ($O(\frac{tk+dk+1}{2k^2})$). For sparse matrices, those comparisons depend on the degree of fill, and the QR factors are generally dense while the SVD factors may not be. Thus, a true comparison requires study of fill in the decompositions. Similarly, the relative computational costs depend as well on fill, rank, and the number of iterations needed to compute the SVD. Furthermore, different rank choices may be required for the different methods. For example, the optimal rank choices differ by a factor of six for the MED collection, and it is unlikely that the QR method could provide any cost benefit in that case. No comparative complexity data are provided in [3], and we are not able to gather them with our dense Matlab prototypes. A more thorough complexity study of these methods will be part of our future work.

10 Summary

Our goal in writing this paper was to improve our understanding of LSA for information retrieval through empirical testing. We set out to address a series of specific questions about the implementation and performance of the method. In this section, we summarize our findings and suggest future research areas.

A primary concern was the reliability of LSA as compared to the full-rank vector space model. From every angle, we found retrieval performance to be strongly dependent on both the rank chosen for LSA and on the document collection used.

These results are somewhat unsatisfying as little can be said about either factor *a priori*, but some general observations can be made.

We found that, at best, LSA with the optimal rank choice delivers modest performance gains for test collections without special LSA-friendly structure. These results echo those in the literature. We saw that the performance gains are a result of LSA's ability to partially overcome the problems of term mismatch between queries and their relevant documents that are endemic in the vector space model. Clearly, further research into both the nature of the term mismatch problem, and how LSA handles it, is needed.

The problem of best rank choice remains open although we have established that the range of 100-300 used in practice and supported by statistical analysis [5] remains an acceptable option. We believe that further research into the connection between rank reduction induced error and retrieval performance will shed more light on this problem.

On the question of how to identify relevant documents, we have made more concrete progress. We have established that absolute cosine cutoffs are unlikely to lead to reasonable retrieval performance but that relative cutoffs are a tractable alternative. Again, what cutoff to use is application dependent, but we have made recommendations both for the case where recall is a priority and for the case where precision is the prime concern.

Finally, we wanted to learn if other matrix decompositions could be applied in place of the SVD. We demonstrated that document retrieval methods based on the QR and ULV decompositions provide competitive performance to the standard SVD-based LSA method. Determination of the true value of these alternatives awaits a careful complexity analysis.

Bibliography

[1] M. W. BERRY, Z. DRMAČ, AND E. R. JESSUP, *Matrices, Vector Spaces, and Information Retrieval*, SIAM Review, 41 (1999), pp. 335–362.

[2] M. BERRY, S. DUMAIS, AND G. O'BRIEN, *Using Linear Algebra for Intelligent Information Retrieval*, SIAM Review, 37 (1995), pp. 573–595.

[3] M. BERRY AND R. FIERRO, *Low-Rank Orthogonal Decompositions for Information Retrieval Applications*, Numerical Linear Algebra With Applications, 3 (1996), pp. 301–328.

[4] S. DEERWESTER, S. DUMAIS, G. FURNAS, T. LANDAUER, AND R. HARSHMAN, *Indexing by Latent Semantic Analysis*, Journal of the American Society for Information Science, 41 (1990), pp. 391–407.

[5] C. H. Q. DING, *A Similarity-Based Model for Latent Semantic Indexing*, in Proceedings of 22nd International Conference on Research and Development in Information Retrieval, Berkeley, CA, 1999, SIGIR.

[6] S. DUMAIS, *Improving the Retrieval of Information from External Sources*, Behavior Research Methods, Instruments, & Computers, 23 (1991), pp. 229–236.

[7] ——, *LSI Meets TREC: A Status Report.*, in The First Text REtrieval Conference, D. Harman, ed., National Institute of Standards and Technology Special Publication 500-207, March 1993, pp. 137–152.

[8] ——, *Latent Semantic Indexing (LSI) and TREC-2*, in The Second Text REtrieval Conference, D. Harman, ed., National Institute of Standards and Technology Special Publication 500-215, March 1994, pp. 105–116.

[9] ——, *Latent Semantic Indexing (LSI): TREC-3 Report*, in The Third Text REtrieval Conference, D. Harman, ed., National Institute of Standards and Technology Special Publication 500-226, March 1994, pp. 219–230.

[10] S. DUMAIS, G. FURNAS, T. LANDAUER, S. DEERWESTER, AND R. HARSHMAN, *Using Latent Semantic Analysis to Improve Access to Textual Information*, in CHI '88, ACM, 1988, pp. 281–285.

[11] C. ECKART AND G. YOUNG, *The Approximation of One Matrix by Another of Lower Rank*, Psychometrika, 1 (1936), pp. 211–218.

[12] G. FURNAS, T. LANDAUER, L. GOMEZ, AND S. DUMAIS, *The Vocabulary Problem in Human-System Communication*, Communications of the ACM, 30 (1987), pp. 964–971.

[13] D. HARMAN, *Overview of the Third Text REtrieval Conference (TREC-3)*, in Overview of the Third Text REtrieval Conference, D. Harman, ed., National Institute of Standards and Technology Special Publication 500-226, April 1995, pp. 1–21.

[14] D. JURAFSKY AND J. H. MARTIN, *Speech and Language Processing: An Introduction to Natural Language Processing, Computational Linguistics and Speech Recognition*, Prentice Hall, Upper Saddle River, New Jersey, 2000.

[15] TITLANDAUER. Personal Communication.

[16] T. LANDAUER, P. FOLTZ, AND D. LAHAM, *Introduction to Latent Semantic Analysis*, Discourse Processes, 25 (1998), pp. 259–284.

[17] T. LETSCHE AND M. BERRY, *Large-Scale Information Retrieval with Latent Semantic Indexing*, Information Sciences, 100 (1997), pp. 105–137.

[18] KITLOCHBAUM AND L. STREETER, *Comparing and Combing the Effectiveness of Latent Semantic Indexing and the Ordinary Vector Space Model for Information Retrieval*, Information Processing and Management, 25 (1989), pp. 665–675.

[19] Medline collection. `ftp://ftp.cs.cornell.edu/pub/smart/med/`. May 27, 1998.

[20] L. MIRSKY, *Symmetric Gauge Functions and Unitarily Invariant Norms*, The Quarterly Journal of Mathematics, 11 (1960), pp. 50–59.

[21] G. O'BRIEN, *Information Management Tools for Updating an SVD-Encoded Indexing Scheme*, Master's thesis, University of Tennessee, Knoxville, TN, 1994.

[22] W. SHAW, J. WOOD, R. WOOD, AND H. TIBBO, *The Cystic Fibrosis Collection: Content and Research Opportunities*, Library and Information Science Research, 13 (1991), pp. 347–366.

[23] H. SIMON AND H. ZHA, *On Updating Problems in Latent Semantic Indexing*, SIAM Journal on Scientific Computing, 21 (1999), pp. 782–791.

[24] *Telcordia Latent Semantic Indexing Software (LSI): Beyond Keyword Retrieval.* http://lsi.research.telcordia.com/lsi/papers/execsum.html, December 5, 2000.

[25] Time collection. `ftp://ftp.cs.cornell.edu/pub/smart/time/`. December 5, 2001.

On the Use of the Singular Value Decomposition for Text Retrieval *

Parry Husbands, Horst Simon, and Chris H.Q. Ding [†]

1 Introduction

The use of the Singular Value Decomposition (SVD) has been proposed for text retrieval in several recent works [2, 6]. This technique uses the SVD to project very high dimensional document and query vectors into a low dimensional space. In this new space it is hoped that the underlying structure of the collection is revealed thus enhancing retrieval performance.

Theoretical results [9, 3] have provided some evidence for this claim and to some extent experiments have confirmed this. However, these studies have mostly used small test collections and simplified document models. In this work we investigate the use of the SVD on large document collections. We show that, if interpreted as a mechanism for representing the terms of the collection, this technique alone is insufficient for dealing with the variability in term occurrence.

Section 2 introduces the text retrieval concepts necessary for our work. A short description of our experimental architecture is presented in Section 3. Section

*This work is supported by the Director, Office of Science, Office of Laboratory Policy and Infrastructure Management, of the U.S. Department of Energy under Contract No. DE-AC03-76SF00098. Computing resources were supported by the Director, Office of Advanced Scientific Computing Research, Division of Mathematical, Information, and Computational Sciences, of the U.S. Department of Energy under Contract No. DE-AC03-76SF00098. Work was also supported by the NSFC under Project No. 19771073 and the National Science Foundation under Grant Nos. CCR-9619542 and CCR-9901986.

[†]NERSC Division, Lawrence Berkeley National Laboratory, 1 Cyclotron Road, Berkeley, CA, 94720. Email: {prjhusbands,hdsimon,chqding}@lbl.gov.

4 describes how term occurrence variability affects the SVD and then shows how the decomposition influences retrieval performance. A possible way of improving SVD-based techniques is presented in Section 5, and we conclude in Section 6.

2   Text Retrieval Concepts

In text retrieval (see [4, 10, 1] for treatments of some of the issues), a simple way to represent a collection of documents is with a term-document matrix D where $D(i, j)$ gives the number of occurrences of term i in document j. Queries (over the same set of terms) are similarly represented. The similarity between document vectors (the columns of term-document matrices) can be found by their inner product. This corresponds to determining the number of term matches (weighted by frequency) in the respective documents. Another commonly used similarity measure is the cosine of the angle between the document vectors. This can be achieved computationally by first normalizing (to 1) the columns of the term-document matrices before computing inner products.

2.1   Term Weighting

In the above description, frequency counts were used as the entries of the term-document matrix. In practice, these counts are typically scaled using various term weightings in order to cancel out the dominating effects of frequent terms. One scheme that is commonly used is Inverse Document Frequency (IDF) weighting. This technique multiplies $D(i, j)$ by $w(i)$ where

$$w(i) = \log_2(\frac{\text{Number of documents}}{\text{Number of documents with term } i} + 1).$$

This scheme gives very frequent terms low weight and elevates rare (and hopefully more discriminating) terms.

In the discussion to follow we will denote by *term matching* the retrieval scheme where IDF weighting is used prior to document length normalization on both the matrix of documents (D) and queries (Q). The matrix of scores is then computed by `Scores = D'*Q` in Matlab.

2.2   LSI

Latent Semantic Indexing (LSI, [2]) attempts to project term and document vectors into a lower dimensional space spanned by the true *factors* of the collection. This uses a truncated Singular Value Decomposition (SVD) of the term-document matrix D.

If D is an $m \times n$ matrix, then the SVD of D is

$$D = USV',$$

where U is $m \times n$ with orthonormal columns, V is $n \times n$ with orthonormal columns, and S is diagonal with the main diagonal entries sorted in decreasing order. LSI uses a truncated SVD of the term-document matrix where D is approximated by

$$D \approx U_k S_k V_k'$$

where $U_k = U(:, 1:k)$ (the first k columns of U), $V_k = V(:, 1:k)$, and $S_k = S(1:k, 1:k)$ (the upper left k by k part of S). This gives the best rank k approximation to the original matrix.

Because a full SVD is not required, the truncated SVD is usually computed by an iterative technique such as the Lanczos method. The SVDs in this report were computed with the PARPACK software package [8] (as well as TRLAN [12] for verification). See [5] for a more complete treatment of the SVD and related decompositions.

The matrix of scores can then be computed by the product $V_k S_k U_k' Q$. Traditionally these scores are computed by first projecting the queries into k-dimensional space (by $S_k U_k' Q$) and then finding the cosines of the angles with V_k. In this representation, the columns of $S_k U_k'$ are identified as the *projected terms* and the columns of V_k are identified as the *projected documents*.[1]

Note that the new representation of term i is $S_k U_k' e_i$ and the new representation of document j is $S_k^{-1} U_k' D(:, j)$ ($D(:, j)$ denotes the jth column of matrix D). Note that because

$$D(:, j) = \sum_{i=1}^{m} D(i, j) e_i$$

the new representation of document j can be written as

$$\sum_{i=1}^{m} D(i, j) S_k^{-1} U_k' e_i.$$

Ignoring for now the diagonal scaling, we see that the *projected documents* are simple linear combinations of the projected terms.

2.3 Evaluation

In response to a query, a text retrieval system returns an ordered list l of the documents where $l(1)$ is the most relevant, $l(2)$ is the second most relevant, and so on. The standard way to evaluate the performance of a system is to obtain these lists on pre-judged queries and compute precision and recall. At point i, the precision is the number of relevant documents in the first i elements of l (denoted by $l(1:i)$) divided by i. This is a measure of the *accuracy* of the retrieval: the fraction of the documents returned that are relevant. The recall is the number of relevant documents in $l(1:i)$ divided by the total number of relevant documents. This is a measure of the *completeness* of the retrieval: the fraction of all relevant documents returned. For each query, these measures are computed at each i from 1 to the

---

[1]There is some disagreement about using U_k', $S_k U_k'$, or $S_k^{-1} U_k'$ as the *projected terms*. In this work we use $S_k U_k$ primarily because the term-term similarity matrix DD' can be decomposed as $US^2 U'$ if $D = USV'$. Hence, the rows of US naturally correspond to the rows of D.

number of documents. Precision values at fixed recall levels (typically interpolated to 0,.1,.2, ... ,1) are noted and then averaged. A sample precision/recall curve for the MEDLINE test set (with 8847 terms and 1033 documents) using term matching and LSI is shown is Figure 1.

In precision/recall terms, higher curves are better as they indicate a higher percentage of relevant documents at each recall level. In the discussion that follows, we will be evaluating various algorithms for text retrieval based on their precision/recall performance.

2.4 LSI Performance

Experiments with LSI have primarily used small data sets. The primary reason for this is the complexity (in both time and space) of computing the SVD of large, sparse term-document matrices. Nevertheless, early results were encouraging. Figure 1 compares LSI using with $k = 100$ to term matching for the small MEDLINE collection. Here, IDF weighting was used and the term-document matrix was normalized prior to decomposition. The cosine similarity measure was used in both cases.

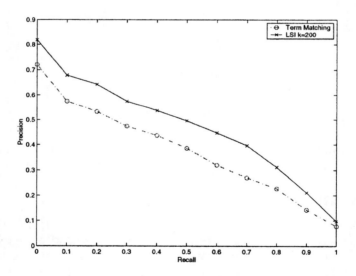

Figure 1. *LSI vs. Term Matching on MEDLINE*

Performance on very large collections is not as good. Figure 2 shows LSI using $k = 200$ on TREC6 [11], a collection with 115000 terms and 528155 documents. Experiments with different numbers of factors up to 1000 have shown similar performance. Note that the computational resources needed for using more than 1000 factors make this impractical for all but the largest supercomputers.

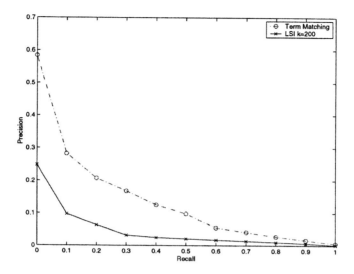

Figure 2. *LSI vs. Term Matching on TREC6*

In the rest of this paper, we will investigate reasons for this drop in performance and attempt to change the projection process in order to rectify this problem. A major factor will be the norm distribution of the projected terms, discussed in Section 4.

3   Software Used

For the experiments in this paper we used the MATLAB*P system [7]. MATLAB*P enables users of supercomputers to transparently work on large data sets within Matlab. Through the use of an external server (that stores and operates on data) and Matlab's object-oriented features, we can handle data as though it were *in* Matlab. In this way, we were able to run our experiments in parallel on NERSC's Cray T3E and no changes had to be made when moving from small to large collections. For example, if A is the term document matrix and Q is a matrix of queries, to investigate LSI we can type,

```
[U,S,V]=svds(A,k);      % Perform a truncated SVD
newTerms=U*diag(S);     % Compute the projected terms
newA=V';
newQ=newTerms'*Q;       % Get new representation for queries
% Use normcols for cosine measure and find the similarities
Scores=normcols(newA)'*normcols(newQ);
```

For the TREC6 collection, computing the SVD above for $(k = 1000)$ takes approximately 104 minutes using 64 T3E processors. Computing and graphing precision/recall curves from pre-judged queries also takes place in MATLAB*P using simple m-file scripts.

4 Norm Distribution of Terms and Impact on Retrieval Performance

The norms (lengths) of the rows of $U_k S_k$ (in addition to their directions) have great influence on the representations of the documents and queries. As Figure 3 and Table 1 show, there is great variability in term norm. In this section we will attempt to explain this variability and its effect on retrieval performance.

Because projected documents and queries are simple *linear combinations* (c.f. Section 2.2) of the projected terms, terms with low norm contribute very little to the representations of documents and queries. The cosine similarity measure comes into play too late: *after* the documents and queries have been projected. Thus, if searching for a term that happens to have low norm, the documents that contain it will have only a small component of that term and be dominated by other terms making it difficult for retrieval.

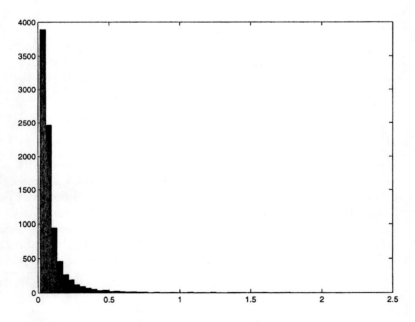

Figure 3. *Histogram of MEDLINE ($k = 100$) term norms.*

Currently, a theoretical explanation for the norm distribution has not been proposed. However, we can empirically study the phenomenon in an attempt to determine its cause. Figure 4 plots IDF weight vs. term norm for the MEDLINE test set. We see that the lowest norm terms have the highest IDF weights. This implies that lowest norm terms are those with the *lowest frequencies* in the collection.

As an example of this, consider the TREC6 query that contains the words *polio, poliomyelitis, disease, world, control, post*. For this query, the word *polio* is clearly the most important word. It has IDF weight 11.75 but norm 0.16 (k=300). The word *disease* has weight 6.17 and a much higher norm of 3.44. It comes as no surprise, therefore, that the top documents returned for this query are all about disease eradication efforts, but for diseases other than polio (malaria, tuberculosis, AIDS, etc.).

The popular TFIDF weighting scheme does little to mitigate the effect of low term norm. Table 1 shows the range of norms and IDF weights for a few test collections. The lowest term norms are typically orders of magnitude away from the highest IDF weights, hinting at IDF's inadequacy. We can therefore see that the effect of IDF is lost after projection.

Because the columns of U_k are scaled by the singular values, these have a contributing effect on term norm distribution and the projected documents. Figure 5 plots the singular values of the MEDLINE and TREC6 collections. It is interesting to note that after an initial drop, the singular values decay very slowly over the displayed range.

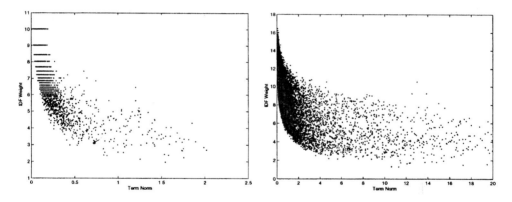

Figure 4. *IDF weight and term norm for the MEDLINE (left) and TREC6 (right) collections. TREC6 terms with norm > 20 (42 in total) were not displayed.*

Collection	k	Min norm	Max norm	Min IDF	Max IDF
NPL	100	$2.5e-3$	$5.4e+0$	2.5	13.5
MED	100	$1.3e-2$	$2.0e+0$	1.9	10.0
TREC6	300	$1.5e-4$	$1.5e+2$	1.3	16.4

Table 1. *Term norms and IDF weights for text collections*

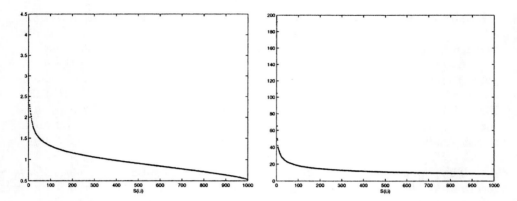

Figure 5. *The first 1000 singular values of the MEDLINE (left) and TREC6 (right) collections.*

5 A Remedy

In this section, we attempt to remedy the situation by recapturing the effectiveness of IDF. We do this by first re-examining the way documents are created in term matching. In term matching, we start with unit orthogonal vectors as terms (e_j, see Section 2.2) that are then scaled using term weighting. Finally, documents are created by frequency weighted sums of these (scaled) terms. When we use LSI, we perform a similar procedure: we create documents by frequency weighted sums of the *projected* terms. The major difference with term matching, however, is that these projected terms are neither orthogonal nor scaled in proportion to any term weights. The non-orthogonality is desirable: the whole motivation is to have similar terms come closer together. However, as discussed in Section 4, the scaling (or norms) of the projected terms can have a negative impact on retrieval performance.

One simple fix is to re-scale the projected terms so that they are all unit vectors. In this way we can benefit again from term weighting. This scheme, denoted by NLSI (for Normalized LSI), is described below:

- Compute the SVD with k factors U_k, S_k, V_k

- Compute the projected terms $U_k \times S_k$

- Normalize the rows of the projected terms

- Project the documents and queries using the normalized projected terms (note that the document matrix already incorporates term weighting, and so we do not need to scale again)

- Find the scores using the cosine similarity measure

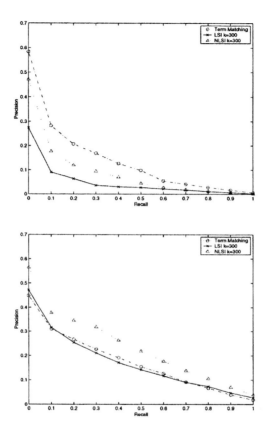

Figure 6. *TREC6 (top) and NPL (bottom) with projected term normalization*

Figure 6 shows the results of using this procedure on the TREC6 and NPL (7491 terms and 11429 documents) test sets. While not a panacea, re-scaling the projected terms has a positive effect on LSI performance for the NPL and TREC6 collections. For NPL, we outperform term matching and for TREC6 we improve on LSI, but still fall short of term matching. For MED, performance seems to depend on the number of factors used as Figure 7 shows. This suggests that we may also need to investigate the orientations (positions in k-dimensional space) of the projected terms in addition to their lengths.

6 Conclusions

LSI attempts to project the documents of a collection into a lower dimensional space in order to improve retrieval performance. This work examines the properties of SVD-based projections in order to determine whether they agree with our intuition

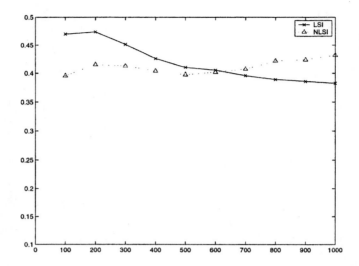

Figure 7. *Average precision for MED with projected term normalization. Each point represents, for each scheme and value of k, the mean of the precision at 11 recall levels (0,0.1,0.2, ... ,1)*

about IR concepts. The lower dimensionality of the space is intuitively desirable; terms that are related *should* be brought closer together (the cluster hypothesis). However, other properties of the SVD may not match our intuition. The main focus of this paper is the examination of the influence of term norm on retrieval performance. We have seen that rare terms (with low norm) contribute very little to the final LSI representation of documents which sometimes results in poor retrieval performance.

The properties described above are by no means exhaustive. Others include the enforcement of orthogonality of the columns of U and V, the distribution of the projected documents along each axis, and the interpretability of the singular vectors as *topics*. All of these are candidates for future exploration in an effort to fully understand the nature not only of LSI, but of other projection-based approaches to text retrieval.

Bibliography

[1] M. W. BERRY AND M. BROWNE, Understanding Search Engines: Mathematical Modeling and Text Retrieval. SIAM, 1999.

[2] S. DEERWESTER, S. T. DUMAIS, T. K. LANDAUER, G. W. FURNAS, AND R. A. HARSHMAN, *Indexing by Latent Semantic Analysis*, Journal of the Society for Information Science 41(6):391-407, 1990.

[3] CHRIS H. Q. DING, *A Similarity-Based Probability Model for Latent Semantic indexing*, In Proceedings of the 22nd ACM/SIGIR Conference, pp. 58-65, 1999.

[4] WILLIAM B. FRAKES AND RICARDO BAEZA-YATES, editors, Information Retrieval: Data Structures and Algorithms. Prentice-Hall, 1992.

[5] GENE H. GOLUB AND CHARLES F. VAN LOAN, Matrix Computations. The Johns Hopkins University Press, 1993.

[6] DAVID HULL, *Improving Text Retrieval for the Routing Problem Using Latent Semantic Indexing*, In Proceedings of the 17th ACM/SIGIR Conference, pp. 282-290, 1994.

[7] PARRY HUSBANDS, CHARLES ISBELL, AND ALAN EDELMAN, *MATLAB*P: A Tool for Interactive Supercomputing*, In Proceedings of the 9th SIAM Conference on Parallel Processing for Scientific Computing, 1999.

[8] K. J. MASCHHOFF AND D. C. SORENSEN, *A Portable Implementation of ARPACK for Distributed Memory Parallel Computers*, In Preliminary Proceedings of the Copper Mountain Conference on Iterative Methods, 1996.

[9] CHRISTOS PAPADIMITRIOU, PRABHAKAR RAGHAVAN, HISAO TAMAKI, AND SANTOSH VEMPALA, *Latent Semantic Indexing: A Probabilistic Analysis*, In Proceedings of the 17th ACM Symposium on Principles of Database Systems, 1998.

[10] GERALD SALTON, editor, The SMART Retrieval System: Experiments in Automatic Document Processing. Prentice-Hall, 1971.

[11] E. M. VOORHEES AND D. K. HARMAN, editors, *The Sixth Text Retrieval Conference*. National Institute of Standards and Technology, August 1998.

[12] KESHANG WU AND HORST SIMON, *TRLAN Users Guide*, Technical Report LBNL-42828, Lawrence Berkeley National Laboratory, 1999.

Experiments with LSA Scoring: Optimal Rank and Basis

John Caron[*]

1 Introduction

Latent Semantic Analysis (LSA) is one of the main variants of vector space methods for information retrieval, and continues to be an active area of research, both in the theory of how LSA works and in the practical applications of the method. Alternatives to the Singular Value Decomposition (SVD) have been explored that offer improvements in storage, speed, updating or other advantages, especially for large datasets. Alternatives to constructing the term-document matrix, such as term-weighting schemes have also been explored.

At the core of LSA is the scoring of a query against a canonical set of documents, using the inner product of their vector representations. Virtually all LSA researchers have assumed a particular scoring function, and alternatives have not been well investigated. In this paper, I define a family of scoring functions parameterized by a *weighting exponent p*, which weights the score by Σ^p, where Σ is the diagonal matrix of SVD eigenvalues. I present empirical findings on how retrieval accuracy varies as a function of p and the SVD approximation rank k, and find that often the standard scoring function, corresponding to $p = 0$, is not optimal.

In Section 2, I review the Singular Value Decomposition, and define LSA scoring functions as a choice of basis for the vector space defined by the document set. In Section 3, I test these scoring functions on standard test datasets for different values of the SVD approximation rank k. In Section 4, I present results from a similar experiment on matching question with answers, within the context of the Frequently Asked Question Organizer (FAQO), a prototype system for technical support that I developed. In Section 5, I summarize related work, and discuss the significance of these results.

[*]University Corporation for Atmospheric Research, and Department of Computer Science, University of Colorado at Boulder. Email: caron@ucar.edu.

2 SVD bases for LSA scoring

Singular Value Decomposition

Any real matrix A can be decomposed (assume $n < m$):

$$A^{(m \times n)} = U^{(m \times n)} \Sigma^{(n \times n)} V^{T(n \times n)}$$

into matrices U, Σ, and V, where $U^T U = V^T V = I_n$ are column orthonormal, and Σ is diagonal with elements $(\sigma_1 \geq \sigma_2 \geq \sigma_3 \geq \ldots \geq \sigma_n \geq 0)$, called the *singular values* of A. The number of non-zero singular values is the *rank* of A.

The first k column vectors of U, Σ, and V can be used to form the matrix

$$A_k^{(m \times n)} = U_k^{(m \times k)} \Sigma_k^{(k \times k)} V_k^{T(k \times n)}$$

which has the important property that it is the best rank-k approximation to A: $\|A^k - A\|_F$ is minimum for all rank-k matrices (Frobenius norm). The matrix $A_k = U_k \Sigma_k V_k^T$ is the *SVD rank-k approximation* to A.

The Term - Document Matrix

Starting with a set of n documents called the *canonical document set*, we extract a set of m terms called the *canonical term set*. We then form the $m \times n$ *term-document matrix A* whose elements a_{ij} are some function of the frequency of the ith term in the jth document.

Any document can be made into a document vector of length m by setting the ith element to some non-zero value if the document contains the corresponding canonical term, and to zero otherwise. If a document contains none of the canonical terms, then its vector is the null vector. Clearly the set of canonical terms determine how and if a document can be represented effectively. Let D be the set of all possible document vectors formed using the canonical term set, and for convenience we will assume that $D = R^m$.

The columns of $A = \{\vec{d_j}, j = 1..n\}$ are the document vectors for the canonical document set. The set of all linear combinations of these vectors defines a vector space $F = Span(A) \subset R^n$. The projection of an arbitrary document vector $\vec{q} \in D$ into F can be found by forming the inner product of $\vec{q}$ with each $\vec{d_j}$. In matrix form: $\vec{q}_{proj} = A^T \cdot \vec{q}$. So A^T is a linear transformation from R^m to R^n, $A^T : D \to F$, which takes a document vector $\vec{q} \in D$ and represents it as a linear combination of the canonical document vectors $\{\vec{d_j}\}$.

Basis sets for Span(A)

The SVD decomposition provides a basis set for $F = Span(A)$, namely the columns of U. To see this, we have to show that any $\vec{d_j}$ can be expressed as a linear combination of the columns of U. If $\vec{e_j}$ is the jth unit column vector, $\{\vec{u_j}\}$ are the column vectors of U and v_{ij} are the matrix elements of V, then

$$\vec{d_j} = A \cdot \vec{e_j}$$
$$= U\Sigma V^T \cdot \vec{e_j}$$
$$= \sigma_1 v_{j1}\vec{u}_1 + \sigma_2 v_{j2}\vec{u}_2 + \ldots + \sigma_n v_{jn}\vec{u}_n.$$

Since the $\{\vec{u}_j\}$ are orthonormal ($U^T U = I \Rightarrow \vec{u}_i \cdot \vec{u}_j = \delta_{ij}$), then the $\{\vec{u}_j\}$ are an orthonormal basis set for F.

There are other possible basis sets for F that fall out of the SVD decomposition. For example, (anticipating the next sections) for any integer b, $U\Sigma^b$ is a basis for F, since each $\vec{d_j}$ is a linear combination of the columns of $U\Sigma^b$:

$$\vec{d_j} = \sigma_1^{1-b} v_{j1}(\vec{u}_1\sigma_1^b) + \sigma_2^{1-b} v_{j2}(\vec{u}_2\sigma_2^b) + \ldots + \sigma_n^{1-b} v_{jn}(\vec{u}_n\sigma_n^b).$$

Since the columns of $U\Sigma^b$ are scalars times the columns of U, they are orthogonal (although not normalized).

LSA Document Retrieval Scoring

Generally we are interested in retrieving documents from the canonical document set $\{\vec{d_j}\}$ that are similar to some document $\vec{q}$ not in the canonical set. To do so, we compute a score based on a comparison of $\vec{q}$ with each $\vec{d_j}$, then return the $\{\vec{d_j}\}$ sorted by highest score. The standard scoring algorithm uses the cosine between two vectors: $cos(\vec{a}, \vec{c}) = \vec{a}^T \cdot \vec{c} / \|\vec{a}\|_2 \|\vec{c}\|_2$, and in what follows I explore ways to choose the vectors representing $\vec{q}$ and $\vec{d_j}$ in calculating the score.

(1) A straightforward approach is to use the columns of $A_k = A_k\vec{e_j}$ as approximations to the document vectors $\vec{d_j}$ and directly take the cosine with $\vec{q}$, so that the score of the jth document against $\vec{q}$ is:

$$score_j = cos(A_k\vec{e_j}, \vec{q}) = \frac{\vec{e_j}^T V_k \Sigma_k U_k^T \cdot \vec{q}}{\|\vec{e_j}^T V_k \Sigma_k U_k^T\|_2 \|\vec{q}\|_2} = \frac{\vec{e_j}^T V_k \Sigma_k U_k^T \cdot \vec{q}}{\|\vec{e_j}^T V_k \Sigma_k\|_2 \|\vec{q}\|_2}. \tag{1}$$

(2) Another approach is to observe that

$$A \approx A_k = U_k \Sigma_k V_k^T \Rightarrow U_k^T A \approx \Sigma_k V_k^T$$

implies that the columns of $\Sigma_k V_k^T$ approximate the $\vec{d_j}$ in the vector space that has U_k as its basis set. The query projected to that basis is $U_k^T \vec{q}$, so:

$$score_j = cos(\Sigma_k V_k^T \vec{e_j}, U_k^T \vec{q}) = \frac{\vec{e_j}^T V_k \Sigma_k \cdot U_k^T \vec{q}}{\|\vec{e_j}^T V_k \Sigma_k\|_2 \|U_k^T \vec{q}\|_2} \tag{2}$$

$$score_j = (\sigma_1 v_{j1}\vec{u}_1 \cdot \vec{q} + \sigma_2 v_{j2}\vec{u}_2 \cdot \vec{q} + \ldots + \sigma_k v_{jk}\vec{u}_k \cdot \vec{q})/norms$$

which gives the same retrieval results as (1) because the $\|\vec{q}\|_2$ in (1) and the $\|U_k^T \vec{q}\|_2$ in (2) are constant for all scores, and so do not affect the document rankings.

(3) Similarly:

$$A \approx U_k \Sigma_k V_k^T \Rightarrow \Sigma_k^{-1} U_k^T A \approx V_k^T$$

implies that the columns of V_k^T approximate the $\vec{d}_j$ in the vector space that has $U_k \Sigma_k^{-1}$ as its basis set. The query in that basis is $\Sigma_k^{-1} U_k^T \vec{q}$, so:

$$score_j = cos(V_k^T \vec{e}_j, \Sigma_k^{-1} U_k^T \vec{q}) = \frac{\vec{e}_j^T V_k \cdot \Sigma_k^{-1} U_k^T \vec{q}}{\|V_k^T \vec{e}_j\|_2 \|\Sigma_k^{-1} U_k^T \vec{q}\|_2} \tag{3}$$

$$score_j = (\sigma_1^{-1} v_{j1} \vec{u}_1 \cdot \vec{q} + \sigma_2^{-1} v_{j2} \vec{u}_2 \cdot \vec{q} + \ldots + \sigma_k^{-1} v_{jk} \vec{u}_k \cdot \vec{q}) / norms.$$

(4) More generally, for an integer p:

$$A \approx U_k \Sigma_k^{-p/2} \Sigma_k^{1+p/2} V_k^T \Rightarrow \Sigma_k^{p/2} U_k^T A \approx \Sigma_k^{1+p/2} V_k^T$$

implies that the columns of $\Sigma_k^{1+p/2} V_k^T$ approximate the $\vec{d}_j$ in the vector space that has $U_k \Sigma_k^{p/2}$ as its basis set. The query in that basis is $\Sigma_k^{p/2} U_k^T \vec{q}$, so:

$$score_j = cos(\Sigma_k^{1+p/2} V_k^T \vec{e}_j, \Sigma_k^{p/2} U_k^T \vec{q}) = \frac{\vec{e}_j^T V_k \Sigma_k^{1+p/2} \cdot \Sigma_k^{p/2} U_k^T \vec{q}}{\|\Sigma_k^{1+p/2} V_k^T \vec{e}_j\|_2 \|\Sigma_k^{p/2} U_k^T \vec{q}\|_2} \tag{4}$$

$$score_j = (\sigma_1^{1+p} v_{j1} \vec{u}_1 \cdot \vec{q} + \sigma_2^{1+p} v_{j2} \vec{u}_2 \cdot \vec{q} + \ldots + \sigma_k^{1+p} v_{jk} \vec{u}_k \cdot \vec{q}) / norms.$$

Using $U_k \Sigma_k^{p/2}$ as basis for F is equivalent to scaling each basis vectors $\vec{u}_i$ by $\sigma_i^{p/2}, i = 1 \ldots k$. Since both $\vec{q}$ and the $\{\vec{d}_j\}$ are projected into F, the effect on $score_j$ is to 1) weight the contribution of the ith eigenvector by an additional factor of σ_i^p, and 2) divide the score by the norm of the jth column vector of $\Sigma_k^{1+p/2} V_k^T$. (Note that the constant factor $\|\Sigma_k^{p/2} U_k^T \vec{q}\|_2$ does not affect the retrieval results). This defines a family of LSA scoring functions parameterized by p, which might be called the *LSA score-weighting exponent*. Note that (2) and (3) are the special cases where $p = 0$ and $p = -2$, respectively.

Almost all LSA researchers use (1) or (2) as the scoring function (also see Section 5), but I have not been able to find a theoretical basis for that assumption. At the heart of LSA is the dimension reduction of the SVD rank-k approximation, which (somewhat non-obviously) provides a better solution for the problems of polysemy and synonymy than representing the document and query vectors in exact form [4], as for example in the vector space model [7]. In this context, the optimal approximation of the documents and queries for the purpose of scoring is unclear. A future theory of how LSA works should hopefully clarify this, and will likely involve some characterization of the statistical correlation between document sets and queries. In the meanwhile, empirical results may be useful. In the next section, I explore the effect of varying the LSA score-weighting exponent on retrieval accuracy on several standard test datasets.

Table 1. *Characteristics of test datasets*

	Medline	Cranfield	CISI	Time
# docs	1033	1400	1460	425
# terms	5696	4516	5483	10595
avg.#terms/doc	50	58	46	199
% non-zero	.87%	1.3%	.85%	1.9%
# queries	30	225	112	83

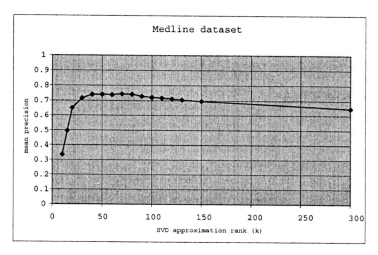

Figure 1. *Standard scoring algorithm (Medline dataset). Performance vs. number of dimensions (compare to Figure 1 of [6]).*

3 Effect of the weighting exponent on retrieval

To examine the effect of the stretching parameter on retrieval accuracy, I created a Java program for constructing the term-document matrix, and used the SVD-PACKC software (las2.c) for the SVD solver [10]. This environment was developed as part of the FAQO project, described in the next section and at [3].

I reproduced as closely as possible the results of Susan Dumais' early work on LSA [6], by using the same term weighting algorithm (*Log(TF) Entropy*), and a similar procedure for constructing the canonical term list. I also normalized the columns of the term-document matrix A, which she may not have.

I also used the same test datasets (available from the SMART ftp site [9]) as she did, and Table 1 shows the characteristics of my document matrices, which can be compared to her Table 1. Figure 1 shows the results of varying the number of dimensions (k), using the standard scoring algorithm (corresponding to $p = 0$), on the Medline dataset. This can also be directly compared to her Figure 1 in [6]. Mean precision is the precision averaged over recall levels of 25%, 50% and 75%. Note that in my Figure 1 it is clearer that the LSA algorithm performs almost identically

162

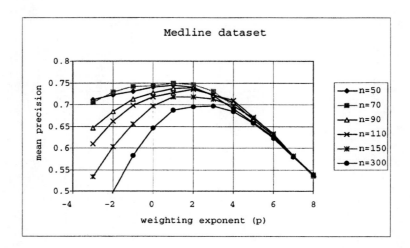

Figure 2. *Medline dataset: Retrieval accuracy vs. p (weighting exponent) for various values of k (SVD approximation rank)*

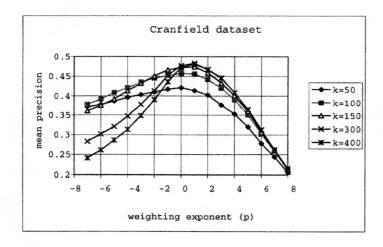

Figure 3. *Cranfield dataset: Retrieval accuracy vs. p (weighting exponent) for various values of k (SVD approximation rank)*

for this dataset for a range of dimensions between $k = 40$ (mean precision $=.7391$) and $k = 90$ (.7276) with a maximum around $k = 70$ (.7435). This figure shows that my experimental setup gives very similar results to that of other researchers.

In Figures 2, 3, 4, and 5, I show the mean precision of the retrieval as a function of the weighting exponent, for various values of k (the SVD approximation rank), for the Medline, Cranfield, Time and CISI datasets respectively. Some comments on these figures:

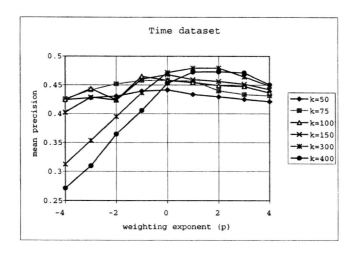

Figure 4. *Time dataset: Retrieval accuracy vs. p (weighting exponent) for various values of k (SVD approximation rank)*

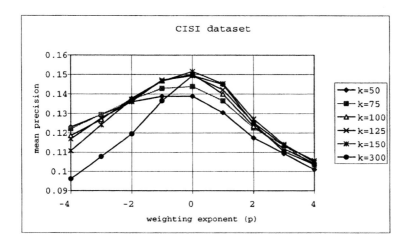

Figure 5. *CISI dataset: Retrieval accuracy vs. p (weighting exponent) for various values of k (SVD approximation rank)*

• These curves are continuous for the most part. While the difference between most of these numbers is relatively small, it does not appear due to randomness. Figure 6 shows a higher resolution plot of the Medline dataset near the optimal $k = 70$. Here some scatter is seen, probably due to the small number of queries, but the shape of the curves as a whole is not random.

• All of the curves for different values of k converge as p increases towards the right side of the plots. This is most clear in Figures 2 and 3, which show retrieval

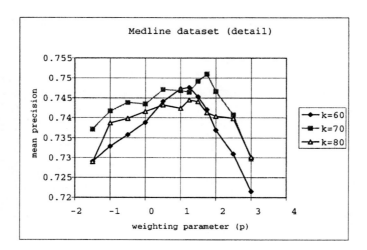

Figure 6. *Medline dataset (detail): Retrieval accuracy vs. p (weighting exponent) for values of k near the optimum.*

results for values of p up to 8. This is further discussed in section 5.

• The optimal value of p depends on k, and on the dataset, and generally increases as k increases. For the limited range of k tested here, the optimal value of p ranges between -1 and 2.

• For the Medline, Cranfield, and Time datasets (Figures 2, 3, 4, 6), at the optimal value of k, the optimal value of p is around 1.75, 1, and 2 respectively. These are respectively 1.0%, 1.2% and 1.7% improvements over the standard basis ($p = 0$). For non-optimal values of k, the optimal value of p can do quite a bit better than the standard basis, e.g., for the Medline dataset and $k = 300$, the optimal basis is about 7% better than the standard basis.

• For the CISI dataset, the standard basis ($p = 0$) is optimal for all values of k tested. At the optimal value of $k = 150$, the standard basis is about 4% better than $p = 1$. It may be noteworthy that the LSA algorithm has the lowest mean precision for the CISI dataset, 3-5 times lower than the other datasets.

4 Experimental results with the Frequently Asked Question Organizer (FAQO)

The Frequently Asked Question Organizer (FAQO) is a prototype system to assist technical support personnel in answering customer questions [3]. It uses Latent Semantic Analysis for matching queries against a database of previously asked questions and answers. It is currently under active development and testing for technical support at Unidata/UCAR.

To evaluate the usefulness of FAQO, the technical support person rates the documents returned. However s/he typically only rates the first 10 or perhaps 20

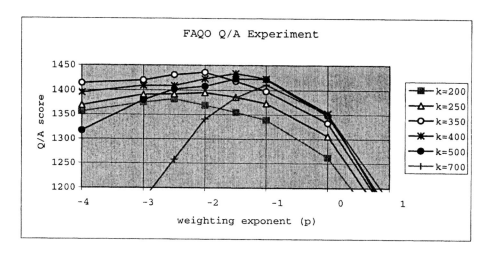

Figure 7. *FAQO QA Experiment: Total Q/A matching score vs.* p *(weighting exponent) for various values of k (SVD approximation rank)*

documents, rather than systematically finding all documents relevant to a query. Therefore, it is not possible to calculate traditional measures such as recall using these ratings.

As an alternative, I developed a simple methodology called *question/answer matching* for comparing LSA scoring algorithms. The document database consists of email messages that often contain a single, easily identified question and answer. A set of these is manually identified and the question and answer are separately tagged. The LSA matrix is generated as usual, except that for the tagged messages, only the answer text is used in the document vector. Each question is then used as a query, and the top 10 scoring documents are returned. For each question, a score of 10 is given if the answer is the first returned document, a score of 9 for a rank-two answer, and so on, down to a score of one for a rank 10 answer. Answers that have rank higher than 10 get no points. The algorithm's overall score is then the sum of these scores.

While this algorithm Q/A score is not as good as traditional recall and precision metrics, the score is simple to do, it plausibly measures the usefulness of the results for a user, and it is not obviously biased towards any particular algorithm.

Figure 7 shows the results of this experiment using one set of emails gleaned from the Java Advanced Imaging mailgroup. This dataset contained a total of 979 emails, out of which 209 emails with clear questions and answers were identified and used as queries. The maximum possible score for the test is 2090.

Unlike the tests using the standard datasets in section 3, here values of p less than 0 were optimal. At the optimal value of $k = 350$, the optimal value of p was -2, which is 7.7% better than the standard basis of $p = 0$. For various values of k, the optimal value of p varied from -2.5 to -1, and again increased as k increased. A weighting exponent of -2 is equivalent to dividing the contribution of the ith eigenvector by a factor of σ_i^2.

In concrete terms, the difference between using the standard basis of $p = 0$ and the optimal basis of $p = -2$ is that 4% more answers were returned within the top 10 documents by the optimal basis (168 vs 159 returned out of 209 total), and the average rank of the returned answers decreased from 1.62 to 1.45 (an average rank of 1.0 would mean that all answers that were returned within the top 10 documents were returned as the top-ranked document).

5 Related Work and Discussion

There is some confusion over the actual scoring algorithm used in the original paper on LSA by Deerwester et al. [4]. Most likely they used the standard method given by equation (2), i.e. used U_k as the basis set, as does Ding [5]. Berry et al [2] do a careful job explaining the difference between (1) and (2). I interpret [1] as using equation (3), $(U_k \Sigma_k^1$ as basis) for their scoring, but this is quite possibly an incorrect reading.

Kolda and O'Leary [8] (p 328) suggest a scoring algorithm using a *split* Σ_k:

$$score_j = cos(\vec{q}^T U_k \Sigma_k^\alpha, \Sigma_k^{1-\alpha} V_k^T)$$

for various values of a *splitting parameter* α. However they did not seem to interpret this as a basis scaling, and I am unclear on the motivation for the split. This formulation is not equivalent to mine, since it does not add scaling factors of Σ_k^p to the score calculation.

Jiang and Littman [7] present a very interesting formulation and comparison of vector space methods, including LSA. They show that the standard vector space model approximates A by the unitary matrix $\overline{A} = UV^T$, which we might write as

$$\overline{A} = UIV^T = U diag(1, 1, ...1) V^T$$

while the standard LSA scoring algorithm is equivalent to approximating A by

$$\overline{A}_k = UI_k V^T = U diag(1, 1, ...1, 0, 0...0) V^T$$

and a third variation, the Generalized Vector Space Model uses the matrix A directly to calculate scores, which of course can be written

$$A = U\Sigma V^T = U diag(\sigma_1, \sigma_2, ...\sigma_n) V^T.$$

This emphasizes that the difference between these methods is their use of the singular value matrix Σ in the score calculation. The weighted-exponent parameterizations presented in this paper can be formulated in these terms as

$$\overline{A}_k^p = U diag(\sigma_1^p, \sigma_2^p, ...\sigma_k^p, 0, 0...0) V^T. \tag{5}$$

Their hypothesis of an *ideal singular value plot* deserves more investigation and may shed some light on what value of p is optimal for a dataset.

Ding [5] constructs a statistical model for LSA in which he shows that the rows of U are the maximum likelihood estimates of the *latent semantic structures* that act as the generators of the statistical distribution of documents found in the document set. An important result is that the statistical contribution of $\vec{u}_i$ is proportional to σ_i^2 (modulo a slowly-varying normalization factor). While the details of the normalization factor make things complicated, he is able to derive the optimal rank for various datasets that is close to the experimentally determined value.

The relationship between optimal rank and optimal value of the weighting exponent, which has been a major feature of the experiments presented here, may contain important insights to the underlying mechanics of LSA. It is certainly noteworthy that the retrieval results converge to a common value for all values of k as the value of p increases (see Figures 2 and 3). As p increases, the factors with larger eigenvalues increase in importance, which probably has the same effect as rank-reduction.

More surprising is the results of Figure 7, in which accuracy is improved by increasing the importance of the factors with smaller eigenvalues (optimal $p < 0$). This effect may have something to do with the correlations between questions and answers in written natural language conversations.

In conclusion, I have defined a family of LSA scoring functions parameterized by a *weighting exponent* p, which weights the score by Σ^p, where Σ is the diagonal matrix of SVD eigenvalues. The usual LSA scoring corresponds to $p = 0$. I have shown experimental evidence on standard test datasets that retrieval precision can often be improved by a few percent using values of p greater than zero. In another experiment, I have shown that values of p less than zero can improve question/answer matching by around 8%.

The optimal value of p is dependent on the dataset, on the SVD approximation rank k, and possibly on other choices of how the term document matrix is constructed, such as term weighting. Therefore, the practical consequences of finding the optimal p may turn out to be small. However, the theory of how and why the SVD algorithm works for information retrieval is not well understood. It is a challenge to theoretical models of LSA to explain these empirical findings.

Acknowledgments

I would like to thank Dr. Elizabeth Jessup at the University of Colorado, Boulder for pointing out the confusion in LSA scoring algorithms, and for other useful discussions.

Bibliography

[1] BERRY, MICHAEL W., SUSAN T. DUMAIS AND GAVIN W. O'BRIEN *Using Linear Algebra for Intelligent Information Retrieval* in SIAM Review, 37:4 (1995), pp. 573-595. http://www.cs.utk.edu/~library/TechReports/1994/ut-cs-94-270.ps.Z

[2] BERRY, M.W., Z. DRMAC, AND E.R. JESSUP *Matrices, Vector Spaces, and Information Retrieval* in SIAM Review 41:2, (1999), pp. 335-362. http://epubs.siam.org/sam-bin/dbq/article/34703

[3] CARON, JOHN *Applying LSA to Online Customer Support: A Trial Study.* Masters Thesis (April 2000). FAQO source code and related documents are at http://www.unidata.ucar.edu/staff/caron/faqo/index.html

[4] DEERWESTER, S., DUMAIS, S. T., LANDAUER, T. K., FURNAS, G. W. AND HARSHMAN, R. A *Indexing by Latent Semantic Analysis* in Journal of the Society for Information Science, 41(6), 391-407 (1990). http://lsi.research.telcordia.com/lsi/papers/JASIS90.ps

[5] DING, CHRIS H.Q. *A Similarity-based Probability Model for Latent Semantic Indexing* in Proc. of 22nd ACM SIGIR 99 Conference, pp.59-65. (August 1999). http://www.nersc.gov/research/SCG/cding/papers_ps/sigir2.ps

[6] DUMAIS, S. T. *Improving the Retrieval of Information from External Sources* in Behavior Research Methods, Instruments and Computers, 23(2), 229-236 (1991). http://lsi.research.telcordia.com/lsi/papers/BRMIC91.ps

[7] FAN JIANG AND MICHAEL L. LITTMAN *Approximate Dimension Equalization in Vector-Based Information Retrieval* in Proceedings of the Seventeenth International Conference on Machine Learning, to appear, (2000) http://www.cs.duke.edu/~mlittman/docs/icml00-lsi.ps

[8] KOLDA, TAMARA G. AND DIANNE P. O'LEARY *A Semi-Discrete Matrix Decomposition for Latent Semantic Indexing in Information Retrieval* in ACM Transactions on Information Systems, 16 (1998) 322-346. http://www.cs.umd.edu/Dienst/UI/2.0/Describe/ncstrl.umcp/CS-TR-3724

[9] SMART DATA ARCHIVES ftp://ftp.cs.cornell.edu/pub/smart/

[10] SVDPACKC MICHAEL BERRY, THERESA DO, GAVIN O'BRIEN, VIJAY KRISHNA, AND SOWMINI VARADHAN *SVDPACKC (Version 1.0) User's Guide* Univ. of Tennessee Computer Science Report CS-93-194, revised March 1996. http://www.netlib.org .

A Comparative Analysis of LSI Strategies

Marco Lizza and Flavio Sartoretto[*]

1 Introduction

Many Information Retrieval Systems (IRS) for automatically retrieving relevant texts from a large collection of unstructured documents are based upon the Standard Vector Space Model (VM) [10]. For a given collection, a set of relevant concepts known as *terms*, is identified. A term-by-document numeric matrix, $\mathbf{A}$, is obtained by suitably weighting the number of occurrences of each term in each document. The j-th column, a_j, represent the j-th document. Correspondingly, for a given query, a vector $\mathbf{q}$ is obtained by indexing its terms. To identify those documents which are relevant to a query, a vector similarity measure is exploited.

The precision of any IRS, i.e. the ability of retrieving only relevant documents, is undermined by *polysemy* and *synonymy*, which permeate the lexicon of each natural language. Latent Semantic Indexing (LSI) [5, 4] was proposed to reduce those negative effects when exploiting a VM–based technique. LSI amounts to devising a mapping, M, from the column vector space, span($\mathbf{A}$), to a *reduced*, or *approximating* column vector space, spanned by an approximation matrix, $\tilde{\mathbf{A}}$. For a given query vector $\mathbf{q}$, its projection, $\tilde{\mathbf{q}}$, over span($\tilde{\mathbf{A}}$) is computed. The *relevance* of each document, a_j, is estimated by a measure of similarity of $\tilde{a}_j$ to $\tilde{\mathbf{q}}$.

Several LSI variants have been proposed, based upon different techniques for computing $\tilde{\mathbf{A}}$. In the sequel we analyze two of them. The former is based upon the optimal rank-k approximation to $\mathbf{A}$, obtained via the Singular Value Decomposition (SVD) [1, 2, 3], which has noticeable theoretical properties. The latter technique relies upon the k-(pseudo)rank approximation obtained via the Semi–Discrete Decomposition (SDD) [7, 8, 9].

Section 2 briefly recalls some concepts on the VM approach and LSI techniques. Section 3 discusses our evaluation parameters. Section 4 analyzes our results. The importance of phrase indexing is shown in Section 5. Section 6 draws

---
[*]Dipartimento di Informatica, Università "Ca' Foscari" di Venezia, Via Torino 155, Mestre VE, Italy. E-mail: {mlizza,sartoret}@dsi.unive.it

our conclusions.

2 Latent Semantic Indexing

Suppose we have a collection encompassing d documents, where t *relevant* indexing terms have been listed. In the Vector Space Model the collection is represented by the term-document matrix $\mathbf{A} = [\mathbf{a}_1 | \dots | \mathbf{a}_d] \in \mathbb{R}^{t \times d}$. Each entry $\mathbf{A}_{ij}$ is a function of f_{ij} (the number of times that the i-th term appears in the j-th document). Indexing is a key point in computing $\mathbf{A}$. Many strategies have been proposed to compute the entries of $\mathbf{A}$. Let g_i be the number of documents where the i-th term appears. Agreeing with [10], an effective indexing strategy is

$$\mathbf{A}_{ij} = f_{ij} \cdot \frac{\log \frac{d}{g_i} + 1}{\sqrt{\sum_{k=1}^{t} \log \frac{d}{g_k} + 1}} .$$

The j-th column, a_j, represent the j-th document, while the i-th row is attached to the i-th term.

A query is encoded by a vector function, $\mathbf{q} = (\mathbf{q}_1, \dots, \mathbf{q}_t)^T \in \mathbb{R}^t$, of $\hat{f}_i$ (the number of times that the i-th term appears in the query). By experiments, we found that $\mathbf{q}_i = \hat{f}_i$ is a simple, yet effective choice. Note that when dealing with real-life collections, both $\mathbf{A}$ and $\mathbf{q}$ are sparse.

We rank documents by computing the *cosine* similarity measure vector, $\mathbf{s} \in \mathbb{R}^d = (\mathbf{s}_1, \dots, \mathbf{s}_d)^T$, where

$$\mathbf{s}_j = \frac{\mathbf{A}^T \mathbf{q}}{\|\mathbf{a}_j\|_2 \|\mathbf{q}\|_2} .$$

The relevance of the j-th document is assumed to be proportional to s_j.

LSI is a technique for reducing synonymy and polysemy problems which affect any IRS system. It is based upon approximating $\mathbf{A}$ by a (reduced) k model $\mathbf{A}_k$, being $k \leq k_{max} = \mathrm{rank}(\mathbf{A})$. Many approximation techniques have been proposed, which produce LSI variants. Here we consider two of them.

In the first one, $\mathbf{A}_k$ is the optimal rank–k approximation, calculated using the well-known Singular Value Decomposition [6]. This technique is quite effective in improving the precision of the base VM model [1, 2, 3]. SVD produces an approximation $\mathbf{A}_k^{(V)} = \mathbf{U}_k \Sigma_k \mathbf{V}_k^T$, by computing two orthogonal matrices, a $t \times t$ matrix $\mathbf{U}_k$ and a $d \times d$ matrix $\mathbf{V}_k$, together with a diagonal $t \times d$ matrix Σ_k. SVD is optimal in the sense that for $k \leq \mathrm{rank}(\mathbf{A})$ [6],

$$\|\mathbf{A} - \mathbf{A}_k^{(V)}\| = \min_{\mathrm{rank}(\mathbf{B})=k} \|\mathbf{A} - \mathbf{B}\|,$$

where $\| \cdot \|$ is the Frobenius norm. The factor matrices $\mathbf{U}_k$ and $\mathbf{V}_k$, are dense, thus in real-life collections a much larger amount of memory is needed to store them, rather than the sparse matrix $\mathbf{A}$.

The second technique is based upon the Semi–Discrete Decomposition [7, 8, 9], which computes a k-approximation to $\mathbf{A}$, $\mathbf{A}_k^{(D)} = \mathbf{X}_k \mathbf{D}_k \mathbf{Y}_k^T$, by minimizing a suitable error measure. The entries of the factor matrices, $\mathbf{X}_k$, $\mathbf{Y}_k$, belong to the *discrete* set $\{-1, 0, 1\}$; k real numbers identify the *diagonal* matrix $\mathbf{D}$. Exploiting a packed memory representation, like that proposed in [7, 8, 9], less memory than for storing $\mathbf{A}$ is required. SDD requires the solution of an integer programming problem, which in principle can be solved by a trivial enumeration. Note that, while SVD provides a *factorization* of $\mathbf{A}$, i.e. $\mathbf{A}_k^{(V)} = \mathbf{A}$ for some k, the matrices $\mathbf{A}_k^{(D)}$ are called *decompositions* of $\mathbf{A}$, since $\mathbf{A}_k^{(D)} \neq \mathbf{A}$, $1 \leq k \leq k_{max}$. Being exponential-time growing, enumeration is not applicable, thus an approximation matrix, $\mathbf{A}_k^{(D)'}$, is computed via a *greedy* algorithm. Though $\mathbf{A}_k^{(D)'}$ is not necessarily of rank k, such algorithm computes the factors as a sum of rank-one matrices, thus in the sequel we call $\mathbf{A}_k^{(D)'}$ a k-(pseudo)rank SDD approximation. A key point in the greedy algorithm is the choice for a starting vector. Four main strategies are proposed in the literature, which are labeled [9] THR, CYC, ONE, PER, respectively. Each one provides a more or less sparse $\mathbf{A}_k^{(D)'}$ approximation matrix, which affects the precision of LSI–SDD in a peculiar way. For brevity, in the sequel we drop the prime superscript, assuming that $\mathbf{A}_k^{(D)}$ stands also for $\mathbf{A}_k^{(D)'}$.

3   Evaluation Parameters

We estimate the efficiency of an LSI technique from the point of view of the user, which would like to obtain ranked lists of documents where he found *ranked first, the largest possible number of relevant items to his query*. Under this assumption, the most important parameter is the *precision* $p_i = r_i/i$ on a given number, i, of retrieved documents, where r_i is the number of relevant documents retrieved. Since precision depends on recall, we consider the *average* precision, defined as the n–point *interpolated precision*

$$P_a^{(n)} = \frac{1}{n} \sum_{i=1}^{n} \tilde{p}(l_i), \text{ where } \tilde{p}(x) = p_j, \ j = argmin_m \left\{ \frac{r_m}{r_d} \geq x, m = 1, \dots, d \right\}.$$

The *pseudo-precision* $\tilde{p}(x)$, is evaluated, rather than p_i, since standing from the user's point of view, *for a given recall level*, we are interested in measuring the precision of the *most efficient* IRS. That system is the one which retrieves the *lowest number* of documents to meet that recall level. Our interpolated precision differs from that given in [7, 8], where the pseudo-precision was defined

$$\tilde{p}(x) = \max_{\frac{r_j}{r_d} \geq x} p_j, \ j = 1, \dots, d,$$

i.e. by maximizing the precision, rather than minimizing the amount of retrieved documents. As proposed in [5], in our experiments we interpolated the precision over $n = 3$ recall levels, setting $l_i = 0.25, 0.50, 0.75$, respectively. Moreover, since each test collection is provided with a set of queries, we considered the average interpolated precision over all queries. For brevity, in the sequel we write P_a,

174

C_{VM}	$2 \cdot t + 2 \cdot \text{nnz} + d$
$C_{\text{SVD}}(k)$	$(2 \cdot (t+d) - 1) \cdot k + 2 \cdot t$
$C_{\text{SDD}}(k)$	$\text{nnz}_X + 2 \cdot t + \text{nnz}_Y$
S_{VM}	$\text{nnz} \cdot (\text{sizeof(int)} + \text{sizeof(double)}) + (d+1) \cdot \text{sizeof(int)}$
$S_{\text{SVD}}(k)$	$((t+d) \cdot k) \cdot \text{sizeof(double)}$
$S_{\text{SDD}}(k)$	$k \cdot 2 \cdot (\lceil t/p \rceil + \lceil d/p \rceil) \cdot (p/8) + k \cdot \text{sizeof(double)}$

Table 1. *Estimation formulas for the computational load, C_A, in FLOP, and storage requirement, S_A, in bytes, of VM, LSI–SVD and LSI–SDD strategies.*

	CISI	MEDLINE	TIME
Documents	1460	1033	423
Queries	35	30	83
Relevant / Queries	49.8	23.2	3.9
Terms	3572	3944	8228
Terms / Documents	44.1	47.9	186.8
Terms / Queries	7.4	10.2	8.0
# nonzero elements	64388	49509	79022
% nonzero elements	1.23%	1.22%	2.27%
Rank	1458	1033	423

Table 2. *Test collections. Stemming with SMART's [11] stop-list was performed.*

dropping the (n) superscript. We also write $P_a(k)$, when we need to point out that P_a is a function of the rank k.

In our context, precision is considered the most important evaluation parameter. On the other hand, storage requirement and computational cost are equally important, when a practically computable model is to be devised. Table 1 summarizes our estimation formulas for the computational loads, C_A, and the storage needs, S_A. Either the base VM model (A=VM), LSI–SVD (A=SVD), or LSI–SDD (A=SDD) procedure are considered. The storage and time needed to compute the SVD and SDD decompositions are not included. They are considered one-time operations, since we deal with static collections. Our formulas estimate the computational cost, the number of bytes needed to store double precision factors and decomposition matrices, in order to rank all the documents in a collection with respect to *one* given query. In Table 1, the whole number k is either the rank of the SVD factorization, or the (pseudo)rank of the SDD decomposition; nnz is the amount of non–zero elements in the matrix $\mathbf{A}$; nnz_X and nnz_Y are the amounts of non–zero elements in the SDD factors $\mathbf{X}_k$ and $\mathbf{Y}_k$; $u = \text{sizeof(double)}$ is the number of bytes needed to store a double precision float.

4 Results

LSI–SVD and LSI–SDD performance have been analyzed on three well–known test collections, whose features are summarized in Table 2. Each *term* is a single stemmed word.

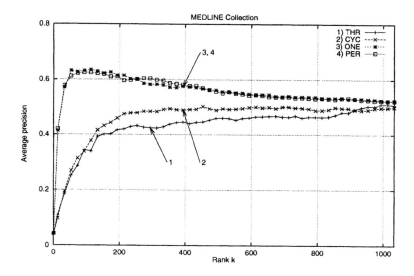

Figure 1. *LSI–SDD average precision, when four SDD initialization strategies are exploited.*

	S_{VM}	S_{SVD}	S_{SDD}	C_{VM}	C_{SVD}	C_{SDD}
CISI	0.78	3.84	0.13	0.14	1.01	0.12
MEDLINE	0.60	3.80	0.12	0.11	1.00	0.14
TIME	0.95	6.60	0.22	0.17	1.75	0.21

Table 3. *Storage requirements, S_A, in Mbytes, and computational loads, C_A, in MFLOP, for retrieving documents relevant to a given query, using VM, LSI–SVD and LSI–SDD, when $k = 100$, $u = 32$.*

Figure 1 shows $P_a(k)$ raised by LSI–SDD, when dealing with MEDLINE collection. A curve for each one of the four initialization strategies is plotted. One can see that using strategies ONE and PER, quite the same behavior is observed, where for $100 \leq k$, $P_a(k) \geq P_a(k_{max} = 1,033)$, as one expects. Dealing with CISI and TIME, our results (not shown here) point out that ONE and PER give quite the same $P_a(k)$ behavior. Unfortunately, on CISI smaller increments in precision are observed when $100 \leq k \ll k_{kmax}$ becomes smaller. *A small decrease* is observed on TIME. These results seem to fit the uniformity degree of our three test collections: on MEDLINE, $P_a(k)$ can increase when k decreases, MEDLINE being a *uniform* collection, i.e. displaying a small dictionary ($t \simeq 3\,d$, see Table 2), featuring a *small* number of synonyms. TIME is the *less uniform* collection, i.e. it displays a large dictionary ($t \simeq 19\,d$, cf. Table 2), and a newspaper oriented lexicon, filled with a *large* number of synonyms. With respect to *uniformity*, CISI lies between the other two collections.

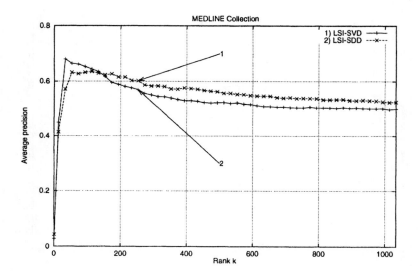

Figure 2. *Average precision of LSI–SVD and LSI–SDD(ONE), on MEDLINE.*

Since we observed that ONE produces more sparse matrices than PER, in the sequel we assume that the ONE initialization strategy is used to implement LSI–SDD system. Figure 2 shows that performing retrieval on MEDLINE under this assumption, LSI–SDD precision, $P_a^{(D)}(k)$, displays practically the same behavior as $P_a^{(V)}(k)$. This result shows that the precision of LSI–SDD is *quite optimal*, being similar to that one of LSI–SVD, which takes advantage of the best k-rank approximation in Frobenius norm.

Dealing with our three test collections, $k = 100$ seems a quasi–optimal value with respect to average precision. This k-value falls in the optimal interval guessed by other authors [1]. Setting $k = 100$, we compare the storage requirement, S_A, and the computational load, C_A, of our base VM system (A=VM), LSI–SDD (A=SDD), and LSI–SVD (A=SVD) strategy. Recall that SVD produces dense factors, whereas the original term–document matrix **A** is sparse. Storage requirement increases so much using LSI–SVD, that it can be up to 7 times that of VM (see Table 3). Such an increase makes LSI–SVD difficult to apply to large collections, encompassing, let us say, more than 10^5 documents. On the other hand, SDD with ONE strategy, delivers sparse factors, which need less storage than the original **A** matrix. Table 3 shows that when $k = 100$, LSI–SDD needs down to 1/6 times the storage for VM. Similar results occur for computational loads. Ranking documents by LSI–SVD, with respect to a single query, needs up to 10 times than using the VM system, while LSI–SDD needs almost the same load as VM (cf. Table 3).

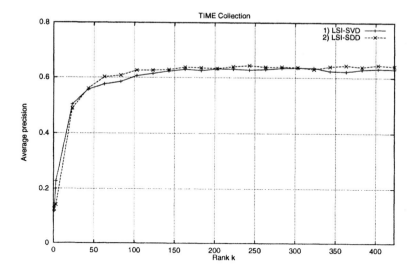

Figure 3. *Average precision of LSI–SVD and LSI–SDD(ONE), on TIME.*

5 Phrase-Indexing

Figure 2 shows that when dealing with MEDLINE, $P_a(100) \simeq 1.3 \cdot P_a(k_{max})$. On the other hand, Figure 3 shows that a reduced model cannot increase precision, when dealing with TIME collection. This result suggests that, when retrieval on non–uniform collections is required, LSI precision decreases when $100 \leq k \ll k_{max}$. In principle, one can guess that other methods to compute a reduced space could provide LSI variants which show improved precision for $100 \leq k \ll k_{max}$. Actually, the optimal properties of SVD suggest that other methods based upon geometric properties of vector spaces cannot provide better precisions. Using LSI, an improved precision is likely to be obtained only when a *better* **A** matrix is computed. This implies working at the indexing phase level. One strategy to improve LSI precision relies upon exploiting *phrase–indexing* [10], i.e. considering not only one-word terms, but also *l*-word sets, or *phrases*. Let LxGy denote such a phrase–indexing strategy, where x is the number of (stemmed) terms, also called the *length*, included in each phrase. The number y denotes the *largest* amount of terms embraced by the first and the last word, also called the *gap*. Our previous experiments exploited L1G0 indexing, i.e. phrases of length x=1 (single words) with no (y = 0) intervening terms. Increasing the length increases the number of phrases, that is the dimension of **A**. Thus it is not advisable to enlarge the length x too much. As a first experiment, we set x= 2. The same arguments apply to the gap. We set the gap y= 3, thus pointing out phrases of length 2, embracing at most 3 inner words.

Table 4 shows the new featuring parameters, when indexing with L2G3 strategy our three test collections. Note that in each collection the total amount of *terms*, which now mean *phrases*, is higher than with L1G0 indexing (cf. Table 2), since

178

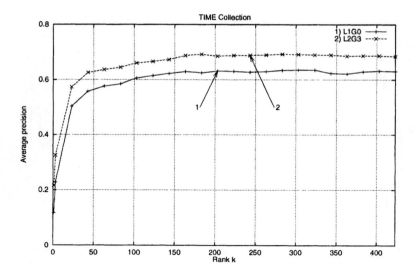

Figure 4. *Average precision raised by LSI–SVD, when L1G0 (curve 1) and L2G3 (curve 2) indexing are exploited.*

	CISI	MEDLINE	TIME
Documents	1460	1033	423
Queries	35	30	83
Relevant / Queries	49.8	23.2	3.9
Terms	6277	4883	12570
Terms / Documents	52.9	50.9	215.9
Terms / Queries	33.4	10.3	9.5
# nonzero elements	77289	52601	91326
% nonzero elements	1.23%	1.22%	2.27%
Rank	1458	1033	423

Table 4. *Features of our test collections. L2G3 indexing.*

besides single words, a number of length-2 phrases is considered.

Let us consider LSI–SVD, which represents the optimal strategy with respect to geometric properties. Figure 4 shows that on TIME collection, for each k value, L2G3 indexing increases the average precision, with respect to L1G0 indexing, thus allowing a up to 9% higher precision at the *working* rank $k = 100$. Other results (not reported here) show that when ranking the MEDLINE and CISI collections, L2G3 indexing does not allow for an useful increase in $P_a(k)$.

Remember that t increases, when switching from L1G0 to L2G3, thus the computational load and storage requirement increase. Table 5 shows the changes using LSI–SDD, while our results (not reported here) show that the precision already resembles that of LSI–SVD. When using L1G0 indexing, the average storage and cost

	S_{VM}	S_{SDD}	C_{VM}	C_{SDD}
CISI	0.62	0.19	0.17	0.15
MEDLINE	0.42	0.15	0.12	0.14
TIME	0.73	0.33	0.21	0.33

Table 5. *L2G3 indexing. LSI–SDD storage requirements, S_A, in Mbytes, and computational loads, C_A, in MFLOP, when $k = 100$.*

ratios are $S_{SDD}/S_{VM} = 0.20$, $C_{SDD}/C_{VM} = 1.12$. Exploiting L2G3, the average ratios become $S_{SDD}/S_{VM} = 0.37$, $C_{SDD}/C_{VM} = 1.21$. The increase in storage requirement is appreciable, but note that the amount using LSI–SDD is again far smaller than with VM. Using L2G3, the average computational cost ratio displays a small increase, which can be rated affordable. Thus practically we can apply L2G3 indexing also on MEDLINE and CISI, though the precision does not improve, while on TIME a non–negligible gain is obtained.

6   Conclusions

LSI is a technique which improves the precision of a VM–based IRS, by reducing essentially the problems due to synonymy and polysemy, via a k-rank approximation of the geometric vector space. We analyzed precision, storage requirement and computational cost of two effective LSI strategies, LSI–SVD and LSI–SDD, when applied to three test collections.

The following points are worth emphasizing.

- LSI–SVD take advantage of an optimal k-rank approximation to span($\mathbf{A}$). However, it is highly storage consuming, up to 7 times the Vector Space Model; the same applies to the computational cost, that can be up to 10 times that of VM. Thus LSI–SVD is unusable on *large* collections, consisting of, let us say, more than 10^5 documents, unless appropriate preprocessing by clustering is performed.

- SDD precision and computational load depend on a *initialization strategy*. That labeled ONE seems to be preferred, since using this strategy the behavior of LSI–SDD average precision vs k closely resembles that of LSI–SVD. On the other hand, LSI–SDD required down to 1/6 of the storage required by VM, and almost the same computational cost.

- Though there is an intrinsic difficulty in predicting the optimal k value, which corresponds to the highest precision, $k = 100$ proved a good choice in all our tests.

- LSI–SVD and LSI–SDD average precision decreases with k when applied to non–uniform collections, that is collections with a large number of terms with respect to the number of documents, and a lexicon filled with synonyms. When combined with LSI, other approximation techniques relying upon the geometric space properties are not likely to provide better precision. To increase precision, the computation of the model matrix **A** must be changed afresh. As an example, small length and gap *phrase–indexing* can increase the average precision of LSI up to 9% on TIME, which was our most non–uniform test collection.

Our experiments show that LSI is not likely to be efficient on large collections, since they are usually non–uniform. When performing retrieval in large ($d > 10^5$) collections, clustering is to be applied first. Then, LSI can be exploited on the most relevant clusters to refine ranking.

Acknowledgments

The authors thank Massimo Melucci for providing valuable hints.

Bibliography

[1] M. W. BERRY, Z. DRMAČ, AND E. R. JESSUP, *Matrices, Vector Spaces and Information Retrieval*, SIAM Review, 41 (1999), pp. 335–362.

[2] M. W. BERRY, S. T. DUMAIS, AND G. W. O'BRIEN, *Using Linear Algebra for Intelligent Information Retrieval*, SIAM Review, 37 (1995), pp. 573–595.

[3] M. W. BERRY AND R. D. FIERRO, *Low-Rank Orthogonal Decomposition for Information Retrieval Applications*, Numerical Linear Algebra with Applications, 1 (1996), pp. 1–27.

[4] S. DEERWESTER, S. T. DUMAIS, AND R. HARSHMAN, *Indexing by Latent Semantic Analysis*, Journal of the American Society for Information Science, 41 (1990), pp. 391–407.

[5] S. T. DUMAIS, *Enhancing Performance in Latent Semantic Indexing (LSI) Retrieval*, Bellcore System Journal, (1992).

[6] G. GOLUB AND C. F. VAN LOAN, Matrix Computation, The Johns Hopkins University Press, Baltimore, second ed., 1989.

[7] T. G. KOLDA AND D. P. O'LEARY, *Latent Semantic Indexing Via a Semi-dDscrete Matrix Decomposition*, Tech. Report UMCP-CSD CS-TR-3713, Department of Computer Science, University of Maryland, November 1996.

[8] ——, *A Semi-Discrete Matrix Decomposition for Latent Semantic Indexing in Information Retrieval*, Tech. Report UMCP-CSD CS-TR-3724, Department of Computer Science, University of Maryland, December 1996.

[9] ——, *Computation and Uses of the Semi-Discrete Matrix Decomposition*, Tech. Report CS-TR-4012, Department of Computer Science, University of Maryland, April 1999.

[10] G. SALTON AND M. J. MCGILL, Introduction to Modern Information Retrieval, McGraw-Hill, New York, 1983.

[11] SEVERAL AUTHORS, *SMART Software*, available via anonymous ftp from `ftp.cs.cornell.edu`, file `\~/pub/smart/smart.11.0.tar.Z`, accessed on February 1, 2000.

Index

184